MOURNING HAS BROKEN

MOURNING
HAS BROKEN

Love, Loss and Reclaiming Joy

ERIN DAVIS

HarperCollins*Publishers*Ltd

Published by HarperCollins Publishers Ltd

First edition

HarperCollins Publishers Ltd
Bay Adelaide Centre, East Tower
22 Adelaide Street West, 41st Floor
Toronto, Ontario, Canada
M5H 4E3

www.harpercollins.ca

Library and Archives Canada Cataloguing in Publication
information is available upon request.

ISBN 978-1-4434-5463-6

Printed and bound in the United States of America
LSC 9 8 7 6 5 4 3

For Lauren
As everything in my life has been and will forever be,
this is for you.

For Colin
May you come to know the sweetness of your mother's heart
and how full it was with love for you.

For Phil
You have beautifully guided this sweet boy into the
world without Lauren's loving hand in yours.
You and Brooke have got this.

For Rob
. . . and I could not ask for more.

CONTENTS

Foreword

THERE IS NOTHING THAT CAN PREPARE YOU FOR life, nor is there a single thing that can prepare you for death—your own, or for one of your tribe, your flock, your family, blood or otherwise. Death comes down either by hammer or feather, neither of which is particularly kind.

What Erin Davis has managed to articulate with her gut-wrenching and brilliantly inspiring memoir dumbfounds me. Page after page is filled with such grace and insight and openness that quite often I was wiping a tear off my cheek or a laugh from the corner of my mouth.

How do you reconcile the sudden death of your only daughter? How do you also navigate a marriage and a job and myriad friendships and errands and appointments and just day-to-day breathing in and out? Erin bares all and in doing so gives us the opportunity to share our own losses—making us feel less alone in our own rivers of grief. That river that winds in and out of our days, stealing sleep and happiness and eventually our mental, physical and spiritual health.

Grief shared is more bearable.

Grief shared heals tender hearts.

Grief shared is a gift that Erin Davis and her beautiful book, *Mourning Has Broken*, give to humans everywhere.

—Jann Arden

Mother's Day:
The Exit Interview

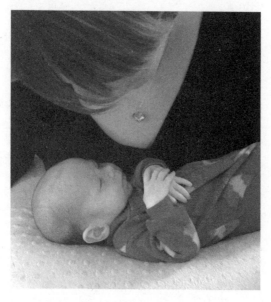

Lauren and Colin, Christmas 2014

MAYBE IT IS, AS WRITER JOAN DIDION so aptly put it, the "magical thinking" of those who grieve—the stories we tell ourselves in order to survive—but in the days and months and years that have added up since the morning our world stopped turning, my husband and I have come to believe that we somehow knew deep down that our time with our only child would be far too short. Perhaps that's why, when she left us, we sought consolation in something with which so many who lose loved ones are not blessed: the absolute surety that we had left no loving word unsaid, no meaningful shared experience denied. In fact, my final tweet about Lauren pared down to 136 characters just some of the immense love and pride I felt on that special May 10, our daughter's very first Mother's Day.

Nothing has made me feel more like a mother than witnessing our daughter @laurenonair grow into the role. So rewarding. #HappyMothersDay

Rob and I called our only child our "limited edition." Just how limited we would find out via a phone call that came in the early hours of the very next morning.

Like her baby, who beamed often and easily, Lauren had been a happy child. Her disposition was as bright as her blonde curls; she loved to sing and lived to make us laugh. Now she was learning that life could hold even more happiness than she'd ever imagined. In a daily internet blog read and heard (in an optional audio version) by thousands of my radio show's listeners, Lauren agreed to answer some questions in the lead-up to her first Mother's Day. Although she sometimes rolled her eyes and graciously passed when I asked her to share the airwaves with me (I thought a mother/daughter podcast would be a great idea if we could figure out the geographical logistics), she surprised me a little by saying "yes" to this request.

I believe that in becoming a mother herself, our daughter began to understand me as more than just the local celebrity she'd grown up with in Toronto. Her son's birth had brought with it, as all births do, a newly added layer of responsibility for and bonding with this little human. Experiencing this meant Lauren was only now beginning to relate to the depths of my love for her, and to understand the ache that simmered in me constantly as I watched her, her loving and tender husband, and their sweet son live their lives a four-hour drive from us.

Just as Lauren saw me in a different, softer, closer light, I was seeing in our twenty-four-year-old daughter further fulfillment of the promise she'd shown from the earliest days of her life, when she shimmered with intelligence, wit and musical brilliance.

We accomplished our audio interview by recording it separately, from two different cities at different times, but very much from the heart and in the most modern of ways. I wrote questions and emailed them to her; she recorded her responses into her own microphone at home, put them into an audio file and sent them back to me. Lucky for me, I had in my home the handiest of handymen: my husband since 1988, Rob, was a radio producer. He seamlessly cut together my recorded questions and our daughter's answers, and together the three of us, in our last collaboration, shared our special Mother's Day interview at www.erindavis.com/erin-s-journals/may-8-2015/just-thought.

First, I asked what Colin had given to her.

Pure joy! He is such a happy baby—his smile is contagious and we've already shared so many laughs together over the silliest things.

He'll cry to wake me up in the morning, but as soon as I poke my head over the side of the crib, his face just lights up. Even when we've had a trying night with Colin, that little dimple will make me forget any frustration we've had at 2 a.m. My husband, Phil, and I talk almost on a daily basis about how blessed we are to have him in our lives.

Colin had been the answer to a prayer that had been whispered for generations in his father's family. He was the first son of a first son of a first son in a chain that can be traced through Japanese history back to the tenth century and Emperor Shirakawa, or so family lore has it. But his nickname, Coconut, was admittedly not quite as noble. As a baby, Colin's mother had become "Peanutty"; "Coco," therefore, just seemed a natural fit for her son! And so it was that Lauren's Mother's Day gift from her adoring husband was a small ceramic coconut, brightly painted and hanging on a delicate chain. I had found it on a craft site and suggested it to Phil, who agreed that it was perfect and ordered it months in advance. She wore it proudly in the family picture she posted on Facebook that day, along with these words:

> *Happy Mother's Day to my mom, Erin—my advisor, mentor and confidante—and thank you to my boys, Phil and Colin, for making me feel like a queen every day of the year.*

Lauren was young, energetic and embracing a full, happy life with her new husband and their soon-to-be seven-month-old son, Colin. When she stepped away from her job as midday news anchor on Ottawa's news and talk radio station, Phil dove in even further to help them make their mortgage payments, juggling three jobs, six days a week. No wonder he was exhausted whenever we came for a visit. But he never complained; marriage and family life were sources of great fulfillment for this soft-spoken thirty-year-old who shared the same passion for radio that his wife and parents-in-law had long held. The plan, moving forward, was for Phil to take over as a full-time stay-at-home father once Lauren returned to her job. Just as she had followed in my footsteps, Phil would be following in his father-in-law's, taking on a role that had given Rob feelings of tremendous satisfaction and accomplishment.

~~~~

LAUREN and Phil looked forward to Sundays as their day to run errands, to unplug and to reconnect with each other. But this one was even more special as their little family celebrated its first Mother's Day.

As Rob and I prepared for an especially challenging workweek ahead—one that had already begun with a trip to a warm foreign land—back in Ottawa our daughter, son-in-law and grandson spent part of the day bundling up and walking to a nearby park. Only three weeks earlier, in that same park, we had painted a cheery family scene: as I reclined on the damp grass, with Colin snuggled in a sling on my chest, Lauren played softball with her husband and dad, something she'd done often with Rob in her childhood (but rarely as an adult). That day, like a scene out of *The Natural* (or perhaps *The Incredible Hulk?*), something remarkable happened: in an incredible show of strength, Lauren hit her father's arched underhand pitch so hard that her aluminum bat broke. Right in half. And in the joy and surprise of that moment, we all laughed so hard that it stirred Colin from his sleep.

The next day, after we'd checked out of our hotel room and stopped in for a brief visit with the sleepy couple (it had been one of "those" nights that are often visited upon new parents), we drove away from their townhouse and pointed our car west for the long drive home. Before we pulled out of the parking lot, I sighed and said to Rob in a sad, soft mono-tone, "That was too short."

How prophetic that comment would turn out to be.

On Mother's Day, the small family shared a rare dinner out. Lauren was intent on being as healthy as she could be in order to, in her words, "be around for a long time" for her son. This dedication was typical of the behaviour she'd shown in the past year: from the earliest moments of her pregnancy, she swore off caffeine, artificial sweeteners, alcohol, her beloved sushi and anything that could possibly harm her child before or after his birth. As she did in everything, Lauren embraced her new status as a mom with enthusiasm, intelligence and a strong sense of purpose. She would do all she could to give her son a head start in life.

In our interview, I asked Lauren if becoming a mother had changed her perspective on the role her mother (or father, even) played in parenting her. She responded that it hadn't yet, but added: "I'm sure in the years to come, espe-cially when he's a teenager, I'll be asking myself, 'What would Mom and Dad do?'"

What would we do? We would just try to keep going for the sake of that little boy, whose cries in the pre-dawn hours woke his father, but not his mother.

The night before, as her first Mother's Day came to a close, Lauren was drifting off to sleep when she heard Colin's cries from the tiny nursery she and Phil had so lovingly decorated and painted in a bright, sunny yellow.

"Right on cue," I can imagine her saying with a half-smile. Lauren had shared with Rob and me how she often marvelled at her son's almost psychic ability to know when his mother was about to close her eyes. It was as though the click of the lamp being shut off was some sort of signal for him to wake up and let his mommy know he was hungry. She climbed out of their warm bed, left her sleepy husband and went to rock and feed their son.

"I love you," she said quietly to Phil. Those were her last words.

The next morning, her heart stilled, Lauren lay lifeless, draped over the side of their bed. The wailing of sirens approaching their home, coupled with the cries of a devastated husband and a hungry boy, signalled the end of her happy life—and what we thought was the end of our world. On that desperately dark morning, our search for reasons, for strength and eventually for hope was about to begin. We would experience the shattering pain of losing the dreams we'd held in our hearts from the moment we learned we'd conceived this most cherished and wanted child. But we would find, also, in the wake of such immeasurable loss, that it truly is possible to keep moving forward until the painful days gradually become less frequent and more bearable. And that there can be light once more.

CHAPTER 1

A Very Special Child
(Just Like Yours!)

Cover of *Today's Parent* magazine, November 1993

O UR HEARTS WERE FULL OF EXCITEMENT THE
morning of May 9, 2015, as we boarded a plane
bound for Jamaica to host the winners of an
annual contest on Toronto adult contemporary radio station
98.1 CHFI. Trip winners were to arrive the next day, but my
husband, Rob, and my radio partner and our producer were
being given a chance to settle in and become familiar with
the all-inclusive luxury hotel a day in advance. The tradition
was to greet our listeners with big hugs, cool towels and
cocktails as they emerged from their air-conditioned buses at
the resort. It was almost always a highlight of these events.

On a few listener trips, we'd been lucky enough to bring
our little daughter along, and I'd even tried to entice her as an
adult to come with us for extra hands-on help. But this year
in particular, she had her own hands full at home with her
new seven-month-old son.

That was fine with me. I knew that when the week was
over and we were on our drive home from the airport to our
cottage (probably in the dark), the journey would be brightened

by a long phone conversation with Lauren, catching up on her week's adventures with Colin and Phil and bringing her up to speed on our trip. And we always had countless emails and texts; her last text had reminded me to have fun and be sure to have "a virgin piña colada for me." That was the plan, anyway. The best part of coming home from a trip was always knowing that Lauren—at any age at all—was waiting to see us or talk to us. Every ending was a new beginning.

Ask any mother if her child is special, gifted or extraordinary in some way (or many) and there's little chance you'll get any response other than "of course!" Even that one on the playground who insists on celebrating the perfect fit of finger and nostril at every opportunity—as well as the child whose knack for public meltdowns makes every outing seem like a (tenser) sequel to the bomb-defusing scenes in *The Hurt Locker*—has a mother, father or grandparent who will attest to just how amazing that child is.

It will come as no surprise that Rob and I were pretty much in awe of our offspring too. And now that we count our time without her not in weeks or months but in years, we have come to adore her even more, if that's at all possible. As the saying goes, hindsight may indeed be 20/20; there is a certain amount of gentle airbrushing that the heart and mind undertake when remembering someone who was so loved.

Just let me give you a few reasons why we felt we had every right to be the proudest parents in North America from 1991 onward.

We knew we had someone special in our midst before she even arrived. At twenty-one, Rob, having considered other options for birth control during his first marriage, had undergone a vasectomy. When we married some twelve years later, Rob decided he wanted to be a father after all. Two vasectomy reversal attempts later, Lauren was conceived. She literally came to be out of joy and laughter (we tried to embrace the adventure of attempting to conceive against the odds, rather than feel pressure or angst), as well as a deep desire to bring a child into our happy little family.

Her arrival nine months later was also comical in its way: my water broke on a busy Saturday in a shopping mall because, well, that's how I roll. We were in the mall on that chilly spring morning to replace a video camera we'd borrowed to shoot aspects of the baby's arrival—modestly, of course. When we tested the camera, we found it to be malfunctioning. Although I wasn't supposed to give birth for three more weeks—Lauren's due date was April 12—we wanted to make sure we had a camera that was in working order when the big day arrived. Told by the department store clerk to go away for a bit while they found a replacement for us, we wandered off.

Rob and I had been sidetracked from our other errands by my sudden desire for an Orange Julius, a fruit-flavoured shake available in many food courts but, as we would learn, not in this mall. We never did find one—because somewhere in the middle of the search, I felt a slow, warm trickle of amniotic fluid beginning to dampen my fleecy track pants. My water was breaking! Rob steered me by the elbow into a stationery store, where I breathlessly asked to use their washroom. Inside the tiny staff facilities, I ascertained that what I thought was happening was indeed occurring. I padded myself up with some toilet paper, took a deep breath and headed back into the mall. Before I did, though, I thanked the people behind the counter for the use of their washroom. I also pointed to their overhead speakers and thanked them for having our radio station, 98.1 CHFI, on in the store, which is also how I roll. Rob and I then returned to that department store with a much more urgent request for a replacement camera. Fortunately, they came through for us. Since labour hadn't actually started yet, we were in a state of "calm before the storm." Perhaps it was shock or disbelief, but we were both remarkably chill about the event that was about to change our lives forever. We drove our minivan home—a thirty-minute trip—where I made a pasta lunch. Then I had a bath, determined to be as well-groomed for the event as possible. "Ready for my close up, Dr. Addison!"

As we made our way back downtown to the hospital we had toured months earlier, reality began to set in. "I'm not ready for this!" I told Rob. Perhaps no couple about to become parents for the first time really is, but goodness knows we were excited to bring home the baby that two or three ultrasounds had assured us was almost definitely a girl.

We arrived at the hospital in the late afternoon and parked our van, its baby seat anchored and ready to protect our precious little one whenever she was ready to come home. We thought it might be in a day or two, but once again, things were not going to run on our schedule. In another one of those "are you kidding me?" moments, as I stood filling out paperwork in the admitting area of the hospital, a radio on a nearby desk was playing my station. Rob's eyes met mine as we heard my voice in a pre-recorded piece saying, "I'm Erin Davis, and here's what's on in Toronto tonight. . . ." Rob turned to me and said, "Guess what else is on in Toronto tonight?" We both laughed quietly.

Except Lauren wasn't going to arrive that night. In fact, at about 11 p.m., the nurses had given me a pill to help me sleep and advised Rob to go home. I strongly objected. It was March, sketchy winter driving conditions could return at any time, and Rob faced a forty-five-minute trip each way. There was not a chance I was going to spend that night alone or risk giving birth solo. So, on a slab of foam we had brought along for just such an eventuality, Rob snored quietly on the floor while I went through what I can only describe as light labour all night. At 4 a.m. the real effort began, and three hours later, there she was—all six pounds and twelve ounces of her, delivered by the ob-gyn who had shepherded me through the pregnancy. How lucky we were that he happened to be the doctor on duty in the overnight and early morning hours of that Palm Sunday, March 24.

Oh, and remember that video camera? Watching the tape later, we discovered that as Lauren emerged, there appeared on tape a burst of static that seemed to stun the camera for a few moments. We've always wondered if it was a sign of the great energy of this powerful being's arrival.

I told you she was special.

The very next day—and every day that week—I was on the phone doing live on-air segments with my radio partner, who was in the studio only a few blocks away. Our producer played especially fitting songs like Stevie Wonder's "Isn't She Lovely" and the Eagles' "New Kid in Town." An ad was placed in the *Toronto Star* the next day, welcoming CHFI's newest listener (a photographer had come to the hospital to take a picture of our new baby—who, of course, seemed to wear a sweet little smile for the occasion). The ad also reminded our audience that I would be broadcasting from home the following Easter Monday.

And I was. Rob had devised a plan for me to do my part of the radio show from our home, through telephone company lines into the house. As a producer, he'd experienced success with this practice—not done *over* the phone exactly, but through phone-line technology that made a news commentator broadcasting from his apartment sound as if he was in the radio station's studios. It's not such a big deal these days, when seemingly everyone with a microphone and some egg carton–like acoustic foam has a podcast, but in the early 1990s it was still pretty recent technology.

To this day I have no idea how it worked; I only know that in these pre-WiFi days, they had to dig into our front lawn to make it happen and that Lauren arriving three weeks early meant that the phone folks hadn't even been summoned to our address yet. We had come up with this show-by-remote solution the moment we got a positive result on our pregnancy test; having just started to gel in the past two years with my radio partner, and with climbing ratings to show for our chemistry, despite the many differences between us, I was reluctant to step away from the show for any prolonged period of time. After all, this was "show business," and at this station, with this partner, I was achieving heights of which I had dared not dream. Top ratings on the top station in the country's largest market? Pinch me.

Doing the show from home would be the perfect compromise: I could sleep in a little later than our usual 6 a.m. start, I would not have to take maternity leave (or the lesser salary that would accompany it) and the show would remain intact, for the most part. I set up cushions as a backdrop to our office desk to absorb sound and eliminate the echo that hard surfaces can cause; my weather forecasts and music sheets would come into our home via fax machine. A talkback line was installed between the radio station studio and our house, whereby I could communicate with our producer and get a "coming up" cue from him as a warning to get ready to go on the air. And we came up with a "code" so that my partner and I knew that a bit or conversation was ending—we'd tell the time. It worked out seamlessly and helped to link our family further to the families (especially other young mothers) who were out there listening. I held Lauren in my arms as I did the show, wearing my often milk-stained terrycloth bathrobe, and occasionally I would answer her mews and cries by feeding her. Imagine how surprised the radio-listening audience would have been at that! On second thought, it might not have been a surprise to every listener; I was told years later by a fellow mom that when Lauren would cry on the radio, *she* would begin to lactate. That is one powerful medium, Mama!

For a radio station that was perceived to be aiming at an older audience—even if we were going after the same twenty-five- to fifty-four-year-old demographic as everyone else—this new arrangement was also a win from a corporate stand-point. Because they'd agreed to the idea and were allowing a new mom to broadcast from home, CHFI was seen as a forward-thinking radio station. This unusual but successful arrangement hadn't disrupted our morning show too much, and everybody was happy—except for the few listeners who called the station to say how terrible it was that they'd made me come back to work so soon after giving birth. These listeners, unaware of our new set-up, thought that I had been forced to return to the studios just a week after having our baby. My goodness. I'm sure there were plenty of media outlets that rushed their on-air talent back to work, but this was simply not the case. I got back on the air as soon as I could because I wanted to. I welcomed this arrangement.

Throughout her life, Lauren was reminded by listeners of just how memorable her arrival had been: at almost every station event (and sometimes just in the grocery store checkout line), people who met Lauren would tell her, "I remember when you were born!" That connection with our little family, felt by so many people, continued throughout her life: from the milestones of marriage and her own motherhood to the day her death was announced on that same behemoth radio station's airwaves. She didn't choose to be born into the spotlight, but she came to understand what it meant to our family—this gift of being cared about by perfect strangers. Her own son has had, and continues to have, this same kindness extended to him.

Whether it was a case of nature or nurture, Lauren was verbal very early—a gift for expression that extended to a singing ability well beyond a toddler's usual scope. At just over two years of age, Lauren was singing—not perfectly, but almost in their entirety—the Canadian and American national anthems (and, yes, there's video proof). I was often fortunate to be invited to perform the anthems at various sporting events, including those of Major League Baseball's Toronto Blue Jays, the Toronto Argonauts of the Canadian Football League and the Toronto Maple Leafs of the National Hockey League. In some cases, the anthems are pre-recorded and lip-synched at game time, so as to preclude any visits by the eff-up fairy. Lip-synching can be tricky, and the last thing I wanted was to be caught "faking it" on the giant stadium screen, so I would practise while driving. Little did I know that, strapped into her seat behind me, my preschool prodigy was learning the lyrics and melodies too. That early work paid off; Lauren and I were thrilled and honoured to sing the anthems together twice at Mother's Day Toronto Blue Jays games before she was even in her teens. Both times, there was a very real risk of me bursting with pride right there near the pitcher's mound. There should have been a tarp ready, just in case.

A child who picks things up so easily can also be a source of concern, although, at the time, we didn't know we should be worried. We ought to have been more careful; by way of warning, my mother often reminded us of the old saying "little pitchers have big ears." Once again, Mom was right. By the time she was safely into her teens, Lauren laughed as she confessed to us over dinner one night that she had frequently been paid off in little erasers and even coins for swearing "on command" for her kindergarten and first-grade schoolmates.

All right. If confession is good for the soul, I might as well lay bare my own now: our little girl learned the most unexpectedly interesting words from her mother, a one-time squeaky clean Catholic school girl who easily leaned into the power of the colourful metaphor in order to fit in with her older colleagues in a smoke- and testosterone-filled radio newsroom. My high-school uniform kilt had barely lost its pleats when, in 1982, at nineteen years old, I found myself surrounded by hot-tempered men who elevated swearing to an art form with cleverly crafted adjectives into which filthy syllables were seamlessly spliced. I often thought it was part of a daring game not to get caught using these words on the air—words that, at the time, had the potential to end a career. Now, of course, you'll hear many of them squiggling from a fellow traveller's earbuds. But then? A kid could earn extra cash or even the precious toy contents of a chocolate Kinder Surprise egg by tutoring peers in the casual placement of a swear word. Did this make Lauren an early paid professional communicator? I'm not sure. What I am sure of is that one of her Montessori teachers had never been overly warm toward Rob and me, and we finally were able to figure out why. To any parents of children born around 1991 who came home with vocabulary skills that extended beyond school curriculum: I'm sorry. Or you're %&*#-ing welcome. Whatever's in order. Ahem. Lauren also had a razor-sharp sense of humour. One example that still makes us laugh, because she did it so often: she'd gaze in my direction and say, "I *love* you!" I'd respond with a gushing thank you. And then she'd say, "I was talking to Daddy." How they laughed about that, those two.

I'd just shake my head, glad to be in on a joke that underlined their closeness while also having a laugh at my own expense. We helped hone that humour, so I didn't mind being the brunt of it so many times. I deserved it!

Her sharpest and often funniest barbs came through a character she created called the Coughing Critic. In a raspy voice, as though she were trying to clear her throat, she'd say things like, "You suck!" at the exact moment she thought the voice in my head might be telling me the same thing—like, say, if I burned something in the kitchen, which is not an infrequent occurrence since High is the only setting I seem to know. The Coughing Critic would chime in with, "You're an awful cook. . . . Why don't you give up?" Honestly, it was hilarious. Lauren would never say these things to me in real life, but when the Coughing Critic was around, it was like having our own Don Rickles heckling from the kitchen table or the backseat of the car, telling us to "turn here" at a doughnut shop on our way to the cottage, or just siding with her dad in a discussion that was about to turn very funny. Since Lauren left us, Rob and I have kept the character alive: not only does it give us a chance to razz each other through an imaginary third party, but it reminds us of Lauren's sharp wit, enabling her to give as good as she got in the teasing department.

Her ability to pick and choose just the right words at the proper moment (even if they were not quite family friendly) made it seem almost preordained that she should follow in my footsteps and choose a career in radio. I'm sure the strands of Lauren's DNA ladder resemble a pair of tangled earbuds. Over the years, Rob and I half-heartedly tried to talk her out of entering a business that often pays its newcomers (and sometimes those who've toiled much longer) wages that are less than she made as a teenager working at Starbucks. With the exception of one notable firing (my own), we did a lousy job of presenting a realistic example of how "tough" a life in the business of radio can be. And while she knew that the days of six- and seven-figure salaries had largely gone the way of the CD players in our studios, she was a born communicator. To quote one of her favourite TV hosts, Dr. Phil, "a racehorse has to run."

Along with that sharp wit, she was fast on her feet and almost preternaturally mature. For two years, I hosted a nightly cable TV show on a community station available in hundreds of thousands of households. In the days before the nine-hundred-channel universe was swallowed up by the internet and the many options it offers, we liked to joke that you had to flip past us on channel 10 to get to something better.

With surprisingly strong ratings for a community television show and good viewer feedback giving us the push we needed, the whole show was a labour of love and a real family collaboration: Rob worked behind the scenes and Lauren would hang out in the green room either doing homework or visiting with staff and guests, all the while absorbing as much of this part of the broadcasting industry as she could. At the age of nine, she even did an entire show, live-to-tape, with every child's idol at the time: Santa Claus. She was already exhibiting skills she would put to use a decade later in her own career.

On the radio, she was a ninth-grade guest on our show during "Take Our Kids to Work Day," and she made increasingly larger appearances on the "Christmas Eve at Erin's" show, a family tradition we felt blessed to have the opportunity to do, sharing in listeners' holiday traditions year after year.

After starting in Montessori, Lauren transferred to the public school system and flourished in an alternative elementary school. We were delighted when she was accepted into an arts high school. Rather than standing out as "different" in a non-specialized school, she was able to join the many kids who sang and danced in the hallways of Rosedale School of the Arts and performed regularly on stage. It was there that she met and became romantically involved with a boy her age who possessed the big voice of Bobby Darin and crooned Sinatra and Nat "King" Cole standards as easily as he belted out show tunes. For a time, it was a match made in musical heaven, especially for Rob and me: many were the hours we'd hear them duetting at the piano or from Lauren's room as they practised for the next big show or simply sang for the love of it. We knew full well how lucky we were to have a teen who was making happy noises almost from the moment she opened her eyes in the morning. We were always thankful.

Later on, we came to cherish even more the many recordings that were made of Lauren singing, some done in professional studios thanks to high-school outings. From Rosemary Clooney and the Mamas & the Papas to Leonard Cohen and Broadway hits, her range of interest was as wide as her talent was deep. She accompanied herself on piano and guitar and took cello lessons as well. But her deepest love was for singing, just as it was for me, although I can easily say that Lauren surpassed my vocal abilities long before she left her teenage years.

We can only hope that she would have found a way to experience the deep joy I felt in my broadcasting career too. She certainly was on a fast track to that end. Lauren had enrolled in a community college to begin (or, since she grew up surrounded by it, perhaps continue) her education in broadcasting. We'd offered her several choices in terms of what she might do when she completed high school: I suggested travel for a year, or perhaps an education on foreign soil. But she was as determined as she was talented, and radio was her career choice.

Did Rob and I try to encourage her to get a university education instead? The answer to that is *no*, and for two reasons. Rob completed a three-year program in university and ended up becoming a successful radio producer before leaving the industry to become a stay-at-home father; I was a product of a two-year program in the community college system and managed to reach the top of my industry. For that reason, I am a full supporter of the style of teaching and learning offered by the community college system and have donated twenty thousand dollars to my alma mater, Loyalist College in Belleville, Ontario, so that other promising young female broadcasters might have the help of an annual bursary to help meet their bills in a notoriously low-paying field. The hands-on and relatively fast-tracked education I received through community college served me extremely well. Why wouldn't we encourage our daughter to follow a similar path in terms of education, if she was determined to get into broadcasting too?

We worried that perhaps my career had set a poor example of the reality that Lauren could expect in the twenty-first-century world of radio. With the exception of one brief but particularly rocky period, what she saw in our home was a life of fulfillment that was rewarding in almost every possible way. Taking trips to luxurious resorts with listeners? Bucket list experiences like meeting one's idols? Why wouldn't someone want to try her hand at a life like this?

But our concerns were for her emotional and financial well-being. The radio industry she was about to enter was far different from the one in which I had admittedly been so very fortunate. When I began in radio, there were few women in the business, but the notion of male/female morning show teams was just coming to the fore. After all, why not emulate in the studio the same dynamic that was probably happening in the family car or over the breakfast table? If you were smart (or, in some cases, just willing to laugh at everything the witty "morning man" said), you could find yourself with an opportunity to prove what you were made of.

Was there discrimination? What do you think? It was the 1980s, and radio was a male-dominated industry; it still is, to a lesser degree, but there are more female executives now, and older women on the scene to whom newcomers can turn for advice and mentoring. But when I began, I felt like the real-life equivalent of silver screen dance legend Ginger Rogers: doing everything Fred Astaire did, as the old saying goes, except backwards and in high heels! I had to work harder even to be perceived as anything near equal to my older, male colleagues, but I also earned every step I took up that ladder. Early in my career, one manager called me the "c" word because I refused to take a lesser role than I'd been promised in our highly touted first male/female morning show in the Detroit radio market; another—after my first show on his station—threatened to break my toes if I ever referred to the station's music as "easy listening" again. (I didn't, and my toes are fine, thanks.) While I'd love to say that those moments from three decades ago aren't likely to be repeated in the era of #MeToo and more attentive human resources departments, the pressures have shifted. These days, there is a climate of constant uncertainty that comes with downsizing and restructuring, as radio stations rely on fewer people to do more work (in many companies), and the mental stress is mounting with every passing year. Of course, this is anecdotal; I only know it from friends and acquaintances who are in the radio business and experience the pressures daily.

I started out as a newscaster and moved into co-host positions in nearly every station where I worked, and the rewards—bonuses, excellent salaries and a high station profile—were eventually worth every breakdown, every dollar and every hour spent in the therapist's office. But what would this industry do to—or for—our daughter? She was soon to learn that the bank vault doors had slammed shut in a business that had increasingly been swallowed up by telecommunications giants. With a few notable exceptions, and many of them are now considering or approaching retirement, there were no more radio headliners being paid the kind of salaries that her mother had earned. One person was now doing the job of several, and making money that often meant a part-time job was necessary if the bills were going to be paid. Contrary, perhaps, to the lyrics of the 1979 song by the Buggles, video didn't kill the radio star—but conglomeration might. Still, despite our only half-hearted warnings, Lauren followed her own star. You can't fight fate, nature or nurture. She had broadcasting in her blood, simple as that.

At the beginning of her second year studying radio, Lauren was given the enticing opportunity to transition from part-time to full-time employment. We offered our advice (that the very purpose of community college is to get you a good job, and this was certainly going to be one), and she consulted other broadcasters for their opinions. Not one suggested that a piece of paper at the end of second year would help her future any more than taking this job doing news at a radio station in the nation's capital.

Okay, not just *a* radio station, *the* radio station at which I began my broadcasting career in earnest. When I was attending Loyalist College, I had worked part- and then full-time at an easy listening music station in Belleville. My sights were set on bigger things, though; almost from the time I began at the station, I was consulting with its news director about where I should go next. Perhaps it was my Armed Forces upbringing, but I was always eyeing my next move. How it came about is a story I love to tell as an illustration of the power of volunteering and the sheer luck that can come with being in the right place at the right time, and being prepared for the next opportunity.

In 1981 I was working at the Belleville station part-time, moonlighting at another job and determined to hold down a 4.0 average at school. My second year of college couldn't have been busier. Mornings, I would attend classes; it was final year, and any afternoon assignments could be completed on my own time, scarce as it was. In the afternoon, I was the deejay on a radio station that played mostly instrumental versions of your mother's or grandmother's favourite songs, a shift that lasted until 8 p.m., when we switched the station over to pick up a national show. A few nights a week, I'd run across the street and, playing in C—the only key in which I can play comfortably—I'd sit at the piano and entertain dinner guests at a French restaurant. Of course, tickling the ivories, even in one key, paid way more than my radio gig. You'd think I'd have taken the money and bought a few lessons, rather than just playing by ear.

In December of that same year, at the end of my course's third semester, I had a week off. I could have gone to my parents' house half an hour down the highway and gotten lots of rest and replenishing—and believe me, that was tempting—but instead, I screwed up my courage and made a phone call, offering to work at a radio station in Ottawa, a three-hour drive away. For free. Short-handed as they were over the holidays, and after speaking with my news director to get a reference, they accepted this rookie reporter. Just like that, when the next semester ended in April, I had a job waiting for me: a position paying fifteen thousand dollars per year as a nineteen-year-old anchor and reporter at the number-one radio station in Canada's capital. I was on my way!

And so it seemed to be a wonderful sign when Lauren was approached to fill the same position on that very radio station just over thirty years later. In a lovely bit of synchronicity, the man who had hired me in 1982 was now morning show host on CFRA. He proudly told listeners of Lauren's lineage and her mother's connection to the station. As flattering as it was to me that he remembered the six months that I was there, and what I went on to do in Windsor and eventually Toronto, perhaps, as it turns out, I was a little too much on Steve Madely's mind.

When the need arose, Lauren would fill in doing traffic on Steve's show. He was openly embarrassed and apologetic when, during an introduction of one of her reports, he called her *Erin* Davis, instead of Lauren Davis. She laughed and said she didn't mind at all. Then it happened again. When I say Lauren got the last laugh, I mean it: he was so red-faced at having called her by her mother's name that he offered on the air to give her five dollars every time he did it. She left work that day with a twenty-dollar bill in her wallet that she hadn't started with. I think Steve and I were more worried about her self-esteem than we needed to be; she found it funny and was quite happy with her compensation. She even hugged him and told him she thought it was a compliment to be called by her mother's name.

Rather than feel threatened, or worry that she would get lost in my shadow, Lauren told me that it dawned on her during her college years that perhaps I was more of a presence in the nation's media scene than she (or even I) had known. "Turns out, you're a bit of a big deal," she said to me one day in her usual teasing way. I was beyond proud to know that my daughter was seeing me through different eyes and would hopefully be seeking my counsel as a mentor and a veteran. Another level, another bond was forming in our relationship, and I loved that we had radio and its many joys and frustrations in common. The medium that had taken me away from her for so many years—first days of school when I was obligated to be on the air during the fall ratings-measurement period, and public events where I was in performer mode rather than that of mother—had also brought us closer together.

In the final Mother's Day card I received from Lauren, she wrote:

> *Thank you for being a limitless source of advice and inspiration.*
>
> *Love, Lauren.*

Sharing my last name may have helped her catch the eye and ear of the station's news director, Steve Winogron, but she earned every word of high praise, every raise and promotion, strictly on her own merits. Steve and I had worked together, having fun and making just a little bit of trouble when I was fresh out of college in 1982. Lauren had barely begun her second year of college in Ottawa when she landed an interview with this high-profile manager. That interview (after which she sent a thank-you note) went well.

Of hiring Lauren, Steve remembered that, sure, she got an interview because she was my daughter and he thought, *Okay, cool, maybe she's got something going for her.*

He told listeners on the day that Lauren died about the hiring process when it came to my daughter. "Very, very quickly, within five, six minutes of our conversation's start, she really stood out as someone who had a bright and promising future, a fantastic attitude. I made it clear to her, 'Look, despite the fact I know your mom and we're in touch from time to time, you're going to stand or fall on your own merits, your own hard work and attitude.'"

So intent was Lauren on not ever being accused of riding my coattails that she even debated dropping the Davis name on the air and taking a different last name. Eventually, however, she decided to keep Davis; she felt that her being in Ottawa and me in Toronto would significantly lower the chances of any such sniping. Even though she told Steve she was proud of and close to me, she was insistent upon being her own person, succeeding or failing on her own abilities.

In very short order, Steve's faith in Lauren was rewarded: she started out doing evenings and quickly progressed to the important midday shift on CFRA. As Steve put it, "I can't remember someone as young as her having so much responsibility and delivering—and, frankly, exceeding expectations."

Rob and I had nothing but the greatest faith in her abilities too. We could see clearly how talented and capable she was; she'd already shown judgment beyond her years as a barista at Starbucks. We lived almost kitty-corner to a Starbucks (like nearly everyone in a city), and at sixteen, while also attending high school, of course, Lauren was their youngest barista. One early weekend morning, she got to the store only to find that the manager had missed her alarm and slept in. Lauren didn't have a key, but she stood outside the store and greeted impatient and caffeine-deprived customers with an apology and a promise that if they returned, they could have a free coffee. I have no idea how or where she came up with that notion, but she was later honoured with the M.U.G. award (a pin saluting "moves of uncommon greatness") for her customer service that day. She would go on to earn another, and I couldn't have been prouder if she'd been honoured with the small white pin that accompanies the Order of Canada. She was much more blasé about it and feigned embarrassment whenever I brought up the pin. Or perhaps it was real embarrassment; that was Lauren. Just like her father, she was able to take almost anything in stride—unlike her more emotional (and some would say overly sensitive) mother.

Early on in her career, on an Easter weekend when we drove to Ottawa to visit her, a real pain in my heart—feelings of sympathy and loneliness—accompanied letting her go to work on the evening shift at CFRA as we wandered the streets of this beautiful, history-filled city. I knew that while we would soon be sleeping in our hotel bed, she'd be updating newscasts and websites, running that big, quiet, dimly lit newsroom all on her own. I remembered how night shifts felt when I first started there in April 1982, and I felt lonely on her behalf. I wish now that I'd offered to go in with a cup of coffee, just to keep her company. She'd have said, "Mo-therrrrrr . . ." and declined. It's not like I had security clearance or anything, but still, I wish now I'd asked. It would have made for more good memories.

Of course, just as was the case when I was working at CFRA, most of Lauren's co-workers were twenty, thirty or more than forty years older than she was. One such veteran of the news-and-talk format was John Brenner. On the day that her death became public, he, too, took to the airwaves to tell listeners how he felt about her presence in the newsroom. He began with noting how professional she was and how she treated her colleagues; he admired how she was so respected and loved by them. John pointed out Lauren's attention to detail and concern for accuracy and facts. Presentation came first; although this was information, she felt that it was a performance as well. He added that she was the "genuine article" and that, as a veteran, he found it remarkable how she rose and excelled at CFRA in such a short time.

At the time of her death, Lauren (who still went by Davis on the air but had taken her husband's last name on all official documents when she'd married twenty-three months earlier) was on a maternity leave from her position as midday news host on the radio station.

This posthumous post on her Facebook page by another co-worker illustrated to everyone what a formidable presence she had already become at CFRA.

Brock McDonough
to
Lauren Shirakawa
May 15, 2015

Lauren,
I don't think anyone who has worked in a newsroom for any length of time would ever call it "easy." I know I'm no exception.

I remember countless times, as a junior reporter just cutting his teeth at CFRA back in 2011, returning back to the newsroom after covering a "heavy" news story and feeling as though I was too overwhelmed by the content to boil it down to 40 seconds of quality on-air journalism. I would be stuck, either too embarrassed or too proud to ask around for help.

However, there would be lucky days when we shared the newsroom—when you and I worked together to produce journalism that I was immensely proud of—and those feelings would disappear with a snap. Regardless of the situation I was dealing with, you would always greet me with a smile, crack a quick joke or two, and in your own beautiful way, give me the confidence I needed to get the job done.

Brock went on to say that Lauren's belief in him helped jump-start his fledgling media career, and that she'd played a bigger part in that career than she could ever have known. Plus, she always made the newsroom fun.

From schoolmates to teachers, from former co-workers to an ex-boyfriend, those with whom Lauren had contact throughout her life made a point of reaching out and telling us how her maturity had affected them. Even her third-grade teacher, Steve Travers, wrote us and said that when the class was in somewhat of an uproar, Lauren's eyes would meet his like she "just got it." A classmate told us of her ability to bring opposing sides together when the situation with a high-school musical cast got a little too dramatic. Her high-school boyfriend, who came out when they were in college together—a situation that gave Lauren the first (and last) true heartbreak of her life—wrote to us in 2017:

> *I just miss her so much today. I feel such a deep-seated guilt for never thanking her properly, making sure she knew how many pivotal moments in my life she helped shape—not least of all accepting myself for who I am. She is still an incredible presence reminding me to stay true and honest in my relationships, now.*

I'm happy to say that we are on the road to mending our relationship with the young man who spent so many happy hours in our home and with our daughter during her teen years, but with whom Lauren had such a painful and acrimonious split. The long path of "what ifs" only leads to a litany of regrets, and the fact that he has reached out to us to share video and audio memories of our daughter and stories in which he reflects upon the job we did in her upbringing has given us comfort. If not a gift from beyond, then certainly a gift from beyond what we had expected.

Did we make mistakes as parents? Undoubtedly; we wouldn't be human if we hadn't. But in the months and short years after her passing, during the hours spent poring over her school projects and the journalling she did, I was touched by the amount of gratitude I witnessed for everything that came her way as a result of the life we'd chosen, the life we'd been given, even though there was always going to be a price. And that price could be summed up in four words: "be on your best." I didn't even have to add the word *behaviour*. She knew. It might as well have been on our family crest.

As for my own childhood, the family motto was probably "Get over it." These were words my mother, who had been born into the Great Depression, lived by. Mom had been thrust into the difficult position of being a wife constantly on the move because of her husband's job, with four daughters (each about two years apart) to raise, often on her own. Being the third of four, I had so little time with my mother that I can count the special times we had alone together on one hand. I cherished those times. As a child and teen, I adored my mom; regardless of what a nerd it may have made me, I'd tell anyone who would listen that she was my best friend. Admittedly, I didn't have a lot of friends, but I put her right at the top of my list. Making Mom laugh was one of my favourite things to do: I'd put on silly voices and imitate Carol Burnett's Queen Elizabeth or Eunice characters from TV to try to bring a smile to her face. It worked so often that humour became one of the strongest foundations of our relationship. I'd usually try to have a joke ready when I called my parents, even up until Mom's death at seventy-nine in 2012. It took the two of us too long to develop the kind of closeness I had wanted so badly, and I vowed to build a special bond much sooner with my own daughter, with time set aside for special one-on-one experiences.

For many years during Lauren's childhood, I was one of the guest hosts on an annual television fundraiser for a major charity. The Easter Seals Telethon provided us the opportunity to give back to our community, as well as to experience and enjoy the excitement of doing live television. It was also a teachable moment: I would take our daughter with me, and she'd help out behind the scenes, working side by side with and enjoying the company of other volunteers, including children her own age who were disabled. I loved that time together and so did she. Lauren got a chance to share in an experience that wasn't all about being "on" but about giving back. About using your small place in the spotlight to help contribute to a larger cause (in this case, raising money for children with disabilities), and about working as a team to do so. A telethon is made up of a beehive of volunteers who toil together to make possible a few hours of meaningful television; every person's role is important. Lauren needed to see first-hand the joy that could be felt by giving of one's time and one's self in order to help others to meet their goals. Year after year, our hours at the telethon gave us that, and we got to do it together. Best of all worlds!

One year, we decided to have a girls' night and booked into a downtown hotel the evening before I was to have an early makeup call and do a full twelve-hour TV shift. As we cuddled in bed (okay, I cuddled and she tolerated) and ate chips, we watched Faye Dunaway chew the scenery in the delightfully campy (albeit scary) *Mommie Dearest*. I remember asking her half-jokingly if I seemed a little less hard on her and less rigid, now that she had seen Joan Crawford.

In her typical teasing form, she smiled and gave me a begrudging, "Well, *maybe* . . . ," and we both laughed, crumbs flying everywhere. But I am sure she felt that those four words she had heard her father and me speak *sotto voce* through clenched smiles were just as effective as anything Ms. Crawford might have said. Those four words: *Be. On. Your. Best.*

That was our code when it was clear that listeners (or others who recognized me from our radio station's TV commercials) were around and looking at us. Call it a sixth sense or a heightened peripheral vision, but I could always tell when eyes were on us or heads had turned. Sometimes my husband would quietly joke, "Well, *she* almost walked into a pole," when we were being recognized. Now, don't get me wrong: I never, ever minded it. These people, these listeners, were the reason we had the life we lived. We were so fortunate to be in a position that people cared or wanted to say "Hello" that I never, ever begrudged them—not once.

Rob and I—and eventually Lauren—knew that it was part of the deal we had made: the radio station would advertise the morning show on television, in print and on billboards, and I, in turn, would be a full-time ambassador for the most-listened-to radio station in Canada. It wasn't a clause in a contract or something we had all agreed to in writing; it was just the way it was. And I couldn't have been more proud than to represent a station that was so much a part of Toronto's very fabric for nearly half of CHFI's sixty-some years.

Okay, I suppose, in a way, I *was* a little like Joan Crawford: fastidiously answering "fan" (I don't like that word and prefer *listener*) mail, which got easier through the years, with the advent of email. Thankfully, I was able to reach out and respond to every one of the listeners who got me where I was. I will state for the record, however, that although, like Joan,

I leaned in to the return of shoulder pads (at five foot ten inches tall, I probably had the silhouette of a corkscrew for much of the decade), I have absolutely no strong opinions on clothes hangers. With a teenager under our roof, we were just delighted when she used them.

Lauren knew that when she heard those words—"be on your best"—she had to do just that: behave herself. No tantrums or outbursts, not that she was prone to them anyway. Was it unfair of us to ask this of a child? While I'm sure there are as many opinions as there are parents, I honestly do not know. I am confident in what worked for us as a family. We reminded her often that, as in all areas of life, nothing was really free; there was a price to pay for the great seats at the musical theatre or the unusual opportunities that this public life afforded us. She knew very early on that there was always a cost, and that we'd have to pay it together.

My reason was not a need to appear perfect, or because I entertained some lofty view of myself that I felt my child should help propagate. I just knew human nature. Many was the time I had sat and heard a manicurist tell me how nasty so-and-so from the TV was (because her cousin had seen her in a lineup at the grocery store), or how someone from another radio station was a lousy tipper or a womanizer or a big drinker or . . . any number of stories about people that may or may not have been true. When it comes to gossip, that rarely matters. As someone whose image was recognizable, I believed (rightly or wrongly) that I was always a face for the radio station to which I was so loyal. Besides that, I was damned if I would let my family be the topic of somebody's dinner table conversation. I wasn't going to give anyone anything to dine on—not if we could prevent it with a simple agreement to conduct ourselves in a way that would make the radio station proud. We knew we were asking a lot of Lauren, but she knew that she was getting a lot. She was not an entitled child, nor did she expect anything. She was gracious, sensitive and grateful, writing thank-you cards and emails to strangers and family alike without being prompted. And she was almost always "on her best."

I had always promised her that, since she had grown up with me for a mother and with this life we all lived out loud, we'd make sure there was always money for therapy. We always laughed together when I said it, but it was true. She was never the born "people pleaser" that I was, always striving for approval and affection; she did things her own way. And yet, there she was as an adult, having chosen to work in a media role in which you literally succeed or fail based on whether people like you. I wish that time and fate had given us the chance to figure that one out together—just who she really was, this very special child of ours, to whom I wrote these words before her second birthday. The note is written on hotel stationery, so I was clearly away again and missing her, feeling guilty about the many miles between us.

My Beautiful Lauren:

Sometimes I wonder how God gave us someone so sweet
Such a droplet of perfection in an otherwise dry and
flawed existence.

Through all our worries and doubts your face shines
An angel permeating the clouds.
And though I know I can't spend the hours with you
I want to—I should—you love me
With the unconditional innocence and trust
That are my gift from you for giving birth.
I would do it a hundred times more
To pay you for the love you've showered upon me.
May I always be deserving—
And you forgiving.

Love, Mommy

CHAPTER 2
We Are (REaL) Family

Erin, Lauren and Rob, February 2013

D ESPITE A LOVE OF TRAVEL, I HAVE HAD NIGHT-mares about plane crashes ever since I was a child: both witnessing them and being in them. To this day, I watch flights coming in and out of our nearby airport (which, as twisted fate would have it, I can see from our living room window) and marvel at the fact that they stay in the sky or land where they should. Planes just scare me.

It stems from a horrific event that marred a favourite family outing, an air show, in Trenton, Ontario, where my dad was stationed. Eventually promoted to lieutenant-colonel, Dad would go on to become a squadron leader there (436 Hercules), and one of his favourite things was to take his family every year to the air show. For a town of fewer than twenty thousand in 1972, the show was impressive, at least to Dad, Mom and their four girls. I believe Dad was proud of the way the people on the base saluted him; he wanted us to see that he had earned their respect, that he was more than just our dad who came home to get laundry done, help Mom with a little discipline where needed, drink up with the boys on Friday nights and then fly away again.

The show was like so many others to which we'd gone or been dragged over the years: static displays of massive aircraft, a glider pilot who wafted through the skies to the tune of "Born Free" while the poem "High Flight" was recited over the scratchy PA system, plus stands where you could get a hot dog or popcorn if you could talk your parents into springing for it. I don't know when, during this particular show, it dawned on this nine-year-old that there was trouble above us, but I do remember I was watching through binoculars when two small Snowbird jets (part of Canada's military aerobatics team) clipped wings in what seemed to devolve into slow motion.

I'm guessing my father had seen what was coming, because he hurriedly made us turn our backs. We all obeyed and did not see lead solo Captain Waterer's small red, white and silver Tutor jet hit the ground in a fiery explosion. But those moments and their aftermath have stayed with me.

Was it because, as a child, a crash is the last thing you expect to witness at an air show? Was it because, until that very moment, it hadn't occurred to me that, as a pilot, my own father was so very vulnerable to forces of gravity and failures of humans and machines? Perhaps it was because we did not talk about it—not one word—at the sombre dinner table that night. When I tearfully told my mother that I wasn't hungry, she told me not to be ridiculous and to eat my dinner. It became clear to me that we weren't going to be discussing the plane crash we'd just witnessed—not then, not ever.

I know now that my mother was probably more shaken than we could have comprehended at that time. How could she not have been? As a pilot's wife, this was a fear she lived with every single day. She knew his life was not all shoe shines and salutes; my mom could tell how rough a flight he'd had both during his time in the Armed Forces and, later, as a commercial jetliner pilot by the perspiration stains on his shirts. She saw marriages around her breaking up and knew of other officers' wives within her circle who had become widows. But she put those fears away. She buried them as best she could and sometimes she even succeeded. For a time I did too.

In my late teens and early twenties, I embraced the risks and adventures that accompanied flying by signing up for every media opportunity to be a passenger in a small stunt plane that came my way, including a chance to ride in a Snowbird as a promotion for the Canadian International Air Show. I was so proud to be among those who hadn't lost their proverbial lunches during a flight, especially once I learned that women had a much better record in that regard than their male counterparts. But sadly, as if to remind me of my initial fears—and suggest that I should not put them away yet—just a few days later, a Snowbird would crash at the Labour Day air show, claiming the life of its young pilot. I remembered the number on its wing; it was the plane ahead of mine as we'd flown over an open SkyDome (now Rogers Centre) and a rapt Blue Jays crowd.

When I became a mother, my fear of flying (and landing) returned tenfold. Suddenly, it struck home that there was someone relying on her daddy and me to return safely. We made sure our wills were filled out. We called our loved ones from the airport. With parenthood, flying had taken on so many more worries and risks.

As Lauren grew, I managed to put those fears aside and embrace the adventure ahead. And there were so many adventures! How could I ever have imagined that the most terrifying thing to happen on one of these long-distance outings would occur not on an airplane but in my "happy place"—near a microphone, getting ready to wake up friendly, sleepy listeners?

Rob and I would tackle our radio station trips (and we must have been on a dozen of them) like a project in those first long hours of travel: I asked our promotions team to take a picture of each winner holding a sign bearing their name when they came to register prior to the week of travel. Using those pictures like the flash cards I'd once employed while prepping for final exams, Rob would quiz me on the names of the winners and their spouses. It was almost foolproof, and something that never failed to impress each listener. They would step off that big bus at the resort and I would hug them and say, "Lisa!" or "Derek!" Surprised, they would quickly look down to see if their nametags were showing (occasionally they were, but even a furtive glance would have given me away); in that instant, they knew I cared enough to learn who they were in advance. And I did care. I loved these listeners. Sure, the week in a foreign land outside of the comfort zone of our studio was a logistical and stressful challenge, but we were so grateful for the chance to bond with some of the people with whom we had shared countless mornings over the years. Besides, it seemed as though *they* already knew not only me and my radio partner and producer, but also my (jokingly) beleaguered husband, Rob. After all, they'd heard all about him for years. And, of course, they'd known Lauren since before she'd been born; we'd announced my pregnancy on the radio as my partner and I did a week of live shows from a frigid downtown department store window in November 1990. Lauren arrived four months later and was immediately nicknamed "Squidget" by my radio partner at the time, the one who described my pregnancy in terms of cattle: "Erin's going to freshen in the spring." Well, I did. And soon, Lauren's coos and cries would be heard on the air, as I did the show with her in my arms.

~~~

LAUREN's being an only child was almost as much her decision as it was nature's. Our determined little Aries made it clear as soon as she could express herself that she didn't want any siblings; I had visions of her mowing me down, like Damien taking down Katherine with his tricycle in *The Omen*. Eventually, it became clear to us that Lauren's desire would become our reality. Although we kept shuffling the deck, another child just wasn't in the cards. Without any sense of loss or missing out, we were contented and grateful to be just three: Rob, Erin and Lauren—or REaL Family, the name our freelance company would come to share.

Despite a work schedule that was taxing and a job that blurred the lines between who I was and what I did, we were afforded wonderful chunks of time for travel. Sometimes it was local: we'd often pluck Lauren from school at noon on Friday to make the more than two-hour drive to our cottage before the rest of the city attempted the same exodus. And we tried to use those car rides to broaden her education: they were spent in a way we deemed extremely productive—introducing our daughter to Beatles music one CD at a time (such a gloriously captive audience we had), and singing silly songs together in three-part harmony:

> *We're going to the cottage*
> *We're going to the cottage*
> *And when we get to the cottage*
> *Then we'll be at the caw-aw-tage!*

Sometimes we couldn't get out of the city early and would arrive at our chilly A-frame on a tiny northern lake after darkness had fallen. On those occasions, while Rob built a fire, I'd turn on the oven and heat a baking sheet to put between Lauren's sheets to warm her bunk bed, removing the sheet before she climbed in, of course. Truly, we were roughing it, *Little House on the Prairie*–style!

Like many who live in the crowded, cranky cacophony of an urban setting, we found ourselves counting down to the end of each week, when we could pack up and escape to a slower, quieter surrounding—one where we were more likely to be awakened by the lonely echoes of a loon's call than the incessant, panicked whines of city sirens. Perhaps it's because the aperture on our mind's eye was closing so gently, but our most vivid family memories were made in our Ontario cottage: Christmas mornings greeted by freshly fallen snow as we scurried to build a warm fire behind those stockings; New Year's celebrations spent laughing in a steaming outdoor hot tub; Easter morning hunts for eggs hidden among neatly stacked piles of firewood; summer days whiled away in slow boats to nowhere, and evenings spent singing while fending off mosquitoes around a firepit under the stars.

Twice, as money allowed, we moved our country life a little closer to the city. The proximity let us skip the long, congested drive back on a Sunday night, when the stiffness in one's neck increased in direct correlation to how close we drew to city limits. Instead, we were able to pack up and depart in the wee hours of the morning, before my radio show. On those coffee-fuelled drives, Lauren, clad in her pyjamas, would climb into the back seat, where a pillow, blanket and warm dog or two awaited. There, with Lauren safely buckled in, they would all sleep for the eighty-minute drive while I tapped on my dimmed computer and Rob navigated dark country highways. We used to joke that at 3 a.m. the only things to worry about on the roads were drunks and skunks. Our Monday morning commutes were, mostly, without incident, and we thank dollar-store adhesive deer whistles for preventing any more animal carnage than one raccoon and a few hapless mice. We can't say for sure that these tiny torpedo-shaped whistles that adhered to our front bumper or side-view mirrors were effective—they might also have fended off elephants, as we never hit one of those, either— but we wouldn't have taken a chance on our dark commutes without them and the high-pitched sound they emitted as the car moved. (And while the jury still appears to be out on the efficacy of these little whistles in alerting deer to a vehicle's proximity, you'll find many motorcyclists who rely on them for that added possible safety factor.)

ERIN DAVIS

Our cottages over the years were where we could be together, just the three of us: no pull of the internet (until much later) or my job, no sharing Lauren with her friends, at least not until their parents considered them old enough to join us. At the cottage, we could always be our true selves: singing, dancing, laughing, watching movies, sleeping in, baking—all without being under the curious eyes of strangers. Yes, passing boat tours would occasionally point out our home to the paying passengers, but that's why I rarely went a day without putting on at least a little makeup. And I always wore a cover-up with my bathing suit.

In a grade school project at age twelve, Lauren described her time at the cottage:

> On the weekend, the cottage is my favourite place to be. There's a load to do, whether it's kayaking on the canal or relaxing in the hot tub. I admit it: we're not really roughing it. But you can do yoga on the front lawn, go fishing, canoeing, cross-country skiing, swimming, water skiing, tubing and a lot more. There's something to do for every season or time of the year.
>
> I hope to keep this cottage until I move away; it's like a vacation spot for me, I love it up there. I wouldn't trade it for anything else, not for a huge amount of money. My heart belongs in the North.

Although her husband told us, after Lauren's death, that she regretted our choosing cottage time for our family over pursuing the invitation extended to her to play rep softball—

something for which she had an obvious talent—I was heartened to find that assignment in a neatly packaged school project binder. It seems that, at least at the time, she had forgiven us and had as soft a spot in her heart for our time cocooned together, away from the demands and noise of the city and the life we'd built there, as we did.

Besides our cottage getaways, long-distance travel always played a significant role in the life of our tight little trio. Perhaps that stems from my childhood, when the smell of jet fuel meant there was an adventure in the near future: a trip west to see my grandparents, or even a move to Great Britain. We moved six times before I was a teen, and I changed schools three times in fifth grade alone! It gave me something to blame for my shortcomings in math—and for that, I'm grateful. Growing up in such a nomadic way can make you shy or extroverted or both, in my opinion: either you're forced into a place of putting yourself out there trying to make friends among a classroom or a school full of strangers, or you retreat into a corner and hope no one notices the "new kid" and makes fun of her. I ended up being a combination of the two: someone who's full on when the curtain opens, but with a distinct hermit-like streak the rest of the time. It's why cottage life suited us so well.

Before we had Lauren out of diapers, we had her in an airplane seat. As a trial, we took part in a brief charity flight from Toronto to Niagara Falls and back that would let her become accustomed to the noise, movement and pressure changes that accompany air travel. She became a seasoned flyer quickly and, thanks to her interest in colouring and puzzles, was easily amused during longer flights. From journeying to Walt Disney World in Florida to joining us on far-flung listener trips with our radio station, Lauren was always ready to pack her blankie and her rolling suitcase and head for the skies.

Twice during Lauren's childhood, Rob gathered up our daughter, her suitcase, a little TV/VCR combination that could run in the car, and a few toys and headed south to Florida, just the pair of them on a two-day drive. I was unable to take March Break off (ratings were taken at that time) and so the inseparable duo took advantage of the free time to visit grandparents who were wintering in northern Florida. They made wonderful memories and ate at restaurants I might have tried to talk them out of (probably way more than I ever heard about)—places with "waffle" or "all you can eat" on the sign. One year while Lauren was with her dad on a road trip, I was hosting CHFI listeners at a Backstreet Boys concert in Toronto. She should have been there! But when it came to a choice between her daddy and BSB, BSB would have come in second. Those road trips just helped to strengthen the bond between Rob and Lauren.

Admittedly, not every family trip was a success. One Christmas, we decided it would be magical to wake up in the Rocky Mountains. We flew to Edmonton, Alberta, took a train to Jasper Park Lodge and spent a week there. Despite the opportunity to ski with her dad on Christmas Day, share a glass-topped train ride through the snow-dusted Rockies and skate with her tentative mother on a silvery lake with a glorious mountain backdrop, this wasn't one of our daughter's favourite family memories. She had arrived at the age of wanting to be where her friends were, and that was not in the mountains. So much for that attempt at a Great Canadian Christmas.

Another trip that began with high hopes but ended up being a distinct "meh" on the scale of teen excitement was one we took to Hawaii. Rob and I decided to treat my parents and Lauren to a stay at a condo in Kona. The crashing waves, dramatic sunsets and staged luau at a nearby hotel paled in comparison to the internet in the condo building's lobby, it seemed. Nice try, folks. Reluctantly, we soon gave up on trying to plan family vacations. Besides, we'd really had more getaways than we could have hoped for, given how busy my work and freelance life was.

That is, until it wasn't busy at all.

Perhaps that's why one trip stands out as a shimmering chapter in our family's story. It came against the backdrop of a very dark and rare period of unplanned unemployment (you'll read more about this later). It was July 2004, and my second consecutive summer off. I had a fill-in position at a new radio station lined up for the fall, so we decided to take advantage of this period without alarm clocks and mandated bedtimes. Apart from the previous summer, when we didn't really feel much like travelling after having suffered the shock and humiliation of my firing, I'd never had a vacation that lasted more than two weeks. While my one-time partner Mike Cooper spent most of his career avoiding a vacation longer than a week, as he (wrongly) feared that was all the time it would take station management to replace him, two weeks was the minimum duration I needed to wind down from a highly stressful existence, and then just begin to replenish and rejuvenate in preparation for my return to work. One particularly short-sighted boss warned me that if I took longer than two weeks, no one would remember my name when I got back. How grateful I was to have the opportunity to prove him wrong. When I actually returned to hosting a full-time radio show after more than a year off the air, we were astonished when it became obvious through radio ratings statistics that audiences had come back with me. But despite this time of uncertainty and concern about our long-term future, taking the opportunity to travel as a family and see some of the world together was irresistible. It was time to stop obsessing and take advantage of the gift of time that we had been given.

After scanning numerous travel brochures, we booked two back-to-back bus tours of Europe, cramming in visits to sixteen countries in the space of one month. Lauren was about to enter eighth grade and wasn't yet interested in boys, the nascent internet or anything but exploring the world with us. It was the trip of a lifetime—hers and ours. Much to her annoyance (and amusement), I'd wake her up every morning playing Ringo's drum solo from "The End" on her backside. In part thanks to some small hotel rooms, we were as close as three people could be, this REaL family of ours. Except for her gradual burnout on touring churches (as they did for many travellers, the letters *ABC* came to stand for "Another Bloody Cathedral" or, alternatively, "Another Bloody Castle"), it was all we could have hoped for.

It was a true gift to us, that month together, on so very many levels. Later, as her high-school studies opened up more of the world to her, Lauren would say, "I've been there!" when new locales and their histories were introduced. We were grateful for the opportunity and the ability to have taken that trip. It served both as a foundation for Lauren's future and as a perfect example of taking lemons and making *limoncello*.

Travelling together was just one way that we tried to seize the day when it came to life with our daughter. We also sought musical experiences that we hoped would become memories to last a lifetime. Lauren had been a Beatles fan since the days we rocked her to sleep to their songs, so it was a culmination of all of our dreams when we steeled ourselves for the exorbitant second-hand ticket prices and bought front-row seats to a Paul McCartney show in Toronto. I'd been unable to buy more reasonably priced tickets on the floor fairly close to the stage, so I bit the bullet. It was one of the best decisions of my life.

As I stood arm in arm with Lauren, tears ran down my cheeks when Sir Paul played "Penny Lane" during the pre-show sound check (attendance was a privilege that came with our front-row seats). Another frill that came with the VIP package we'd bought was vegan dinner before the show. It was tasty enough, I suppose, but our appetites had really been whetted for a quick appearance by the man for whom we'd adopted Meatless Mondays in our own home. Alas, it was not to be. It's probably for the best: I likely would have turned into a blathering version of Chris Farley's interviewer in a famous *Saturday Night Live* skit: "So, remember when you were with the Beatles? That was awesome!" Just as well.

Later, as we sat only a few feet from one of the greatest songwriters and showmen of our time, Paul made eye contact with and winked at Lauren while he sang. As if to prove to us (and everybody else there) that this was all really happening, the giant screens flanking the stage flashed our beaming faces as we sang along with the outro of "Hey Jude." While we'd end up regretting that moment of unexpected exposure the next day, that night our feet didn't touch the sidewalk as we made our way home through the busy Toronto streets. I expect that sharing that experience with us meant as much to our nineteen-year-old daughter as she meant to us. When she was ten years old, she'd written in a school project:

> *Since I was two years old, I have been trained to say that the Beatles were the best band in the whole wide world! Later in my life I realized they were. I stand by what I say. While other kids my age are into the latest bands, I'm booming "Strawberry Fields Forever" on my stereo.*
>
> *I will continue to love the Beatles for the rest of my days. I will play the Beatles for my children and their children and their children. The Beatles are a true legacy that needs to be recognized by more people today. The Beatles will rock on in my heart for an eternity.*

As if to remind us once again that there's always a price to pay for the gifts we've been given (even though in this case the tickets were not gifts, but the ability to afford them most certainly was), I received an email the morning following the McCartney concert. A man who was sitting far, far back in the massive Air Canada Centre wrote me a letter dripping with disdain, and in a tone so angry it made me shake as I read it at work in our radio studio. Because we'd been shown sitting in the front row, the man assumed that I hadn't paid for but had been given those precious tickets—or, worse, that we were occupying seats meant for our radio station's listeners. He couldn't have been more wrong, and I let him know that in an email response sent shortly after I'd read his. We had paid dearly for those seats and—until he'd written to us—had felt nothing but joy for having done so.

Wrong as it was, I let that man's incorrect assumptions and misdirected anger at being, as he later put it in a letter of apology, "on the outside of the bars looking in" taint the perfection of that night. I know full well that letting it bother me to this day is my own fault, and that I'm forgetting the "it's his movie" lesson don Miguel Ruiz taught us in that tiny gold-mine of Toltec wisdom called *The Four Agreements*. I should forgive—or at least forget—someone's taking an exquisite, golden moment in our family's life and tarnishing it with his own dark and bilious thoughts. Let's just say that, as with so many other things, I'm working on it. And those efforts to set aside the vitriol of strangers would be strenuously challenged again, in ways Rob and I couldn't have imagined, during our darkest days after Lauren's death.

From the early years of her education, I tried to share with our daughter *The Four Agreements* and many other words of wisdom. I would often tell her that the things people call her or think of her are none of her business, and that their perception of her is not truth. If I needed to really make my point, I would use a line that I often thought would make the basis for a good children's story one day—a story I would call *You Are Not Purple*.

At its heart was a metaphor I would share with Lauren. If someone at school said that she was stupid or that her name was funny, I would ask her, "Are you purple?"

After the mandatory eye roll, she'd say, "No . . . but . . . ," and I'd ask her again. And again.

Until she got what I was saying: "They might as well be saying that you are purple. You and I can both plainly see that they're wrong, because you are not purple. So why would you listen to what they have to say?" I hope that helped her; I'd like to think she would have tried to pass that same lesson along to her own little boy.

There are many lessons that I've learned through years of therapy and searching for ways to survive in a business where you are targeted for having an opinion, for being successful, for being a woman—just for being *you*. Just as people can like or love you without knowing you, they can also dislike or hate you: the yin and yang of the universe, as always. And it was this Buddhist-based philosophy of lightness and darkness working together that we tried to instill in our daughter. Most of all, though, I hope we were able to show her the importance of giving, of volunteering, of showing compassion and empathy. We only wanted to raise a good human being, someone who made the world better by being a part of it. In keeping with Lauren's spiritual but not religious upbringing, we attended yoga classes together, hands touching during the quiet moments of the corpse pose, Savasana. On long car rides to the cottage, we'd sometimes discuss the "never judge" mantra I tried (mostly in vain) to adopt when I dipped my toes into the popular teachings of Deepak Chopra. She got used to the smell of Nag Champa incense in the house and cottage, the ever-present candles and India-influenced music on the stereo that meant I was probably in a good mood, centring myself (or something). Lauren and her dad waved goodbye to me at least a half-dozen times as I embarked on retreats in Sedona and Tucson, Arizona, and Essex, Connecticut, where I tried to seek answers from within (as well as above) and equip myself with tools to grapple with and ease the stress, anxiety and depression that would so often come home to wipe their grimy boots upon my heart and mind.

There's little doubt that depression runs like a rivulet of thick, black sap through the veins of my family tree. My maternal grandfather, an accomplished western landscape artist, suffered from dark mood swings—so much so that he built a studio apart from the small house he shared with my grandmother in the flood-prone lowlands of a small Alberta oil town. There, he could escape to paint, to listen to his music, to read his Zane Grey western novels, to score musical parts for his dance band and to brood, coming out occasionally for meals and brief, terse conversations with my tough-as-nails grandmother.

Just like her dad, my mother was an accomplished painter. Also like her father, she was prone to depression and mood swings that were alleviated in her later years when she saw what antidepressants did for me and other members of our family. Before I learned about serotonin levels and heredity possibly being the cause of Mom's moods, I attributed the darkness in her to the fact that she was so often a single parent; my father was frequently away, leaving Mom to raise four daughters on her own. How she and so many other Armed Forces wives in the same predicament didn't end up stuck in the bottom of a martini shaker is beyond me. But she knew that between parenting and her job as a registered nurse, she had no time for that kind of escape—or, really, much fun at all. Our somewhat peripatetic life of being transferred among provinces and even countries left Mom without a strong social network. Prone to introversion, she didn't make friends easily. She was often alone, seemingly disappointed in her life and depressed.

As you might imagine, that made growing up around our mother a challenge: Which one of us—me, one of my three sisters or our often-absent father—was she angry with? What had we done to incite it? And would it be better to disappear until her mood passed, or to try to find a way to make her happy? Being raised by someone who can be emotionally unpredictable puts a child in the position of Junior Storm Watcher: Are there clouds forming? Which way is the disturbance moving? And how do we best avoid being affected by whatever is coming our way? My best tool was humour.

I've come to realize that Mom's tendency toward occasional emotional darkness, which was likely as prevalent within her DNA as her blue eyes, and my inherent need either to stay under her radar or make her laugh helped hone a sense of humour that would serve me well in both my career and my own future survival. So did being the third of four children, constantly trying to come up with new ways to get my parents' attention. I wasn't alone in these attempts, and this built a kind of division-forming rivalry between my siblings and me. Whether by design or accident, my sisters and I didn't grow up supporting and loving each other; instead, we competed over who could earn the highest marks or the loudest and most numerous accolades. It was a no-win situation: even if you came out on top—and each of us did, in our own ways and times—there was little recognition that you'd done so. What were you going to accomplish next? If you achieved 90 percent, what happened to the other 10 percent? I thought that was a joke or a cliché until Dad asked if we wanted to be passengers in a plane in which the pilot only knew 90 percent of how to land. Good point, but . . .

The effort on my parents' part at equanimity among the offspring was still going strong well into our adult years. A clear illustration of this came in 2015, when the Toronto Blue Jays invited a few Rogers media personalities, myself included, to join our dads in a Father's Day discussion about parental pride. My father, flown in from several provinces away, answered the producer's question about why he was proud of me by saying that he had four daughters of whom he was equally proud. He listed off their accomplishments (and, eventually, my own) as I sat there sinking into my seat. It wasn't that I was embarrassed or disappointed; I just knew that—after all of the time, effort and expense they'd put into getting Dad to the Rogers Centre to film this bit—they weren't getting the tape they wanted. Dad had spent his entire fifty or so years as a parent trying to distribute whatever praise there might have been on an equal basis. TV cameras or not, I was still only one of four: seemingly nothing less and nothing more. Having had only one child, I can't say whether I'd have been any different.

I believe it is every parent's hope to improve upon the methods by which we were raised, and perhaps be the mother or father we wish we'd had. I like to hope I would have encouraged each child's fulfillment as an individual without nurturing a sense of competition. Is that possible, I wonder, or is it in a child's nature to try to outdo a sibling? As I say, I cannot know.

~~~

WHETHER my own mom and dad nurtured our sibling rivalry or it arose on its own, perhaps it was because of that ongoing struggle to stand out that each of us has excelled in her own way: my eldest sister by five years achieved firsts as a woman and musical conductor in the Canadian Armed Forces and is now a fully accredited gemologist; my next oldest sister, three years ahead of me, has battled systemic lupus erythematosus since her midtwenties with success and determination (and got to sing with her choir at Carnegie Hall!); and my younger sister by three years achieved rock star status in the field of sales and marketing. We all worked hard in our attempts to make our parents proud, but we fell short when it came to building close bonds with each other—bonds that for so many siblings come, well, naturally. My mother's greatest wish in her later years was that her "girls" would get along. And, in truth, we did, for the most part, and continue to do so to this day. We just aren't super-close—reverberations of childhood bitterness on many of our parts, I'm guessing. Perhaps that's one of the reasons why, on several occasions in her teen and adult years, Lauren looked at the conflicts that arose among my sisters and me and expressed gratitude that she was an only child.

Despite those occasional exclamations and her insistence from such an early age that she did not want siblings, Lauren wasn't always happy being a "limited edition." We were fortunate that she had a second cousin five years her senior who would gamely go along with us for trips to the cottage, playing the role of big sister. Lauren never wanted a younger sibling—just an older one! All of the benefits without the conflict? Quite a great arrangement, we thought. Whether it was an occasional would-be older sister or experiences we hoped would be indelible, Rob and I gave Lauren everything that we could, without going so far as to "spoil" her (or so we hoped). Our mantra was that if we were going to say "no" it had to be for a reason, and not just "because we said so." We tried to parent her with reason, understanding, discipline and mutual respect, but not with fear or deprivation imposed just for the sake of authority. We taught her that actions always have consequences and that the feelings of others should always be considered first and foremost. We were also adamant that she should never, ever take for granted the many gifts and good fortune with which our family had been blessed. And that awareness extended to her own expectations.

We always told her—both when she was a teen and later, when she was an adult living on her own—that we truly loved to give her things (especially surprises, like the puppy she received on her seventh birthday), but that we would stop the moment she started to "expect" them. She took that rule to heart. When Lauren moved to another city to start college and eventually her career in radio, Rob and I were comforted, and lucky enough, to be able to provide her with a townhouse to share with her boyfriend at the time, as well as another paying tenant. We wanted her to be safe and renting from us, rather than at the mercy of some stranger as a landlord; we knew Rob could take care of her needs, even if it meant she was Skyping us images of a stove that wasn't working or a furnace that needed some kind of tweaking. And she was, as always, grateful.

In 2013, Rob, Phil, Lauren and I were able to pool our efforts and ideas and give Lauren the wedding of her dreams. The fact that we have a long-time family friend who also happens to be an event planner (and just two years later would be called upon to aid with funeral plans) certainly helped.

In addition to the wedding, we helped Lauren and Phil with the purchase of their new home. All cash wedding gifts (which was what they had requested) were matched by us; that was our promised gift to them. Soon, the young newlyweds were planning on building a future in a small new home on the outskirts of Ottawa, the city where they'd met at college. But with the exception of the wedding money they received, they were intent on making their own way in every sense. Lauren was responsible, thrifty and appreciative of everything that she had, no matter how little or how much.

We felt no need to hold back with Lauren. Not with money, not with love, not with experiences. Why would we? Everything we'd worked for and possessed would one day go to her anyway, we figured; why not be benevolent when we could all share in the enjoyment of what we'd earned, and see how much of an impact those gifts would have on her life?

But perhaps there was more to it than just wanting to feel the joy of giving. Did we have a sense, somehow, that there was an expiry date on the time we'd have to share our gifts—whether making possible a trip to the Yukon, about which she'd done a school project and with which she was fascinated, or a pilgrimage to Strawberry Fields in New York City's Central Park, to leave a guitar pick in memory of John Lennon? As we look back on our twenty-four years together, we consider that maybe we had a premonition that our time with Lauren was going to be limited. Perhaps on some level, she did too.

Rob and I hadn't considered that Lauren would want to take on motherhood—at least not right away. She'd never babysat and had never been one of those children who gravitated toward babies or even playing with dolls. She saw them as somewhat perplexing and occasionally nasty little creatures who cried, were disagreeable and needed changing all of the time. In some ways she was right, but when you have your own, it's a whole different game of crying and stomping and pooping. You love them so much you just don't care.

Although the expansion of their little family was obviously not about us, the timing of Lauren's pregnancy, a year and a half after she and Phil married, came at a sensitive moment in her father's life: when they told us, Rob was less than a week away from turning sixty, and he was not taking it especially well. A seventeen-year-old goalie trapped in the body of a silver-haired man (who still plays hockey two or three times a week), Rob was already quietly reeling from the gut punch of hitting a new decade when Lauren and Phil sat us down in the living room of the cottage where we'd gathered a huge family group less than two years earlier, on the morning after their wedding. This time, though, they weren't opening a gift—we were: a small hand-painted frame with BABY on it and a picture of an ultrasound inside.

I realize now that due to some sort of state of shock and disbelief, we weren't as outwardly elated about Lauren's announcement as she and Phil had undoubtedly hoped we'd be. When we figured out what the gift symbolized, my hand flew to my mouth. "Oh!" was all I said. And then, in that split second, I realized there would be no "take two." Making matters worse, I knew we'd already failed to provide the Hollywood moment that was supposed to be our reaction when they'd announced two years earlier that they were engaged. I still shudder over that misstep on our part and remember it clearly.

Lauren had called from Ottawa and asked us to go on Skype. But I'd been having trouble with it for a few days and said I'd rather just chat by phone. So she proceeded to tell us that she and Phil were engaged!

Rob and I stared at each other in silence for what I'm sure was far too long, or at least felt that way to both parties in this conversation. For a great many reasons, most of them having to do with her age and our lofty dreams for her, we had neither expected nor welcomed the idea of Lauren marrying someone she had met such a short time before. But who were we to talk, having gotten engaged (the first time) three weeks after our first date? Fearing I would put my foot in my mouth, I took a breath and said, "Honey, we're going to have to call you back, okay? This is a big surprise."

She said, "Um, well, sure," clearly disappointed that we weren't elated.

We hung up and took a deep breath. It wasn't that we didn't approve of her choice of husband—far from it—we were just caught completely off guard. It hadn't occurred to us that Lauren would want to settle down so quickly, and with just the second man (and, as it turned out, the first straight man) with whom she'd had a romantic relationship. It all seemed so sudden. From where we sat, it felt as if she was rushing into the union after her husband-to-be had comforted her in the aftermath of a nasty breakup with her high-school sweetheart, live-in boyfriend and musical collaborator. Was she sure? Did they really know each other well enough?

We called Lauren and Phil back within five minutes to congratulate them both with what I hope was enough enthusiasm and sincerity to make up for the fact that we'd cut the first call short. I just wanted to make sure that, in my shock, I didn't say the wrong thing, or words that would be brought up in heated moments in the years to come. Goodness knows I have a long memory when it comes to things that have been said in the heat of the moment, and I had no doubt Lauren did too. After all, there was my reaction three years earlier to her telling me she'd decided to get a tattoo. We laughed about it later, but it served to underline how careful I learned to be about blurting out an opinion.

Lauren's teen years were much like mine in terms of not having a rebellious or "I hate my parents" stage, though that's not to say she didn't exercise her independence or push boundaries. Of course she did. But that came when she moved out and decided to do what so many young men and women are doing: she got tattoos. With the first few—Japanese symbols of harmony on her inner forearms and a heart/bass-clef combination on her foot—she would call the day before and tell me what she was getting. When she realized that all I was going to do was try to talk her out of it she stopped asking my opinion, and that's when I stopped offering it. After all, what would be the point in criticizing her decision after something that permanent had been done? Her tattoos all turned out to be tasteful and discreet, and in the end, they were her choice.

Now she was sharing with us news that would again deserve a measured and careful response. Don't get me wrong! We wanted Lauren and Phil to know how very happy we were that they were happy, and that we would support them in any way they wanted. We just needed a little time to get used to the idea, was all. I don't know what the timeline is to get "on board" with the notion of your only child taking a spouse—and one whom you really hardly know—but I would like to think that we did so without too much delay. We wanted the world for her—just as all parents do for their children.

Those same thoughts about using carefully chosen words ("be on your best") were exactly what went through my mind when we were told we were going to become grandparents for the very first time.

Months earlier, during one of the few occasions upon which we had talked about maternity leaves and family planning, I had gently expressed to Lauren my private hope that she and Phil would hold off until they'd had some significant time to really get to know each other. Although I wouldn't have put it so bluntly to her, I wanted to make sure that this was a union that was going to last. Of course, as I told her, we supported her in her marriage and respected the hard-working, loyal and soft-hearted man she had chosen. We made sure she and Phil had the wedding all four of us wanted her to have, and we did everything we could to show her new husband that he was welcome in our family. We so hope that he felt a part of our tight little unit. I know he understood that she was Rob's and my world. How do you watch your child step into a huge new chapter of her life with no worries or cares? Still, we knew she'd be fine. They'd be fine.

With every passing year, our love for and bond with our son-in-law has become stronger. Distance and his demanding work schedule meant that we'd hardly had a chance to get to know him before everything was shattered; this new family arrangement—without the bond of Lauren's love and understanding cushioning us all—was not how things were supposed to be. Explaining what we meant when we spoke in the code of a language we'd built in love over twenty years with our girl. Unveiling our intentions—always good—when it came to their little family. "You take care of your people and I'll take care of mine" was Lauren's philosophy when it came to parents and in-laws. But now we found ourselves trying to communicate directly with someone in a dynamic none of us had signed up for. Fortunately, time has opened more doors—including of communication—between the quiet, thoughtful man Lauren chose and the parents that were chosen for her. We have come to love and understand each other even more than we did in the beginning, sharing in the knowledge that, above all, our deepest affection lies with that sweet little boy that Lauren carried with such care and loved so very much. With a tie that strong, we all know that we can weather everything, and that our bonds will only strengthen with time as we move into the future together. We are thankful every day for little Colin and for the beautiful job Phil is doing in raising him with a steady, loving hand, endless patience and a love and devotion unsurpassed by any father for his child. Come hell *and* high water—quite literally.

~~~

MY other concerns about becoming a grandparent were based in fear instead of reality, and it is with some shame that I share this with you. In Toronto's youth-conscious business of radio, there were, I believe, no other grandmothers doing morning shows, and I was afraid of suddenly appearing to be aging out of our demographic, even though I was still well within the twenty-five to fifty-four age group that we pursued so diligently. Rather than embrace this as a challenge and opportunity to expand and change minds about what a grandmother looks, sounds and acts like in the twenty-first century, I feared the snide comments and the rampant ageism that pervades the world of women in media. My fears were not without justification: after all, when I'd been let go at forty from my job at the same station (to which I returned joyfully two years later, as you'll read), the radio industry gossip boards and websites were filled with comments about me being old and "menopausal." As if what's happening with someone's menstrual cycle has anything to do with job performance! Talk about misogyny. Besides, I *wasn't* menopausal—although I suspect those making the comments had limited experience with females (perhaps through online porn or video games) upon which to base their assessment. Whatever.

When I was let go, I'd felt that it was, at least partially, for age-related reasons. That suspicion was seemingly borne out when one of the managers said he was bringing in the new morning team—and I kid you not, this is the word he used, whether ironically or accidentally—to "youthanize" the station. Actually, from a ratings standpoint, what happened next could more accurately be described by the homonym of that word.

From age forty onward, I believe I was in my prime as a broadcaster—strong enough, finally, to stand up for myself and to defend my opinions. I was fortunate to be able to prove my worth to myself, and anyone signing my paycheque, every day until I decided, at age fifty-four, to step away from my career and the spotlight that had accompanied it. I had always meditated on the universe giving me a sign so that one day, as designer Bill Blass so perfectly put it, I would "know when to leave the party."

There were several clues that the party was winding down. Things had changed in my workplace: my close friend and amazing partner of eleven years had left the show to spend time with his wife of over forty years (and childhood sweetheart), who had been diagnosed with cancer. I should take a moment to point out how rare it is for a radio host still to be with his or her first spouse after several decades. Especially when you're talking about a host like Mike Cooper, who had every temptation thrown at his feet during his years as a hotshot rock jock whose boy-band good looks and deep voice made him a woman-magnet for decades. (With a wink, he'd want to make sure you know that he still gets propositioned in the Home Depot he frequents in small-city Ontario.) After Mike left, work suddenly began to feel like, well, work. The easy ebb and flow, give and take, and laughter were no longer as frequent or as genuine; the trust, compassion and honesty I'd felt from my partner had disappeared with him, and I found myself unable to go in and just have fun. Much of it had to do with where Rob and I found ourselves in our lives: I was just tired. Tired of trying to choreograph and learn new dance steps, tired of donning the happy mask, tired of being tired. Some people listening thought that I was sad (or that I should be, anyway), and so that is what they heard. But they were wrong. I was finding joy in the day-to-day routine and comfort of a radio show. But eventually, even that ran its course.

The beginning of the end of my time on Toronto radio came on November 9, 2016, the same morning the world was coming to grips with the news that a reality TV show host had, it seemed, been elected US president. That was the day I had to announce that I was leaving CHFI. In no way were the two stories comparable, of course; it was just unfortunate timing, from an emotional point of view. I was already distraught about current affairs and wasn't quite ready to deal with what I was going to be saying about my own life that depressing morning, but the date had been selected by those above me, who had planned a multi-level public relations operation to coincide with my news. So, things went ahead as planned, and it was announced that my final show would be broadcast on December 15, live from a ballroom in Toronto's castle-like landmark, Casa Loma.

Through the hard work of dedicated co-workers and our dear friend and producer Ian, the final show was just as perfect as it could be—even with a nasty snowstorm preventing some faraway guests from making the trek downtown in the wee hours of that Thursday morning. With echoes of our wedding day, for which I rented my dress, I borrowed a gorgeous black ball gown for the event. After all, I reasoned, when was I ever going to need a ball gown again in my new "reWired" life? It was a beautiful send-off, featuring videos from entertainers with whom I'd crossed paths over the years as well as mayors of Toronto and nearby Markham. At the end of the show, after I'd said my goodbyes, the strains of the Beach Boys classic "God Only Knows" filled the room. In a moment inspired by Kristen Wiig's final appearance as a cast member on *Saturday Night Live* in 2012, I was danced out of the ballroom by a chuckling Mike Cooper, then our sweet, tearful producer Ian and, finally, by my dear, handsome, tux-edoed Rob. Emerging from the dim ballroom with its regal dark-wood walls into a brightly lit solarium in this elegant castle, I sobbed as the song ended and we stopped dancing. These weren't tears of sadness prompted by the end of my career; instead, they were, as the saying suggests, an expression of gratitude for the fact that it had happened.

Getting up at 3:15 in the morning to do something you no longer feel absolute joy in doing is not what you work thirty-five years for. I felt that I'd done what I needed to do: I'd proved that you can survive anything and do it with humour, tears and what I hoped was some form of grace. It was time to let someone else awaken to three alarms and head off to work each day in the dark, dodging the drunks and skunks and planning every single day around how much sleep you'd get in a nap or at night. It was time for a new dawn, and I planned to sleep through it as often as possible. And it was all made necessary by the events of that one May morning when we thought all we'd have to worry about was the quality of the broadcast going back to Toronto from a beautiful Jamaican hotel.

One and a half years later, Rob and I had arrived at a place of peace about the changes that lay ahead. The only truly sad note that morning was the feeling of missing the one person whose absence had somehow made all of this change necessary: our Lauren.

CHAPTER 3

The End of the Beginning

Lauren and Phil, summer 2014

THIS LISTENER TRIP WAS STARTING OUT AS SO very many others had: we'd landed safely on Saturday, been transferred smoothly to a beautiful, lush resort on the island paradise of Jamaica and been welcomed like VIPs. By the following night, we had greeted our listeners with cool towels, cocktails and a cake that had *Happy Mother's Day* written on it in icing. We had shared time at the microphone introducing ourselves and our staff and expressing our hopes that our guests would join us at six the next morning for the show that was being broadcast back to Toronto.

As night fell, partner Mike, producer Ian and I felt well prepared for the shows ahead. We'd taped a bit with a bartender—we'd nicknamed him "Dr. Phil"—who had a remedy for every ailment we brought up: rum. Mike (whose wife's illness had forced him to travel solo this time) joined Rob and me for dinner at a teppanyaki restaurant where the chef splattered me with hot oil while flipping his utensils. It's funny the things you remember from those benign moments before your life changes forever.

For months after our daughter's heart stopped beating I would awaken from a restless night's sleep and look at the clock wondering, *Is this the time she died?* It was as though I felt I should have known, somehow, that our daughter was leaving this earthly realm at the exact time that she did. How could I have slept through the tearing away of part of myself from this life? How could any mother? *How did my heart not stop too?* I wondered again and again. I asked myself and the universe how my own life could have come to what seemed like such a screeching halt without my even stirring in my bed. *I was her mother. I should have felt it happening. I was there when her life began, and I wasn't with her when it ended. I didn't even know.*

At the time that Phil was trying to wake Lauren and then frantically calling 911, Rob and I were trying to get just a few more hours' sleep before one of the more stressful aspects of an already tightrope-walking-over-hot-coals kind of job: doing a live radio show from a foreign country in a hotel ballroom filled with fifty or sixty contest winners, and a much larger radio audience at home. Along with co-host Mike and producer Ian, and with headphones on, listening to instructions from our home base in Toronto, we pounded back coffees like shots at a bachelorette party and got ready to begin the first of that week's live remote morning broadcasts. Deep into preparation mode, I barely noticed when our lead promotions staffer approached the head table broadcast set-up with a concerned look on her face. (I wouldn't have been alarmed at her expression even if I had noticed; worry is a constant state of being when you're staging a remote broadcast. In fact, it's pretty much a job requirement.) As Rob sat near me, helping to download show material onto my computer, Jackie Gilgannon stood in front of the table and addressed the two of us.

"There's a Patricia somebody on the phone from Toronto who wants to talk to you," she said in a vaguely confused voice.

"Shirakawa?" I asked, knowing that Lauren's stepmom-in-law was the only Patricia who might be trying to reach us.

When Jackie nodded in the affirmative, we both wondered aloud why on earth Patricia would be calling during a broadcast. Rob rose to take the call in the lobby. In what is— or was—so typically "me," as God is my witness, I thought it was some kind of good news. That's my nature: like the kid who's digging joyfully through the manure pile because she's sure there's a pony down there somewhere, I'm always expecting something wonderful to happen. After all, that's how my whole life had unfolded. And so it didn't occur to me to worry when five minutes ticked by and Rob hadn't returned.

One, maybe two songs played. I don't remember if we did a live break or were waiting until after the 6 a.m. news to begin our broadcast. Often we would record that first half-hour while we tested the transmission lines and found our footing. Finally, standing up at the table, I said to no one in particular, "Where the heck is he?" There were stories to track down and print and, as always, preparation to do. Like an unpaid extra staffer on the show, Rob was always my right hand on these trips, if only to help keep me fully caffeinated (bless him), just as he did at home, day in and day out.

I recall moving through that ballroom filled with sleepy but happy listeners, many of whom raised their coffee cups in anticipation of a fun show and smiled as I passed by, offering up a cheery, "Good morning!"

In a few moments, that party trick ability to recall details and each listener's name would fail me; quite frankly, I'm not sure it has returned to this day. Maybe it never will, and I suppose I'm grateful for the inability to remember some of the worst moments, but I've managed to piece together what happened next by sweeping up shards of memories and trying to place them into some kind of cohesive order. Because outside those ballroom doors, our life—one blindingly bright, shimmering and perfect orb of music, laughter, joy and fulfilled dreams—shattered on the humidity-dampened tiles of a hotel lobby floor into more razor-edged pieces than we could ever count or hope to reassemble.

This is where things start to slow down, where I can watch it happen from above again and again. The instant that everything changed. But this is how those shards appear.

When I emerged from the ballroom and into the hotel's dimly lit lobby, I spotted Jackie again, tears streaming down her reddened cheeks, her eyes filled with what I can only describe as horrified compassion, her mouth open in shock.

Hmm, I thought, *this isn't good.*

By then I was convinced it was bad news (does any good news come at six in the morning when no one you know is expecting a baby?), and my mind started to race. As we do when we're trying to make sense of an unexpected experience, I rapidly sorted through the people to whom this bad news might be connected: Had something happened to my eighty-two-year-old father? No, that would result in a call from one of my three sisters. This was Patricia Shirakawa calling. Our son-in-law's stepmother at the time. It had to be about Phil's dad, Kevin. That was it, I decided. Had to be. But why would Patricia call while we were doing a live radio show *in another country* to tell us about one of our in-laws?

Shoulders slumped, Rob was sitting on a bench opposite the front desk, which was empty except for one or two staffers who had pulled the early shift or were perhaps still working the overnight. The graveyard shift. How inadvertently appropriate.

As I approached Rob, I couldn't see his face; the lights were low. The only sounds were of birds and tree frogs.

"Is Kevin okay?" I asked him gently.

Rob responded, "It's Lauren."

"Lauren? What's happened? What is it?"

And looking up at me, tears on his face and his voice choked and high, he said the words he knew would deliver as much pain to me as he had only just begun to bear: "She died in her sleep."

Rob tells me I repeatedly cried out, "No!" He recalls how the sounds of our anguish echoed through the open-air lobby and into the pre-dawn darkness of a tropical morning. Fearing, I suspect, for the hotel guests' peaceful sleep as much as our sanity, a staff member gently told us she had opened the luggage storage room next to the front desk, if we needed privacy.

As if going into some kind of autopilot mode, remembering the "be on your best" mantra, I shook off the suggestion and said that I was okay. I took a big breath and headed

85

back toward the ballroom, where listeners awaited and, at the other end of our remote connection, a Toronto audience was waking up with an expectation of our usual blend of friendly and laughter-filled conversation, information and adult contemporary hit music. Rob followed close behind. I wonder what our faces must have looked like. Because I swear to you, what was going through my head was that I had a job to do, a lot of people were counting on us, and I would sit down and do that radio show.

Now, I know that a statement like that ought to be accompanied by the oft-used needle-ripping-off-a-record sound effect. But when a bomb suddenly goes off next to you, you cling to the steadiest and most stable thing you've got. For me, that was the day-in and day-out of a radio show, the place where I had to be positive and focused. Where I wouldn't have to think about what had happened to our family, to Phil's family and to our worlds. Admittedly, the show wasn't going to rescue me on that day, but in time it would.

I made my way behind the broadcast table to where our producer, Ian, sat, wondering why we'd left the room. Off air, and in as calm and emotionless a voice as I have ever used, I spoke these words: "Well, Lauren's dead."

Ian's face—and that of Jackie before him—would come to be among the first few of many that day that would reflect back to us the utter impossibility of what had happened: an awful, slicing shock that I wasn't able to begin to comprehend. Ian had known Lauren since the day she was born; his mother had moved into an apartment across the street from our home north of the city so that she could care for

Lauren when she was a baby. Ian and his wife, Anita, were so fond of our daughter—a mutual affection—that we'd asked them to raise her if anything happened to Rob and me. I am so sorry for the cruelty with which I dispatched such awful news to him. "Don't f—king kid about something like that!" he snapped.

I'm sure there was a gentler or better way to have shared the news, but in that instant, I wasn't able to grasp it. I know I also told my radio partner in that first minute; I just don't remember the moment. Mike's response—echoing almost everyone else we told that day—was to keep repeating the word "What?" as though somehow the brain could not comprehend what the ears had just taken in. Like Ian, Mike knew and loved Lauren. She was as much a part of our radio station's family as I was.

Despite my numb insistence that we do our remote show that morning from Jamaica, rather than leave the station and its sponsors in the lurch, saner heads (which would be all of them) prevailed. Mumbling apologies as we passed by our listeners, Rob and I retreated to our room.

Those first moments alone, keeping our voices down so as not to bother other hotel guests, are a blur. I know I kept asking what was to become of us—as though I knew full well there would be no living without our Lauren. We lay on the bed and cried in each other's arms. We hugged, we cried some more and then I wailed into a pillow. Rob rubbed my back and tried to comfort me as best he could, broken as he was.

We soon realized that there were people we would have

to tell—people who needed to hear this horrific news from us. And quickly.

Our first concern was those friends and family who might find out about Lauren's death through social media, radio or television. Unbeknownst to us, Lauren's sudden death was about to make national headlines, and within an hour her name was trending on Twitter. Although she was described in many headlines and stories as my daughter, she was an accomplished broadcaster in her own right, on maternity leave from her news duties at that Ottawa news/talk radio station.

The first person we called was the one most likely to learn of Lauren's death through media, social and otherwise: my long-time friend and media sister Lisa Brandt. Lisa was doing her morning radio show in London, Ontario, and I knew she would be among the first to see the news come across "the wire," the antiquated term we still use to refer to information channels. She refused to believe what we were telling her. Lisa loved Lauren. I had confided in my friend during Lauren's teen years, and also during the early days in her radio career. The news of Lauren's death hit her hard; she had to leave her own news and co-hosting duties mid-show.

Then we called Rob's older sister, with whom Lauren had shared so many wonderful sleepovers. We are forever grateful to Sue for agreeing to make the ninety-minute drive to Ottawa to be with Phil and Colin, since she was the family member who lived closest to them. When Sue arrived, the police were in the midst of attending to the bedroom where Lauren's body still rested, and she marvelled at the compassion of the liaison officer who was comforting Phil. Sue also bore witness to the quiet kindness of the Salvation Army and Red Cross workers who slipped in with groceries and made sure a distraught father had what he needed to care for a small baby.

I called my three sisters, and two of them sprang into action. Cindy and Heather paid my elderly father a pre-dawn visit to spare him what we feared might be a potentially lethal shock over the phone. You see, not even two years before, my father had stood up beside the minister at a small country church near our cottage and helped to marry his granddaughter to her dear Phil. Using a silk rope, he literally "tied the knot" loosely around their clasped hands. Only five months earlier, we'd all shared Christmas together. Dad couldn't make sense of it; it just couldn't be his granddaughter who had died.

Gradually, we got through what we thought was the entire list of people who needed to be notified, with one most unfortunate exception.

There is a list of regrets that I harbour from that darkest of days (led, of course, by Lauren's death itself), and a sin of omission is one that stands out. My aunt and uncle, who happen to be near Rob and me in age, and are extremely close to us as a family, have three children, all just a little older than Lauren. In fact, their youngest daughter, Karen, is the one who was Lauren's so-called big sister and had spent a lot of time with our little family when we all lived in the Toronto area. Because they were living in British Columbia at the time, three hours behind the Ottawa and Toronto time zone, it was the middle of the night, and my sisters thought that perhaps Laura and Vern shouldn't be awakened with the news of Lauren's passing. Unfortunately, by the time they opened their Facebook pages a few hours later, Lauren's death had already been widely posted. That is how they learned of their dear great-niece's passing. Just add that to the litany of regrettable events on that awful day.

Arrangements were made for Rob, me, Mike and Ian to return to Toronto that afternoon. Jackie and the rest of our station staff would stay in Jamaica to entertain listeners during the week-long trip they'd won. The swift and horrible changes that had been made to everyone's plans that morning cast a pall over their free vacations, no doubt, but we were heartened to see pictures of listeners raising a glass to us.

While we awaited our transfer to the airport, Rob and I called Jackie, Ian and Mike and invited them to join us in our room, if they wanted to come by. They did; we shared fruit slices and copious carafes of coffee. I can't remember what we talked about, but the heavy weight of shock had settled on us all.

Soon it was time to leave the resort we'd called home for such a short time. Before we left, Rob and I took a walk down to the ocean we had gazed at, numb, from our balcony that morning as we'd made our excruciating phone calls. Truly, fortune had bestowed upon us a most surreal backdrop for the black cloud that had descended on our lives. The calm ocean, the skies dotted with soft whiteness, the warm sunshine and light breezes were all so violently out of tune with the crushing devastation Rob and I were feeling. Silently, hand in hand, we made our way along a boardwalk and then a pier jutting out into the impossibly turquoise Caribbean waters. I was struck by a feeling of nausea, as though I'd been delivered yet another gut punch by the reality of the morning's events. I asked myself how the worst possible thing in the world could happen to us in one of its most beautiful settings. I felt an urge to find a way off the pier so I could stand in the ocean or feel my feet in the sand; do something—anything—to immerse myself in the grace and warmth of this place that might provide a soft memory to take with me into the days and weeks ahead. Yet in the next moment, I wanted to fall to my hands and knees and just scream until I had no more voice. I needed the world to know that this person stepping mindfully along the pier with her husband was definitely not okay. That she was losing her mind. That it was never going to be okay. That our lives were over and, from that moment onward, anyone who saw me was looking at a dead woman walking.

But I did none of those things. Checking my watch, I sighed to Rob that it was time we went back. Like zombies, we waited in our room until the bellman arrived to take our bags, and then we quietly shuffled back to that cursed lobby—where we discovered that the drama in that particular part of the hotel wasn't yet over.

As we were getting set to climb into the van taking our small, nearly catatonic party to the airport, a large man, whose eyes were almost equally as expressionless as ours, demanded to see my transfer ticket. I wasn't even sure I understood what I was hearing, or what he was asking.

"I need to see your ticket. You cannot leave without it."

I told him politely, and in as coherent a way as I could manage, that I didn't understand; we didn't have any tickets. He didn't seem to hear us, and he sternly demanded the tickets again.

I decided to try to reason: I elaborated and told him that we had just learned of our daughter's death a few hours earlier, and we were leaving right away on an unscheduled flight home. He just kept looking through me, as if this were a dream, and said, "I need to see your ticket." As I repeated that I didn't have one, and wasn't sure what he was talking about, he once again repeated his automaton-like demand. I couldn't quite believe what was happening. Why was he doing this to us?

It was at this point that Jackie, from CHFI promotions—who, along with a travel agency representative, had come to see us off for our hastily arranged trip home—completely lost it on this man. Charged with helping to get thousands of winning listeners to and from resorts year after year, she had dealt with more red tape than most of us have to climb through in a lifetime. I was proud of her for the way she tore into this man for his lack of sensitivity and comprehension of the fact that we did not have, in her words, "any f—king ticket!"

I have often reflected with genuine wonder and gratitude upon the way Jackie handled our tragedy that morning, as well as the demands put upon her in the week that followed. She stepped up in a way that no one ever should have to, and, to make matters even more precarious, we would later learn that she was in the very early weeks of her first pregnancy! How glad we are that the shock of what happened on that trip did not interfere with her own good health and safe delivery, some eight months later, of a beautiful son named Jackson. Throughout our decade of working together, I always felt something of a maternal closeness to Jackie (perhaps it was because she was not much older than my own daughter). And on that awful day, in the worst of circumstances, she was as compassionate, professional and, yes, belligerent as any child would be on behalf of a mother who had been left nearly witless with grief.

I do not recall how the issue of our missing tickets was resolved—I was too mortified that it was even happening to pay attention after Jackie took control—but, finally, we did board that small van and headed off to the airport.

As our group sat near our gate in the Sangster International Airport departure lounge, we tried not to attract any attention as our tears flowed. We were still unaware that people in Ottawa and Toronto were beginning to feel the shock waves that accompanied the news of Lauren's death. In our nation's capital, prominent politicians tweeted their regrets. As a member of the Ottawa media, Lauren had become a familiar figure, further proof to Rob and to me that she was, indeed, making her own mark. She had no shadow of mine to worry about.

~~~

As the day went on, compassionate tweets were posted by members of competing media conglomerates in both Ottawa and Toronto. The news was shared on morning breakfast TV shows. Across the country, our daughter's death was included in news crawls and website feeds.

Of all of the stories we heard about people's reactions that day—and we'd hear of so many in the weeks and months to come—without a doubt this one touched Rob and me the most. Back in Toronto, a woman who heard about Lauren's death on the radio pulled over to the side of the road and sobbed. Another motorist, seeing her distress, stopped her car to see if she could be of help. When she learned the cause of the first driver's tears, they both stood there, hugging and crying.

This public outpouring of grief set the tone for a display of sadness that would continue for weeks at the radio station and among its family of listeners. Once the initial disbelief wore off, that widely spread cloak of grief would serve as an immense source of warmth, comfort and strength for us. I continue to hear from listeners who think of Lauren whenever they receive or donate blood. I'd made it known that this was a favourite cause of hers; she gave blood on the very day that she was eligible after giving birth. We hadn't been able to donate Lauren's organs upon her death because of the extent of the autopsy that her body would undergo in order to try to determine how a seemingly healthy twenty-four-year-old woman had died, so we hoped this would be the next best thing. What a lovely legacy, the knowledge that people giving life to others do so as they remember our daughter. It makes me so proud, and I know that Lauren would be grateful—and incredulous.

While we were *in* the air, back at my radio home, hosts

were *on* the air explaining what had happened. Julie Adam—senior VP of Rogers Radio, my boss and my friend—joined our midday host, Michelle Butterly, and spoke on the edge of tears, her voice filled with emotion.

MICHELLE: *We have received some absolutely devastating news today, and Julie Adam is here to share it with us.*

JULIE: *It is with a very heavy heart and great sadness that I share the news today that we have lost a member of our CHFI family. Lauren Davis, beloved daughter of Erin and Rob, passed away suddenly this morning.*

MICHELLE: *We are heartbroken . . . beyond belief, and we can't imagine what Rob and Erin are going through right now, and their family and their friends.*

JULIE: *It's devastating. We got the news first thing this morning, just after 6 a.m. As you know, Erin and Mike are broadcasting live from Jamaica with a planeload of CHFI listeners. And we got them on a plane right away—Erin and Rob, Mike Cooper and the General [Ian MacArthur]—and they are en route back to Toronto. Erin and Rob will, of course, be going to Ottawa to be with Lauren's husband's family to make arrangements. We are all shocked and saddened. There are no words to express how everyone is feeling today.*

MICHELLE: *The shock is beyond. I met Lauren when she was eight. Lauren was eight years old when I started here. A lot of CHFI listeners were around when Lauren was born and remember when Erin was pregnant with Lauren and when they were on the cover of* Today's Parent *together. There's no words, no words for this.*

JULIE: *I think, as everyone knows, CHFI is a family— our team is very close, and the love for Erin and Rob and Lauren spreads wide across the Rogers Radio organization. This is a very difficult day for our team; as you can imagine, our on-air hosts are working very hard to be professional and to keep their emotions at bay because they have a job to do to entertain the listeners. But I would ask that you understand if we're not as peppy as we usually are; that's the reason. We do thank the CHFI listeners for your unwavering support; we know you're going to do whatever you can to help Erin and Rob get through this. And if you'd like to pass along any condolences, you can do so on our Facebook page or on CHFI.com.*

MICHELLE: *Thank you.*

JULIE: *Thanks, Michelle.*

The interview ended with the playing of Sarah McLachlan's "Angel." It's one of the saddest and most beautiful pieces of radio I've ever heard—that perfect combination of real emotions and just the right piece of music. Time and time again over my career, I'd striven to come up with the same type of heartfelt and real moment. I just wish this one hadn't been about us.

~~~

IT'S remarkable the things that come back to you through the heavy grey fog of shock and pain. One of the small acts of kindness that we experienced that awful day came during our hastily booked trip home. A flight attendant leaned over and told Rob and me that she could block off the lavatory entrance area near the cockpit if we just needed to be together behind the curtain. It wasn't as if we'd been moaning and crying loudly on the trip home; the most any fellow travellers might have seen would have been me dabbing at my eyes or blowing my nose. I might just as easily have been watching *The Notebook* on my iPad. No, it was just an extremely compassionate gesture on the part of the WestJet crew. I'll always remember it with gratitude.

Like a bitter bookend to the "I need to see your ticket" man back at the resort, a terse welcome awaited us upon our arrival home; in retrospect, though, it was completely understandable and should almost have been expected. When we collected our luggage at the airport in Toronto, we were pulled aside by Canada Border Service agents; I'm sure we were flagged for having been in Jamaica for just two days. I remember Rob and me telling the officer the reason for our sudden return and still not quite believing the words as they came out of our mouths. Fortunately, he did believe them, but not before a cursory search of our luggage. I recall being treated with courtesy and even a semblance of understanding and being sent quickly on our way. The radio station had arranged for a car to meet us at the airport, and had even offered to provide a ride to Ottawa the next day if we were too distraught to drive. We assured our bosses that we'd be fine. As we would soon learn, long car rides turned out to be a great chance to talk and cry and shake our fists at the sky.

A few minutes after we entered our downtown condo and put down our bags, the phone rang. It was a *Toronto Star* reporter asking if I'd answer some questions. I took a deep breath and agreed. After all, speculation about the cause of Lauren's death had already begun on our radio station's Facebook page (among other sites, of course). I understood that. First of all, it's the internet. Second, like nature, the truth abhors a vacuum. If there is a paucity of facts, people are going to start to make up details and post sheer conjecture, especially when a healthy young woman dies so suddenly, so senselessly.

I set aside my worries about how it might appear—a grieving mother agreeing to an interview—and decided to try to fill the void. I sat down with phone in hand and told the reporter the few details that we knew at such an early stage. Then came the reporter's apologetically posed but inevitable question about her state of mind: Was she suffering postpartum depression? Truthfully, I hadn't been expecting that association, but my years in media should have prepared me for the likely link in people's minds between the words "died suddenly" and suicide. It's often a euphemism used in obituaries and news articles, and I get that. In an even tone, I responded, "absolutely not." I told the reporter that if our daughter had died by suicide, I would most definitely be forthright and say so. My career was built on honesty and transparency. Through our positions in the media, Lauren and I both were vocal advocates of open discussion of mental health issues, including my own. I stated unequivocally that we had no idea what had taken our daughter's life.

In the days ahead, I had a spectacular life to celebrate in two cities, and plans to make to do just that. I also had my mourning husband to console and support, and the shared job of figuring out what we were going to do, moving forward with our lives as people who are no longer parents, who no longer have a child to carry their name, their dreams, their genes into a future without them—you know, the things people expect when they have a child. It's funny how these things come at you when your mind stops churning and the facts of your new life start to worm their way in. You realize that everything has changed, and the way you thought the steps and stages of your life were going to go has suddenly been upended. I thought there would be someone to whom my mother's silver and china would go. Someone to whom I could pass on my wedding rings and other special things I'd long ago envisioned giving to our daughter before I died, just to see her enjoyment. Like an unusual sapphire-and diamond-adorned ring.

In 1986, about a month before I began dating the man who would become my husband, I had bought this piece of jewellery. Tired of waiting for someone to come into my life to buy me the gifts I found so hard to give to myself, I spotted a sparkling dark blue sapphire and diamond ring that looked somewhat like an eye. It certainly caught mine. After giving myself the "you're worth it" pep talk, I bought the ring and wore it every day for years, even after Rob had given me an engagement and then wedding ring to wear on my left hand. When Lauren was a teen, I asked her if she wanted that ring, and she gave me an enthusiastic response. I joked with her that I'd be keeping my eye on her, through that piece of jewellery.

Lauren wore the unusual ring every day, even on her wedding day. Twenty-three months later, she was wearing it the morning that she died and, fortunately, it wasn't necessary for it to be cut off her long fingers. I'm grateful to Phil for returning it to me; I wear it almost as often as Lauren did.

But when I look at that ring, I'm reminded of so much, the past as well as the future: I wonder to whom that ring will go next. When you lose your clear path to what lies ahead (or at least, what you envision your future will be), you stumble, trying to discern where the new lines on the road may be. You rewrite your wills. You dread Christmases that bring you more pain than joy, leaving you to throw up your hands and say, "Aw, fa-la-la-la forget it!" and just want to fly off, escape to someplace warm, where you and your husband can be anonymous and just cry in private. You wonder just what you worked for all of those years as a parent; what it was you were trying to build. The entire snow globe that held your little family is suddenly, unexpectedly pitched in a slow arc into the air and then hit so hard it could split an aluminum bat in two. Except there are no pieces left to pick up because, for a time, it feels as if it's all gone. All of it. And it becomes very difficult to remember the point in everything you've worked for. You can't look ahead and you can't look back; all you can see is where you are at that very moment and all you can do is try to keep breathing. It all feels like the quicksand we used to see in the *Tarzan* TV shows when we were kids. For me, that had always been the scariest part of those episodes. And now I was standing in it, or rather sinking . . . sinking.

I think back to the words that I said quietly to my husband as we walked from our hotel room back to the lobby and the shuttle that would eventually take our grieving party to the airport in Montego Bay.

"This is who we are now," I muttered.

"Sorry?" Rob replied.

"This is who we are now. We're those people. We're the ones who've lost a child. This is who we are."

We are members of a club with dues so high you never, ever want to pay them, but now we're members for life. And we found ourselves invited to join an especially elite chapter of the club: the one for parents who have lost their only child. And look! The clubhouse even has a stage. Because when we pull back the curtain, this whole ordeal is about to be played out in public.

This was not the first time that the CHFI morning show had also become a mourning show. In 1991, six months after the arrival of our child, my radio partner at the time was grappling with the death of one of his children. I recall a conversation we had a short time after he lost an adult child to suicide, in which he asked if I thought he should talk about his son's death on the air. I was young and had yet to learn the many lessons about sharing oneself publicly and connecting with listeners on a deeply personal level. I had given the man's question some thought long before he asked it, and my response signalled caution: Did he want to become Pagliacci—the laughing, crying clown—in people's eyes? Did he want to risk his popularity, or just keep up his facade of humour and continue to make people laugh?

It shows what I knew then. How lucky I am to have learned enough in those ensuing decades to be able to be honest and real with our listeners. Because, like that co-worker who quite rightly ignored my questions and did the right thing by being open with his audience, I too found a form of freedom in speaking of and writing about my story, my trials, my deliverance. Although the idea of sharing something that personal had scared the younger broadcaster and person I was at the time of that conversation, stepping through that fear and being real, raw and truthful with our audience allowed them to feel safe enough to reach out to me and, in so doing, offer me a form of comfort and ultimately salvation. So much for "be on your best." I am so grateful to have felt secure enough to be openly vulnerable and human.

CHAPTER 4

Saying Goodbye

Lauren on her wedding day, June 22, 2013

I N RETROSPECT, I AM NOT QUITE SURE WHETHER our hastily arranged flight from Montego Bay back to Toronto was the shortest or the longest trip of our lives. I don't remember much, other than that kindness from the flight attendant who offered Rob and me privacy. She probably offered us a drink too, and I'm sure it was only the support of Rob and our radio friends that kept it from even entering my mind as a possibility. How lucky I am that the devious-snake part of my brain didn't whisper to me that this was the best possible excuse to numb myself, if only I would take it. I had logged nine years of sobriety by then and somehow it was staying intact—so far.

As much as I would have appreciated the opportunity to deaden the pain that was setting in along with the realization that all of this was actually happening, there was much to do, and I was grateful for a clear head. We hurriedly and haphazardly unpacked our beach and party clothes and threw together what we thought we would need for who-knows-how-long in Ottawa. After a sleepless night, we were up at dawn the following day, a Tuesday. We headed into the sun for the long and tearful journey to be with Phil and Colin.

While we drove, people in search of details about our daughter's death and our own well-being were going to the journal I'd posted hurriedly on my website the night before.

Hello, Dear Friend.

I feel I should write you a goodbye for now, as I will be taking leave of this space until my heart no longer feels filled to bursting with sadness, tears and the awful pain of being ripped away from my flesh, my own.

You will likely have heard by now our tragic news: our dearest, sweetest, kindest daughter Lauren went to sleep on Sunday night—her first Mother's Day— and did not wake up to her baby's cries and husband's nudges on Monday.

The world will keep turning—a 7-month-old baby will grow surrounded by limitless love and support— and we will search forever to find answers to something that is so unspeakably wrong that none will ever suffice.

Thank you for reaching out through Twitter, on CHFI Facebook, in email. I will answer what I can, when I can. Know that I have seen them, and we've taken them in, as best we can.

In the meantime, Rob and I, Phil and our families need some time to try to make sense of the death of a healthy, happy, beautiful young mother.

Sounds like a lifetime, doesn't it?
I'll be in touch when I can. And thank you again.
She was our world.

Erin

How grateful I was to have a place to tell people what had happened—or at least as much as we knew. Of course, that didn't stop some from jumping to the wrong conclusions, but at least we tried, through the journal, the newspaper interview and, of course, the airwaves, where my colleagues at CHFI told listeners of Lauren's sudden and inexplicable passing.

As we drove up to the house, we saw Phil sitting outside on the steps, watching his phone and smoking from the first pack of cigarettes he'd bought since quitting over a year earlier at Lauren's insistence. She wasn't going to risk having third-hand smoke from clothes or hair coming in contact with her baby, and Phil agreed. As it turns out, a police officer on scene during those early hours of investigation gave Phil his first puff of relief upon his wife's death. Not one of us could or would blame him for seeking some kind of comfort; we could all relate. Rob and I took up smoking steadily again in the early weeks and months after Lauren's death as well. With almost every new cigarette I lit, I said, "Sorry, Loo," knowing how distressed she'd be at our starting again after all of the years we'd butted out. It took a few months for us to stop, once and for all.

After that first night without Lauren, spent in a hotel while police investigated their townhouse, father and infant returned to the cozy new house with its boldly painted rooms where Lauren had died such a short time earlier. Understandably, his warm mother gone from his side, his routine completely upended, Colin was, at times, as inconsolable as the rest of us.

We had checked into that same hotel, but we spent that first evening visiting with Phil and the baby. At one point while Colin dozed in his father's arms, I stepped away to go downstairs to the baby's nursery. Just a few weeks before, I'd sat and rocked in this previously cheery and sunny mustard-coloured room—decorated with framed Beatles lyrics, stuffed animals and books—looking on with immense pride and love as my little girl laughed and changed her freshly bathed and lavender-scented baby boy. Her joy was so immense it was palpable, and I loved being asked to help dress him in his cozy sleepwear before she began the ritual of turning on a night light and soft music, and then rocking him while feeding. Lauren and I were becoming closer than we had ever been. On this evening, though, the room reminded me of how much had been snatched so cruelly from every one of us in that house.

I lay down on the carpeted floor of the room, crying into the crook of my arm, sobbing over the desperation of the whole situation. I guess I wasn't crying as quietly as I thought. When Phil came down, baby in his arms, to console me, I gathered myself and my dignity and stood up. As we turned off the light to leave the room, Colin said something he'd never said before, despite Lauren's ongoing efforts to have him mimic her. Very clearly, Colin said the word "mama." It's entirely possible—likely, even—that at seven months old, his lips had just made that sound quite by accident.

I looked at Phil in disbelief. "Did he really just say that?"

His eyes as wide as mine, Phil shook his head and said, "That would be too sad."

Then again, what wasn't? Years would pass before he would say more than just a few discernible syllables.

Rob and I had checked into a room that became our home base for making arrangements and fielding calls and emails from concerned friends and co-workers while we awaited permission to take our next shaky steps. It took four days for the coroner's office to release Lauren's body to the funeral home; despite his initial suspicions, the coroner was completely at a loss to explain how an otherwise healthy twenty-four-year-old woman could simply stop breathing. On Friday of the same week that had begun in Jamaica, we found ourselves in a funeral director's office, holding a paper bag containing the pyjamas our daughter had been wearing when she died, along with a dryer sheet that they had tossed in; funny, the things you remember.

Although we had all agreed upon cremation for Lauren's body, we had also asked to see her before that took place. It was a tall order, especially considering the extensive autopsy that she had undergone, but we were determined to have one last visit with the body we had made and that had held such an incredible spirit.

As we numbly watched Colin sleeping peacefully in his baby carrier in an office corner, Phil was first to go and say goodbye to his wife. After ten minutes it was our turn. The young, gentle-mannered funeral associate led Rob and me down a hallway to a private visitation room. She opened the windowless oak doors and told us that she would be right outside if we needed her; as we closed the doors, we could see her taking a seat in the hallway.

Across this sparsely and simply furnished room, resting on a platform, was a rectangular plywood box. A panel of wood covered the lower part of our daughter's body to just below her chest; her hands rested atop one another on her torso. She wore the dark blue stretchy Calvin Klein pyjamas we'd given her for her birthday just two months earlier—the ones I knew would make nursing Colin a little easier. For this day, I thought they would be somehow comfortable for her (yes, I know how illogical that sounds) and easier for the funeral home to do whatever needed to be done. Anyway, it made sense to us.

I haven't seen a lot of open caskets in my life, but I remember that when our friend Kathy Morrison died of brain cancer in her forties, she appeared in her casket very much as she did in life: beautiful. Peaceful. Our Lauren was not so fortunate.

Despite what I'm sure was the funeral home staff's best attempts at cosmetically hiding it, we could easily make out the raised ridge that ran across her forehead where the coroner had opened her skull and closed it again. Although it shouldn't have been a surprise to us, it somehow was. Of course, on a conscious level, we knew there had been an autopsy—one that provided no concrete answers, to our great distress and chagrin—but I suppose, in the interests of preserving what little sanity we were clinging to at the time, we had chosen not to think about its invasiveness to our daughter's body. The funeral home's cosmetologist was able to camouflage the facial bruising Phil said he had seen the morning she died from where she'd lain on her side for hours before he discovered her, partly off their bed. Her chest was stuffed to the point of looking barrel-like, no hint of shape beneath her dark blue buttoned-up pyjamas. Truly, the staff had done all it could, we knew, but this was not our daughter, so bursting with passion and sparkle and laughter and music. So full of life.

Yet, it was all we had left, this damaged vase. It was to us as though a once-beautiful vessel had tipped and broken, its formerly colourful blossoms spilled out and left to wither. Despite valiant and honourable attempts to glue the vase back together, the shattering had been utterly and horribly complete. The vase was simply no more. It would hold no more flowers.

As Rob and I knelt in front of the box holding her body, we sobbed quietly so as not to be heard by the woman in the hall (*be on your best*) and talked to Lauren in hushed tones of our pride in all she was and had accomplished, in her beautiful spirit and her generous heart. We promised our daughter that we would help her son to grow up to be the boy and man she would want him to be. We stroked the cold, smooth and pale young skin of her hands, those hands that were the first thing the delivery nurses commented on when she was born twenty-four years earlier. "Look at those fingers!" they'd said, marvelling at their length. We called them "piano fingers," so delicate and long were they. She had such beautiful hands, and she used them to span octaves on a keyboard, form bar chords on a guitar and reach for distant notes on the long, smooth neck of a cello. How we loved those soft, sweet hands.

Then Rob and I did something we hadn't done with Lauren since she was a child.

I'm not sure if it's something other families do, but we had a fun game we called "twenty kisses." To be truthful, I think I made up this game so that Lauren would let me shower her with the affection and love I so badly wanted her to accept. Her tendency to deflect my admittedly over-the-top gestures (impromptu songs and poems that included her name; high-pitched calls of her many nicknames that echoed through the house) was, in a way, part of our dynamic: she knew how much I loved her, how desperately I wanted that same love in return, and she would get a kick out of pretending to withhold it, just to bug me.

This time, this last time that Rob and I played "twenty kisses" with our girl, I leaned down to kiss her firm, cool skin. Then Rob did, and we alternated our light pecks on her cheeks and on her ridged forehead, now wet with our tears, until we'd done it a total of twenty times. How we wanted to stay and just keep kissing. But that clenching pain in the pit of our stomachs told us that the lady outside, and back in her office, Phil and the baby, had probably waited for us long enough.

Reluctantly, we said our last goodbyes, and I groaned as we backed out of the room with the slow, heavy steps of a death march that you'd expect to accompany one of the worst moments of two devastated people's lives. I wished with all my heart that, like Abraham Lincoln had done with his own deceased son, I could steal back in and cradle her body, holding and rocking her in my arms again one more time. But despite the incredibly cruel twist our lives had taken, the real world still turned, time kept its constant pace and there would never, ever be enough hours in which we could say goodbye, no number of tears or words that could be shed and said that could make leaving Lauren any easier. And so, with one last look at the beautiful girl with whom we'd shared so much love, we took a deep breath, opened the door, stepped into the hall and prepared ourselves for our next steps: the public goodbyes. We would make preparations and then head back to Toronto to pack, to prepare a visual element for the first of her two services and to spend some time in our own bed. After saying our private farewells, it was time to do this publicly.

~~~

I KNOW that Lauren was with us on our journey to Ottawa for her memorial on May 19. How? She told us. Sitting in the passenger seat as I tapped away on my laptop, I received a Facebook notification that Lauren was "poking" me. Now, I know that there is likely some logical explanation for that poke at that particular time, but I have no idea what it might be. And I might point out that it never happened again. It doesn't seem illogical then to choose to interpret that timely little random social media gesture as Lauren's way of getting through to me to say she'd be at our side for yet another excruciating day. But that wasn't the only way she tried to get our attention.

As we travelled the four-lane highway on the outskirts of Ottawa, while I continued to marvel at what had just shown up on my computer, we were passed by what we remember to be a white car. The colour of the car matters little, compared to its licence plate. Rob pointed it out to me; I'd been looking down at my computer screen, answering listeners' emails.

"Did you see that?" he asked with incredulity.

"See what?"

"That licence plate. It said PURE JOY."

For a moment, the two of us were speechless. Those two words were exactly what Lauren had said when I asked, during our Mother's Day interview, how she felt about motherhood. Pure joy.

We don't know why we saw that licence plate at that time on that road on that day. But we do believe Lauren was again reminding us that she was with us and always would be. And, oh, how we needed that nudge and the accompanying feeling that she had her arms around us and would hold us up during the difficult hours, days and years to come.

We had spent the days between Lauren's passing and the first of the two memorial services preparing a digital photo display with the same dedication and attention to detail that we'd brought to planning her wedding less than two years earlier. Rob and I tackled the gruelling task of putting together the right pictures to show during musical selections, as well as a continuous stream of pictures from various moments in the lives of her and her family. And the technical gods were not playing nice.

I don't know if you've heard of Mercury retrograde, or if you believe it's a thing, but many people do, including us. According to multiple sources, it's an astronomical phenomenon that occurs a few times each year, and it can have mysterious and negative effects on many forms of communication and technology. We were right in the thick of it for the entire second half of that month. Computers would unexpectedly and inexplicably shut down, screens would freeze, work we'd done would disappear and we were seriously worried that we were going to lose everything.

Our technological challenges did let up briefly, however, when Rob was able to hack into Lauren's laptop and retrieve pictures and music files. He figured it out simply by looking up online how to do it. I shouldn't have been surprised: this is the guy who once managed to crack the combination on luggage we thought was ours, only to find that we had inadvertently picked up someone else's identical new set of London Fog bags on the airport carousel. Getting into Lauren's files was just a different sort of challenge, and one for which we had Phil's kind blessings.

Through it all, Lauren gave us strength. In fact, many days after her death, Rob told me that she came to him one evening in our cottage kitchen, where so much love and warmth (and Lauren's baking) had been shared. He says he heard her say, "I'm sorry you have to go through this, Daddy." In those early days of preparing for her memorials, she made her presence known in the most unusual of ways. We were lying in our bed in a room overlooking a spring scene on Lake Simcoe. On his laptop, Rob played me the audio he'd prepared for the memorial, with Lauren's voice singing, then talking, and baby Colin full-on belly laughing. It was so perfect and so sad that I just held a pillow to my face and screamed. A full-out, wall-shaking cry that was the one and only time I let out that rage and sadness. My throat felt raw, and my first thought was, "Okay, that wasn't smart . . . ," since my voice was—and to some extent still is—my living. But I had to release that terrible pain somehow.

Rob, otherwise paralyzed by his horror at not being able to help ease my pain, held me as I sobbed. And then, as each of us did so many times in those early weeks and months, I sat up, dried my eyes and took some deep breaths. But I smelled something unusual.

I asked Rob if he smelled anything, and he echoed what he thought the aroma in the air might be: the smell of baking. Something warm and sweet, like a cake or rolls or cookies. But here's the thing: our neighbours at the cottage several metres away weren't home that day. No one came to our door. I don't bake; Lauren was the one who would put my mixer to use and toss and replace my ancient baking powder and ingredients to suit her needs. The sweet, comforting aroma came to us when our hearts were the closest they'd come to breaking. If there's a Cinnabon in heaven, I'm guessing our daughter came from there to visit. At least, that day she did.

~~~~

THERE are a few things from the first gathering in Ottawa that will always stand out in my memory. First, the persistent wails of Lauren's inconsolable baby, his bottom raw from the sudden change from breast milk to formula. Colin was giving voice to the stabbing pain we were feeling in our hearts. Understandably, his overwhelmed father had forgotten to replenish the supply of diapers in Colin's bag, and no one staying with or helping him had thought to prepare for the day in that way, so a quick trip to the store was necessary before the actual memorial began. Fortunately, there were plenty of arms eager to try to console the little boy dressed in a sweet outfit of dark pants, a dress shirt and button-on tie. I recall being in a total fog, wandering the aisles of a store looking for something a seven-month-old should wear to his mommy's memorials. What an obscene thought! It reminded me of the oft-played "Christmas Shoes" song where the little kid wants to buy shoes for his dying mother so she can look nice when she meets Jesus. I mean, what on earth is the point in any of it?

And yet, as I shopped, I looked at the other mothers and grandmothers sharing the aisles of the store with me. I thought, *If they only knew* . . . What pain we were going through. How awful life can turn in a heartbeat. How lucky they were. *If they only knew.*

The second thing we recall, and something that genuinely surprised us, was the number of people who came to console Phil and remember Lauren: some two hundred people stood (while Phil, Rob and I sat facing them) for the casual forty-five-minute service. We'd debated whether holding two services was perhaps too much, but our worries were unfounded. Their friends and co-workers in Ottawa—the city they called home—deserved a chance to say goodbye to Lauren on that Tuesday afternoon, just as our own friends and families would ten days later, some 450 kilometres away.

We sat there, Rob, Phil, Colin and I, facing the crowd of sad friends and family who had gathered to hear tributes, and to add their own, for our dear girl.

As pictures of Lauren at many stages of her life quietly rotated on screens in the funeral home, we remembered a twenty-four-year-old mother, daughter, wife and broadcaster. Morning host (and my former boss) Steve Madely, who'd accidentally called her "Erin" on the air, told that story and shared how Lauren was discovered while attending a local college. At our request, Steve also read the achingly sad "Stop All the Clocks" by W.H. Auden, also known, appropriately, as "Funeral Blues."

That sombre piece, featured in both services, set the tone perfectly for the depths of our grief and seeming hopelessness; however, we endeavoured to turn that tone to one of hope later in the service with a Celtic poem called "She Does Not Leave."

Her friends and co-workers spoke tearfully and with fondness of her passion, preternatural maturity, preparedness, eloquence, enthusiasm, fearlessness and kindness. They talked about her humming quietly to herself in the newsroom in the midst of a flurry of breaking-news activity. When a co-worker mentioned it, Lauren was startled and asked if she should stop. He told her to continue. Somehow it gave those in the newsroom the sense that it was all going to be okay and that they were family.

They spoke of an Ottawa police officer hugging and consoling one of Lauren's tearful co-workers on the street outside their radio station. They mentioned Lauren's insistence on helping out the Salvation Army with their kettle campaign and of donating blood as regularly as she was allowed, even jokingly competing with another on-air staffer who also gave blood as soon as the designated waiting period was over. (In Canada, we volunteer to give blood; there's no remuneration except for perhaps a cookie and some juice and a really good feeling.) Co-workers and friends shared how, after Lauren's passing, callers spoke to on-air staff of feeling that they knew her from listening to 580 CFRA, where she did a daily midday news package, just as so many more felt they knew Lauren in Toronto from listening to my stories of her, and those told in her own clear voice during the course of her childhood and young adult years.

Rob and I had carefully prepared remarks for the memorial, but doubting that we would be able to deliver them coherently, at least at this point in time, we had recorded them in our home studio. It turned out to be a wise choice. We sat, heads bowed, as our recorded voices spoke of gratitude for the fact that she did not die after her husband had slipped away to work; she hadn't been carrying her baby on the stairs or driving with him in the car when her heart stopped. We talked of the beauty of Lauren's spirit, the countless reasons we loved her and how proud we were of our girl. We looked ahead at the impossible notion of life without Lauren.

Our underlying theme was the question we had asked ourselves so often, and now more than ever: "*Why couldn't she wait?*"

Then it was her husband's turn to speak. Also a broadcaster (he and Lauren had met in Algonquin College's radio course), Phil smoothly and seemingly calmly delivered his remarks off the cuff and spoke of how Lauren was his everything, how easily and wholeheartedly she had embraced motherhood and, in a vein similar to our own, how impatient she was! To illustrate that point, he lightheartedly asked for a show of hands to see if any other husband had been proposed to by his girlfriend. There were great laughs when Lauren's father—my Rob—raised his.

"That makes total sense," Phil exclaimed, eyebrows raised as he laughed when he looked at Rob and me. And then, in a moment of extreme tenderness, Phil shared with us Lauren's last words to him, spoken just after midnight that Monday morning of her death: "I love you."

As Phil ended his time at the microphone, he thanked everyone gathered in an even and measured voice and attributed any strength he might be showing to his son, Colin, and the job he had ahead. Phil gave a beautiful tribute to our daughter and their lives together, and we were so proud of this young man who had had such unthinkable tragedy thrown at him in the past eight days.

With the help of my one-time co-worker and Lauren's boss, Steve Winogron, we ended the Ottawa gathering by introducing a recording of Lauren's own beautiful voice.

During high school, she and her bandmates had gone on

a school trip to Memphis where, at Sun Studios, they had recorded an album. Although the musicians had moments where they were uncharacteristically out of time and out of tune ("hungover" was the excuse Lauren gave for her school chums' performance), Lauren's vocals were just about perfect: throaty, laid back and, as always, perfectly on key. If she'd been indulging too, it wasn't obvious in the recording. The song was "Dream a Little Dream of Me," and Rob had produced the piece to include, during a bumpy instrumental break, a clip of Lauren talking in that Mother's Day interview with me about what motherhood meant to her.

Although I had prepared for it days earlier with those screams into the pillow, it was as big an emotional blow as you might imagine, hearing her singing and then talking about the baby who had cried throughout the gathering. Poor Phil broke down for the first time in the entire service; we had inadvertently overlooked letting him know this moment was coming. He told us through tears that he missed hearing her voice as much as we did. And that moment of great sadness in listening to Lauren's clear, strong singing voice, and the clip of her eliciting their baby boy's belly laughter as she described her joy, served to underline not only the enormity of our shared loss but also just how tragic the whole situation truly was. A baby without his mother, a husband without his young wife, two parents without their only child. The layers were thick and dark.

Like the sweetness of that phantom whiff of baking, the very real smell of spring lilacs in the air alleviated our heaviness in the first days of mourning. Even though we knew for a fact that the best part of our lives was ending, life began anew around us in the form of blossoms erupting on branches throughout a city known for its trees, flowers and landscaped beauty. I recall taking breaks during the preparation for Lauren's cremation and her memorial and strolling across the street from the funeral home to a little park dotted with fragrant trees. As I gathered the perfumed purple masses into my hands and pulled them to my face to take in their scent, I asked Rob how the world could be so beautiful and so awful.

His answer? "It always has been."

Love. Loss. Lilacs. Lauren. Life itself. So much beauty, and so unimaginably awful. More than once on a long drive to or from Ottawa, I told Rob that had she died in the grey darkness of November, I don't think I could have survived it. The hope of spring helped carry me through that May. Now, though, May is a month so rife with razor-edged memories—not to mention the full weight of Mother's Day, whatever that's supposed to be to me now—that it brings more sadness than hope. But I do believe it will get easier. These are still early times, after all.

That evening, after the memorial, we gathered at our hotel restaurant and bar on the outskirts of the city with a few close friends and co-workers who'd driven from Toronto to be with us on this difficult day. We ate a bit of dinner and shared a few inappropriate but blessedly welcome laughs. You can always count on radio people to make you laugh under the worst circumstances; call it gallows humour if you will, but it makes life a little more tolerable when all hell and the worst of humanity are thrown into your face and you have to share it with people who are counting on you to make sense of it all somehow, or at least give them the details so that they can. I was grateful to be able to do something besides cry and grieve. And soon I was able to turn around and make our friends laugh too: when our server told us that the kitchen was out of whatever special was up on the board, I looked up at her and said, "Well, that's the WORST thing that has happened to me ALL DAY!" She didn't get it, but we all did. You have to laugh or the awfulness of it all could kill you.

One of those people who laughed along and was at our side in so many ways during the early days of our grieving, including at the first memorial and the gathering that followed, was my boss, Julie Adam. Julie figured prominently in our family's life in so many ways, but one of the most welcome benefits of our years spent working together was the friendship that grew among us. As such, she was one of the few people outside family to witness a time when Lauren broke the rules. But luckily for Lauren, Julie would soften the terms of our daughter's punishment—something for which Lauren would always be grateful.

During the early years of social media, we had made it clear that Lauren was not to use MSN. We were unsure about the safety of the messaging application on her desktop computer, and we forbade her to use it. But the lure of the connection to her friends was too strong, and she did go on MSN. One evening—after we'd found her using it earlier and had issued a warning—we heard the tattletale "ping" coming from her bedroom.

Our caution was the result of the many stories we'd heard (and which I'd shared with listeners) about the dangers of strangers on the internet. We didn't know enough about MSN, and although Lauren downplayed our concerns, we had made a rule in an effort to protect her. When we heard proof that she'd disobeyed, we grounded her: no using her computer, and no attending an Elton John concert to which I'd been given tickets.

There were many tears and pleas, and she even hand-wrote a letter of apology (which I have kept) expressing her regret at having disappointed us. Her efforts proved effective: when Julie asked if she could take Lauren to the concert instead of us, we felt it was a bit of a win on both sides. Lauren got to go, and we got to stick to our guns by not taking her. And to be honest, I was honoured that my boss wanted the company of our teenaged daughter.

Looking back now, I'm glad that Lauren made her own choices, even if I didn't immediately approve of or appreciate them. Rob and I might have been disappointed by her decision to dye her hair pink, get a tattoo or contact her friends on MSN, but it was all part of growing up. We now cherish those acts of everyday rebellion and are as proud of her feistiness as we are of her graciousness and generosity.

~~~~

AFTER one more night in Ottawa, it was time to head back home to Toronto and begin the task of planning a second memorial, without letting much more time pass. We struggled to find a place to hold it, as May is the time for graduations and weddings and there were very few suitable options available. We needed a venue large enough to accommodate our friends, co-workers and acquaintances, as well as those listeners with whom Lauren had a relationship. Eventually it was suggested we try Koerner Hall, an acoustically acclaimed concert venue with seating for a thousand or so and a wide, deep stage. As it turned out, we were able to book it for the afternoon of May 29, ten days after the Ottawa gathering. Fortunately for us, the woman who was in charge of the hall just happened to have worked with me twelve years earlier in a production of *Cinderella*. She remembered Lauren coming often to rehearsals and performances, enthralled with the musical comedy as well as the backstage workings of a professional show—and more than a little in love with the actor who embodied Prince Charming. We were grateful for this connection to help walk us through planning our event and to have found what looked to be the perfect setting.

Clearly, this memorial was going to be less casual than the first. Being in production mode and planning for another gathering was really a saving grace, and Rob and I were both grateful for the diversion: an opportunity to focus not on the totality of our suffering but on making this the best tribute to our daughter's brief but shining life that we could.

We spent many hours during those ten days between memorials scouring through and choosing photos to go along with lyrics to songs that were to be performed live, as well as for Lauren's own recording of "Dream a Little Dream." We enlisted the help of our friend Allan Bell to aid us put this together. An event planner and professional hospital and charity fundraiser, Allan had turned Lauren's wedding in an otherwise unremarkable hotel ballroom into a sheer white and sparkling setting. His love for our family and sense of— for lack of a better word—show would come in very handy for the May 29 event. As had been the case at her all-too-recent wedding, Lauren's goodbye celebration featured several Beatles songs. Our friend and fellow *Cinderella* performer, musician, director and writer David Warrack, took his seat at the shiny black grand piano under a spotlight at centre stage. Near him stood solo artist and lead singer of the band Lighthouse, Dan Clancy, also a family acquaintance; the two performed Billy Joel's "Lullabye" and the Beatles' "Golden Slumbers." A large black and stainless steel urn shaped like a sleek blackbird (in honour of that favourite and familiar Beatles song that Rob had taught Lauren on guitar) sat on a table onstage next to a microphone bearing her radio station's call letters, its head bent as if in sorrow.

A warm and down-to-earth minister, Susanne McKim, who had performed Lauren and Phil's wedding ceremony, oversaw our goodbyes to her. Our mutual co-worker from Ottawa, Steve Madely, spoke again, and then we heard "Stop All the Clocks," this time recited live by my radio partner and our close family friend, Mike Cooper. There was also a live rendition of the traditional Celtic blessing "She Does Not Leave," read by Lisa Brandt, my fellow broadcaster, my friend and a mentor to Lauren, and accompanied, quietly—perfectly—by David Warrack playing Billy Joel's "Dublinesque."

She does not leave, she is not gone, she looks upon us still.
She walks among the valleys now, she strides upon the hill.
Her smile is in the summer sky, her grace is in the breeze.
Her memories whisper in the grass, her calm is in the trees.
Her light is in the winter snow, her tears are in the rain.
Her merriment runs in the brook, her laughter in the lane.
Her gentleness is in the flowers, her sigh in autumn leaves.
She does not leave, she is not gone, 'tis only we that grieve.

This time, Rob and I spoke at our daughter's memorial in
person. We used many of the same notes we had written for
Lauren's Ottawa gathering, and had only fleeting moments
where emotions risked closing our throats. I recall walking
up the stairs from the audience at Koerner Hall and onto the
stage. As I stepped up to the podium, I took a deep breath. I
began by saying the words I'd always used in the studio when
there was a challenge at hand: "We can do this." And we did.

I told our friends and family in the auditorium and
watching online (both live and later on) that Lauren had
never worried us: she didn't do drugs, didn't drink and always
made sound decisions. She was everything we wanted in a
daughter, and we took comfort in knowing that she knew
we felt this way every day that she lived. I joked that she
grew up knowing there would be a therapy fund for her if
she ever needed it. But she was so well-adjusted, it turned
out she didn't, and we had Rob to thank for that! I said that
I'd learned at her Ottawa memorial that although Lauren
had worried she wasn't going to be good enough to get into
Algonquin College's radio course, her professor said she was

the best student ever to have gone through the program. Then I apologized if that sounded boastful. Throughout the time I had at that podium, I kept asking: With her short courtship, her desire to get into her career as soon as she could and, of course, her untimely and tragic passing, "Why couldn't she wait?" (In the months ahead, I would come to believe there was a preordained response to that question.) I shared the things for which we were grateful, both about Lauren's life and even her death. But I also took the opportunity to thank my husband, Rob, publicly for the amazing job he'd done as the stay-at-home father to our daughter.

> *Lauren did what Lauren wanted to do . . . and nothing held her back. And you know, she had her priorities straight—family first. Phil would take on four jobs: two minimum wage (the radio ones), one volunteer (again, radio) and a night job as a server/manager at a restaurant to allow Coco to have a full-time mom for a year. And somehow, our brilliant girl and her smart, hard-working new husband found a way to save money. To buy life insurance. To make sure their little family would be taken care of . . . no matter what.*
>
> *You see, the plan was for Lauren to return to work after her year's maternity leave, and Phil would take on the role that Lauren's own father had joyfully fulfilled: stay-at-home dad.*
>
> *Lauren knew what a solid and powerful relation-ship could come of this kind of arrangement . . . and I will tell you that it was Rob who fed and dressed Lauren*

before she went to school each day. He made her lunch.
He also made her the butt of school jokes when he put a
weenie in a thermos of hot water, complete with dental
floss, so she could fish it out and put it in an already
dressed hot dog bun.

Rob's influence on Lauren was felt long after she
began her life with Phil, and here's an example: in their
home, Lauren has rigged up this hose sprayer through
their toilet plumbing, complete with shut-off valve and
Teflon tape, for rinsing cloth diapers. She was a smart,
smart girl, and she learned well. She had the best pos-
sible role model in her daddy.

Then I moved aside and stroked Rob's back as he stepped
up to the microphone and spoke to the hushed gathering.
He told Phil that he was taking on the most important role a
person can ever have, and one that he had relished so completely: that of full-time father. He said to his son-in-law
that having seen how he'd handled parenting Colin single-
handedly over the previous eighteen days, he knew for sure:
"You've got this."

Just as he had ten days earlier, Phil took the stage and
spoke eloquently and from the heart. In a strange twist—and
as if to underline how public a life his wife and her family
lived—this time he wore a suit that was sold to him by a man
in a Toronto-area store who, when Phil gave his name at the
counter, recognized it from hearing about his wife's death on
the radio. I'm sure Phil was as blindsided as he was touched
by the man's kind words of condolence.

At this second memorial, the grieving widower's soft words weren't punctuated by the wails of his small son; baby Colin was backstage in Koerner Hall's comfortable green room with his paternal grandfather, nursing on a bottle during the heart-wrenching proceedings as Grandpa followed the memorial on a television monitor.

It was a marked difference from the Ottawa gathering, when Colin's cries had given voice to our feelings and underlined the uncertainty, the hornet's nest of questions to which we had no answers: What was to become of this sweet baby and his father? What was to become of us, two shattered parents who were now childless? Who were we now as a couple? Would I return to work? How would someone so completely shattered ever take up the mantle of morning show host again—and would it be appropriate? We'd get answers to almost all of these questions in time. Everything would take time. But the first order of business, now that we had said our goodbyes to our dear Lauren, was to continue to survive publicly and to start to heal privately.

CHAPTER 5

No Easy Answers

Lauren and Colin

BEFORE WE HAD EVEN HAD A CHANCE TO HOLD Lauren's first memorial we began searching for answers to the question on the mind of everyone who knew and knew of Lauren: How could a seemingly healthy twenty-four-year-old simply die in her sleep? The word *why* became a mantra that ran through my brain with what seemed like every second thought; I screamed it into a pillow and sobbed it onto Rob's shoulder within moments of retreating to our Jamaica hotel room. From May 11, 2015, on, I could almost see that one-syllable word hanging over our heads. I heard it in my restless sleep like an earworm, a pervasive melody that refused to cease. Everything about Lauren's passing defied logic: the fractured lines of the natural life order wherein a parent is expected to die before their offspring; the sudden, freakish and fatal thunderstorm that struck her down in the midst of what would have appeared to be the sunniest time in her life. Nothing about her death was expected, dreaded, understood.

Crime procedural television dramas like the massively popular *CSI* franchise have conditioned us to expect answers in an hour. But life, as we have all come to know, rarely mirrors television, and anyone involved in the real world of crime-solving will tell you that scientific investigation is necessarily painstakingly slow. Although a crime was never suspected, our situation would be no different: it would be months before we could hold a neatly printed, clinically worded copy (in the most literal sense) of the coroner's report in our hands. And had ours been the storyline of a TV show, no writer would have conjured up such an inconclusive final scene (not if he or she expected to be hired again). We were given no explanations. Only possibilities. In an age where we can turn to pocket pals like Siri or Google for resolutions to almost every big question or trivial pursuit, we found ourselves with only suspicions and no concrete answers. A big question mark came within the first twenty-four hours, when my friend wrote to inquire as to what Lauren had been taking to help her in her struggles to breastfeed. If you were going to drop in a plot twist, this would be the one to add.

～～～

IT seems almost impossible now, as parents, to look back and realize how much we did not know—and didn't even know we didn't know. Yes, there was always that readily available advice from our own mothers, mothers-in-law and even grandmothers—the sisterhood of those who'd gone before and had so much more experience and knowledge than we did as new moms, and who were more than anxious to share it. But it is difficult to measure how quickly that steady stream of advice became a firehose as soon as every know-it-all, every been-there-done-that-got-those-stretchmarks, got a megaphone and a soapbox with the arrival of the internet.

Not every opinion needs to be expressed, especially when it comes to issues about which people know little or nothing. But who are we kidding? This is the twenty-first century, when it's perfectly okay to argue facts and science with opinions and feelings, and when being offended is considered by some to equal being right. People seem to search the internet only for answers with which they already agree. And in no subject on this wonderful worldwide web are there more opinions than on parenting in general and motherhood in particular (with the possible exception of politics).

So let me share a story from back in the day, before everyone had access to all the answers (or purported to have them already), when we fumbled along and did the best we could by using good old instinct and a new parent's handbook. In our house, as in so many others, we consulted the paperback version of Dr. Benjamin Spock's *The Common Sense Book of Baby and Child Care* when the questions were too numerous or embarrassing to pick up the phone and call Mom. That was until, of course, Dr. Spock's parenting methods were blamed for turning out a bunch of spoiled tyrants. So, did we toss our paperbacks and search for other experts? Of course not! We furtively consulted his book and didn't dare tell *our* parents that we were going to go ahead and raise a hardened criminal behind their backs! Oh yes, we were rebels, all right.

More than once in my own early stages of motherhood, the burgeoning internet, had I consulted it, might have come in most handy. The clearest possible illustration of that comes via the incident involving our tiny daughter's bum. Lauren was only two months old when I noticed a little pink bump near the top of her bum crack. Okay—no laughing here—I will confess to you that I thought it was some remnant of our evolutionary development: the last vestiges of a tail, perhaps? (I thought you said you wouldn't laugh!) After all, are we not still natural works in progress? I had three wisdom teeth instead of four and always considered that an express lane on the evolution highway. Yay, me!

Thankfully, a well-timed visit from my mother changed my mind about Lauren's "tail." I asked Mom, a retired registered nurse, to take a look at the bump, which, in a few short days, had become redder and was seeming to cause our baby discomfort. Mom said that it looked like a cyst, and since it was late in the evening, we loaded up our cranky baby and off we went to the emergency room. Sure enough, it was a pilonidal cyst, something known to war veterans as "jeep seat," and that usually occurs in people between the ages of fifteen and thirty-five. (Word to the wise: if you google *pilonidal cyst*, please take my advice and *do not* look at the pictures that will inevitably pop up.) A quick anaesthetic, removal of the cyst and a stitch, and she was as good as new, albeit with a tiny scar to remind her of her earliest encounter with a scalpel. As I say, there's no doubt I could have used the wisdom of the internet in that case, but at least I had the option of consulting my mom. And I was grateful.

These days, though, we have information coming at us from every direction, and on multiple devices. There's so much peril attached to the constant barrage of opinion and criticism, and as media savvy as our daughter was, she was anything but immune to it. As empowering as the internet has been in this age of social activism, it's been equally debilitating for those who are scared, confused, searching and emotionally vulnerable, like new mothers. I was astonished to learn that our daughter, all ready to embrace the experience of motherhood, was bitterly disappointed when after only one push in labour, the umbilical cord around her baby's neck necessitated an emergency C-section.

For two weeks—or maybe more—Rob and I had been anxiously waiting, phones fully charged, for the day that Lauren or Phil would call and tell us their baby was on his way. On Canadian Thanksgiving weekend, we had an early turkey dinner, eating at about four o'clock in the afternoon of Saturday, October 11. As a fire crackled in the hearth, we were just finishing our dinner when the phone rang. It was Lauren.

"Do you feel like driving to Ottawa?" she asked, a smile in her voice.

"Are you kidding? We're on our way!" Within half an hour, my sister and her family were headed to our lake house to clean up dinner leftovers, take care of our two little dogs and hold down the fort as we embarked on an increasingly dark four-hour drive to Ottawa. We were guided by a pumpkin-orange moon slung low in the sky, and it wasn't until we were about forty-five minutes away from the hospital that the moon disappeared from view and a gentle rain began to fall. We had just pulled into a coffee shop parking lot for a comfort stop when my phone rang. It was Phil telling us that it looked as if Lauren was going to be undergoing a Caesarean section. We told him not to worry, told ourselves the same, and drove as quickly as we could (and only slightly over the limit) toward our daughter and son-in-law. We could hear the concern in Phil's quiet voice; no matter how many books you've read or classes you've attended, there is nothing that can prepare you for a sudden emergency surgery.

We stayed positive for the remaining leg of our drive, trying not to slide into the places that the mind goes when what should be a normal birth suddenly goes sideways. We hear of this happening all the time (in 2018, tennis goddess Serena Williams shared her story of undergoing a C-section when doctors spotted distress in her baby's heart rate with each of Serena's contractions). Had Colin been starved of oxygen? What did this mean for his health, and for that of his mother?

We pulled into the dark, wet hospital parking lot and sprinted to the entrance. Instead of the perfectly orchestrated moment of meeting our grandson and congratulating an exhausted and elated daughter, we were met by a tired but relieved husband and told that Lauren was still out; we'd have to wait for a bit to hold her and coo over the new arrival together.

After we'd hugged and held Phil for what seemed like minutes and he told us all was well, we finally got to see our beautiful grandson in his incubator, decorated with a cut-out turkey with the name COLIN neatly printed on it. The poor sweet boy's unusually long feet were still a greyish-blue hue.

But, we were told, a new son—and grandson—had arrived safely. We all felt so blessed, so happy.

The next day, Rob and I took a bottle of alcohol-free champagne, a teddy bear and a bouquet of roses to Lauren's hospital room. Still a little out of it from the previous night's anaesthetic, she smiled blearily at us, so proud of the little boy who'd come into the world with considerably more drama than any of us had wanted or anticipated, but seemingly safely nonetheless. She held Colin in her arms as he tried to feed in those early hours of life; later, while we shot pictures and video, all of the grandparents gathered and took turns holding this beautiful little creature, the first grandson in any of our lives.

Despite knowing how necessary and possibly life-saving that Caesarean section was, Lauren harboured regrets for the rest of her short life about not having given birth naturally. I can't say for sure, but I believe that those feelings may have stemmed from the prevailing online attitude that it wasn't a "real" birth experience unless you pushed. I would remind her how truly fortunate she was to have gone through but one contraction, and how she would probably have an option to give birth naturally if she chose to have another child down the road. How much she took my words to heart, I'm not sure; after all, I wasn't really the poster child for doing things the hard way when it came to giving birth. You see, the moment I found out I was expecting Lauren, I asked my chuckling doctor if I could just go ahead and book my Caesarean delivery then and there, as though it was a mere matter of finishing up with a pedicure and scheduling another in a month or so. And that's why *this* chicken crossed the road, or at least tried. To get out of labour, *dahling!* As it turns out, I needn't have worried; I sailed through pregnancy, labour and an anaesthetic-aided birth. To paraphrase the Nancy Sinatra hit, "These hips were made for birthin'."

Lauren put the most pressure on herself, and felt the most disappointment, where breastfeeding was concerned. Looking back, I realize now that she simply did not come from a long line of big milk producers. Who knew this was even something that can run in families? Even if this lactation limitation had dawned on me while Lauren was pregnant or nursing, I don't think I would have told her, lest it add to her feelings of discouragement. But as was the case with her blue eyes, Lauren came by this limitation naturally: her cousins, her mother, even her grandmothers (on both sides) and at least one great-grandmother struggled to provide nourishment the way nature intended.

I tried to assure her that retreating from her breastfeeding battle and choosing formula was not the worst thing that could happen. She herself had arrived three weeks early, and we almost immediately began augmenting her meals with formula delivered via a tiny tube taped to her daddy's finger. If she didn't put on weight, they weren't going to let us go home together—and we wanted to leave! So we embraced what the hospital's kind nursing staff offered us as an option and gave her what we felt she needed: a combo meal to go . . . home. There was no judgment that we perceived at that time: the nurses simply offered it as a way to help our baby put on weight. And there was another benefit to that tiny tube, either taped to my breast or to Rob's pinky: the fact that her dad fed her as often as I did, even in those early days, was probably a harbinger or at least a symbol of the unusual closeness that this daddy/daughter combo would share, in large part because he was the one who woke, fed and prepared her for her day, every morning, while Mommy was on the radio.

Lauren fought so hard to feed Colin. She shared with me during evening phone calls her nervous countdown to each doctor's appointment, and she would report in to me regularly about his weigh-ins, literally frustrated to tears. His continued failure to grow at a rate that she and her doctor considered normal or satisfactory worried her and her husband. From what she told me, this was truly the only source of any sadness or consternation in her new calling as a mother. Somewhat reluctantly, she admitted to me that she felt as if, for the first time in her life, she might be on the verge of sliding into depression. Her tears mixed with her baby's as she struggled to give him the nourishment that he needed when he needed it, which was at all hours of the day and night. And I can tell you from the early days and weeks after Lauren's death, a baby cries harder when you're rocking him and crying too. It's as if the shaking of your chest as you sob transfers straight to that baby in your arms. I can only imagine the pain she felt at not being able to feed her sweet boy, and they cried together.

I was reluctant to push Lauren or even nudge her in any direction; she was the kind of daughter who did not take well to advice that she didn't want to hear. She would call from work when she needed help with the pronunciation of a foreign newsmaker's name or from home when an appliance wasn't working and she needed her dad's help. But if Lauren had her heart or mind set in one direction, you might as well have been talking to the wall. So that's why I didn't come straight out and tell her to stop fighting and supplement with formula. Believe me, I've asked myself a thousand times why I didn't try harder, but deep down, I know the answer: she'd have taken out her frustration with the entire situation on me. So instead of going hard with the formula suggestion, I continued to try to encourage her in any way that I could: we talked about natural herbal supplements like fenugreek and blessed thistle, and she took them right away. Her breastfeeding buddy—someone with whom she was teamed up by the city's public health department—cheered her on, encouraging her not to give up and to keep trying to breastfeed, even when Colin's weight was on a low percentile for a baby his size and age. On top of that, one so-called friend boasted of having enough milk for both of their babies, while Lauren struggled to produce enough just to keep her own baby growing and healthy. Thanks a lot! Her frustration mounted and she found herself at her wits' end. What more could she do? Soon enough, Rob and I would pick up that heavy yoke of frustration, sadness and desperation as we, too, searched for answers to questions arising from a seeming breach of the laws of nature: as sure as a mother should be able to produce the milk her infant needs, parents should expect that their child will live a full and long life. How could this all have happened?

Our initial, unending "why?" soon turned to "how?" We knew from conversations Rob had had with the coroner in the first forty-eight hours after Lauren's passing that getting a response to this deeper question would not be a speedy process. There were numerous tissue samples to examine, tests to run and possibilities to rule out. Those in the coroner's office promised to be thorough in their efforts to give us answers, and we have every reason to believe they were. But very early on, the coroner was examining whether a drug that Lauren decided to take in her desperation to augment her milk supply might somehow have interacted with an undiagnosed heart defect.

She would have had no reason to be tested for any possible heart problems; even before surgery for gallbladder removal just a few years earlier, she had not had an electrocardiogram. Now, given that the drug she was prescribed, domperidone, is believed to interact with abnormal cardiac rhythm in some patients, we wish that the test had been run. Had those results shown a problem and been part of her medical records, she might not have received the prescription.

I found out about domperidone's history only one day after Lauren died. My friend Lisa Brandt emailed and asked if, by any chance, Lauren had been using it. I remembered our daughter mentioning that her cousin was taking it for her own problems breastfeeding, and my own dad was on it for a short time because of a medical gastrointestinal problem. Its similarity to the name of a favourite champagne, Dom Pérignon, had made it immediately familiar. When I called Lisa and told her that Lauren was indeed taking the drug, Lisa's response was "Oh my GOD!" Delivering what was the second biggest shock I would get that week, she told me that she had been taking it for a medical issue. She'd stopped, cold turkey, when a story came across her news desk that in 2004, the US Food and Drug Administration, which had not approved its use in the United States, issued a warning specifically to nursing mothers about the potential harms, including the reported risk of cardiac arrest from intravenous use. In late 2014, in the United Kingdom, it was withdrawn from the market as a non-prescription drug, and British doctors are instructed not to prescribe it without conducting a medical assessment of their patients to determine if it's suitable for them because of the risk of cardiac side effects.

Lisa also told me about a young woman at her radio station who said she had been taken off domperidone after heart tests had revealed a pre-existing murmur. The woman, who was Lauren's age and also had a young son, had been taking it to encourage breast milk production. The drug is approved in Canada for certain gastrointestinal conditions, but its use in stimulating lactation is "off-label." Health Canada and the manufacturers have advised that the drug may have cardiac side effects in certain patients.

As soon as I got off the phone with Lisa, I contacted Lauren's cousin Meaghan, herself a young mother of a son just a few months older than Colin. We talked about her own situation.

There certainly is a lot of pressure. I never felt pressure from others, but from myself. Breast is best! What parent doesn't want to do their absolute best for their child?! I struggled so much with both of my babies to nurse them. When it came to the decision to formula feed my second child, I felt horribly guilty. I felt like we wouldn't bond, he wouldn't love me, that I wasn't giving him what was best. . . . The list goes on. I personally don't care what other people think, but I have received more looks and "side eyes" from pulling out a bottle to feed my baby than I ever did pulling out a boob! It's crazy! There's a huge divide between moms that formula feed and those that breastfeed. "Fed is best" is an idea movement that is making progress now, and that's where I stand.

"Fed is best." Have you ever heard of this? Until my niece mentioned it, I certainly hadn't, or I most definitely would have looked into sharing the website www.fedisbest. org with Lauren. After having read more about it, how I wish the organization, founded in July 2016 in the United States, had been in existence during the time of her struggle, just to offer Lauren an alternative point of view to consider when it came to her and her baby.

～～～

WE were even more devastated now; as grieving parents—admittedly not scientists—it seemed *possible* to us that our daughter had died taking something exactly as it was prescribed. I can tell you in all honesty that in the days and months following our daughter's death, with all of the emotions we slogged through, truly the only time we were angry at our situation was when we learned that a prescription drug our daughter was taking perfectly legally in Canada was not approved in the United States and was strictly limited in the United Kingdom.

Could it be that Lauren's passing was not just some horrific accident of nature but caused by something completely preventable? This became the question that moved to the forefront of our minds. The coroner had voiced his preliminary suspicions to both Rob and Phil, but we held onto hope that perhaps we'd finally get some answers with the official coroner's report.

It was April 2016 when a copy of the report was mailed to us. Receiving it was one of those life moments that takes you out at the knees. After my radio show, I had made the short walk from the station to our condo across the street and was in a cheery mood. Another harsh Toronto winter was finally leaving town and spring was in the air. I said hello to our building concierge and, as I usually did, got the mail from a small room adjacent to the lobby. As I sifted through our mailbox contents, ready to pitch junk mail and flyers into the recycling, I stopped when I saw the official Ontario emblem on an envelope from the Office of the Chief Coroner that had been curled to fit into the box.

I felt an icy shock run through my entire body. I numbly closed the mailbox and took the elevator to our floor. When Rob greeted me inside our apartment, he could tell by my face that something was wrong.

Wordlessly, I slapped the envelope onto the kitchen counter, its contents potentially as toxic to me in that moment as a letter sprinkled with anthrax. And with that, I left the room to take off the workday's clothes, leaving Rob to open the grey envelope.

Receiving something bearing an official government insignia tends to make us stop what we're doing. Is it a bill? Did we mess up our income tax filings? Do I have to do something about my health card or driver's licence? These questions and so many more will have the time to run through your mind before you can open it. But I can't say that anything can prepare you for something with the word *coroner* on it. There can be no more stark a reminder that someone close to you is gone.

Rob picked up the letter and opened it.

This is how our marriage has always worked: when there's negotiating with bosses or agents that has to be done, it's Rob's job. While I string words together and share them for a living, his end of the bargain has been to take care of the heavy lifting: the business end of things. To this day, I have not laid eyes on the actual report; Rob has always said that I don't need to see it. He carries with him a burden, a weight that he hasn't made me share, and I am grateful to him for that and so many other things. He spares me pain when he can and, if he feels he needs to, takes it on himself. He saw from my face when I came through the door that receiving that letter took me back to the hour when we first learned of Lauren's death. The passage of those eleven months had helped us to stop thinking every minute of every day about losing Lauren. As we continued to learn new ways to survive this grief, this pain, we were able to imagine that our daughter was still alive and happily sharing the raising of her son.

I've often been grateful that we were spared the pain of her living with us at the time of her death; I frequently hear from parents who struggle with the constant physical reminders of their child's absence. We were able to shove reality to the side, and every day we got a little better at suspending reality. That shroud of shock that helps you to survive the first days and months after losing someone you love eventually wears thin. But the longer you can keep reality at bay, the easier it is to keep going.

It's not like we were delusional, even though every day I would click on an app on my phone, inviting our late daughter to join me for a drawing game we'd been playing just the day before she died. (I've since stopped, but only because the app rebooted and wiped our history.) But you do what you have to do in order to keep functioning in some version of what the world expects from you, and despite the constant reminders of her death because of well-meaning and kind-hearted listeners and journal visitors who would reach out to me on social media, I was able to do that pretty successfully some of the time.

Rob and I already had a rough idea of the letter's contents thanks to a call from the coroner to Phil several months earlier. How grateful we were that Dr. Earle so often took time out of a busy and undoubtedly harrowing day to keep grieving loved ones informed. Somehow, though, we knew that seeing his words more formally and in writing would make the stark facts even more difficult to digest. And perhaps worst of all, we didn't get the answers we sought; the report only raised the same questions again.

The doctor and his colleagues did every test at their disposal. They suggested that one of the possible causes of Lauren's death was an undiagnosed congenital heart disorder and another was that medication had interacted negatively with her heart rate or rhythm. A third possibility, and the one the coroner listed first—chronic meningitis affecting the brainstem—wasn't even heart-related. The report recommended that all of Lauren's direct relatives be tested for heart irregularities; Colin has been tested and all is well.

But try as he might, the coroner was not able to find one certain cause among these three possibilities, and Lauren's cause of death was officially "undetermined." He didn't have the answers we so desperately sought.

It's in our nature as humans to try to make sense of the inexplicable. Ancient civilizations, after all, created gods to explain thunder, lightning and natural disasters. We cautioned ourselves about linking Lauren's death to a medication, but at least in our minds, there was no other answer that made sense. Rob has an unusually slow and abnormal heartbeat; one surgery he was scheduled for was nearly cancelled because his doctors thought an electrocardiogram showed he had suffered a heart attack (he had not). I have a slight heart murmur. Did Lauren inherit one or both of these traits and could they have contributed to her death—with or without a possible medication interaction?

Today we find ourselves in the uncomfortable but inescapable place of not knowing the answers to our questions about what killed our daughter. But we hope we will gradually come to a place of peace in knowing that we cannot always know why. It is not a matter of "closure," a word that gets used so very often after the death of a loved one. No, knowing how she died will never explain to us why she had to be taken from us at such a young age—or at all. Things happen in life that we simply have to accept (or lose our minds), and all we can do is take what we have been given, make the best of everything within our power, love and appreciate her son for the gift that he is and continue to keep living in a way that honours his mother's memory: with laughter, with love and with the occasional well-placed expletive. Because honestly, can you blame us?

CHAPTER 6

Moving Forward: Life After Lauren

Lauren's last pre–maternity leave broadcast on 580 CFRA

THOSE EIGHTEEN DAYS BETWEEN LAUREN'S death and saying goodbye to the guests who joined us for her second memorial (and, later, at a hotel bar just across the street for some tears, some laughs and a lot of hugs) were tremendously busy. There were the four-hour commutes between Lauren's home and ours, the hours spent in bed alternating between crying and sorting through the pictures on my (and her) computer that would be used for the services and, of course, the overall business of putting together two events to honour our daughter and, more importantly, to give her friends and ours, plus family and other loved ones, a chance to grieve her and share their great sense of loss over this wonderful human being.

We called the shock that befell us after losing Lauren a blessing and, really, we did feel grateful to be in that state for about a year. Often we would say, "Boy, if this ever wears off and what has happened really sinks in, we're in big trouble!" But the layer of stupefaction lifted as gradually as a fog over our beloved Lake Simcoe after sunrise. We were allowed to step back into our lives in a slow, even pace—another debt of gratitude for which I'll never be able to repay my employers. While Government of Canada labour laws dictate that only three paid consecutive working days off are to be allotted in the death of an immediate family member (beginning the day after the death), my bosses made it clear that I was to take as much time as I needed while beginning to recover from Lauren's death. In early days, the question "Will she come back at all?" was raised. Initially, I wasn't able to say when that return would be, but I knew that, as radio had been the river upon which my entire adult life had flowed, there was a certain inevitability in the fact that I would return to the medium that had given my family and me so very much.

In the same way that listeners had celebrated Lauren's birth, her marriage and the arrival of her son, they mourned with us and showered us with kindness. They sent us hand-knit prayer blankets, as well as books about how to deal with the grief and how to survive the loss of a child. We were sent countless cards, many with long, handwritten letters express-ing sympathy and, in the case of those who had also lost a child, empathy. We were warmed and touched by the many different ways in which people we had never met reached out through email and messages left on one of the radio station's voicemail lines that had been dedicated especially to those who wanted to connect with me, Rob and Phil.

We later learned that, in an act of unexpected—but most appreciated—generosity, more than two hundred dollars was collected for Lauren and Phil's baby among the listeners we had left behind at that Jamaica resort on May 11. That money would be used to pay for the formula that was now needed to nourish Lauren's seven-month-old. We would witness this kindness and generosity again and again in the days and months to come: beautiful, sweet gestures from friends and strangers alike. Even Rob's hockey buddies in Toronto took up a collection to help Phil and Colin; one of them, actor/comedian Seán Cullen (he of *Last Comic Standing*, *The Producers* and Corky and the Juice Pigs), was particularly affected by Lauren's passing and, even though he'd never met her, wanted to host a fundraising show to help Lauren's boys. It was really the most astounding thing to experience, and I'm grateful we were in the moment enough to see what was happening around us. We would share these stories of generosity with Phil, and all he could do was shake his head in amazement. Lauren had grown up around these kinds of people; she knew how much a part of our family they were, and vice versa. I can only imagine how dumbstruck Phil was to be a part of this largesse. It's almost impossible to believe if you haven't worked to cement these ties for your entire career. Radio can be far more than a one-way medium, and we had long appreciated the benefits of that fact that were manifest in so many ways, now more than ever.

It was all *so* astounding, in fact, that my mentor—respected author and international radio consultant Valerie Geller—was moved to respond that the experience I had with our station's listeners made her reconsider her long-time belief that, as much as those of us who have been fortunate enough to make a living in the medium do adore it, radio does not love you back.

She explained: "I did pivot a bit on 'radio not loving you back. . . .' But it's not the industry, which can be cold, heartless and wonderful (but hey, maybe that happens in life as well). It is the kindness and caring of the people who listen, whose lives you've connected with and touched each day, when you've literally become a part of the cast of characters in their world. THOSE people CAN love you back. . . . It's the people radio gives us (not the delivery system or the business around it) that can and do love you back."

Two days after Lauren's Toronto memorial, Rob and I more or less ran away from home: we pointed the car south, then east, and headed for a small town in Connecticut. Fortuitously, I'd gone there the previous year, searching for a place where I could go "inward": I practised meditation, Skyped with an addiction expert in California, did copious journalling and met a life coach who helped me find answers to many of the questions I was asking myself about my present and future as they pertained to my career. Ellen Wasyl would become a friend in need one year later. Even under the worst circumstances, I was grateful that Rob could meet this woman who reminded me of the actor Laura Dern and was a font of positivity, compassion and inspiration. She still is, to this day.

What I learned in our week there is what I already knew: there is no set timetable or spreadsheet for how—or how long—one is to grieve. There are schools of thought that say six months, and others that are as specific as four years, as though anything as pernicious as the pain of a broken heart can possibly be measured or timed!

When recovering from the same surgery, people do so at different paces—and there can be complications. Grief isn't any different. In fact, in the years to come, we would learn about a psychotherapy model called complicated grief therapy. Bodies heal differently; some never do. As much as our "are we there yet?" and TL;DR (too long; didn't read) lives demand or even expect a GPS for the route and duration of this trip through hell, we have to face it: there is no one-size-fits-all when it comes to grief. Add to that the completely unnatural order of things when a child predeceases his or her parents, and it's like trying to recover from a knee replacement surgery where you've woken to find that your new joints bend the wrong way. It's going to take a long time to learn how to move in the direction you need to go. You know you've got the equipment to do the job successfully, but it's just all wrong.

And of course, there was the undeniable fact that people, as kind-hearted and well-meaning as they were, would always be reminding us of the tremendous loss we'd suffered. An encounter in Lake Placid, New York—where we stopped for a night on our way home from New England—provides an example of not only how far-reaching our grief was but also how small a world this truly is. As Rob and I perused the pottery in a quaint gift store on the town's main street, a woman I thought I'd seen peeking at me over the shelves said, "Erin Davis?"

When I smiled and said yes, she told me that she and her husband were on their honeymoon and had watched the video of Lauren's memorial online just the night before. As she and I stood there with tears in our eyes, Rob couldn't help but joke that there were definitely better ways they could have been spending their honeymoon! We all laughed—and Lauren would have agreed. But such was the openness of every facet of our lives, our very public lives. Just as people remembered hearing on the radio that our daughter had been born, they were there with us when she died and when we were saying our goodbyes. We were, and remain, grateful.

Of course, reminders come in all ways, at all times. Many of them are unexpected, while others are as set in stone as the calendar. Some came via occasions we'd antici-pated with joy until now—like birthdays, weddings and Christmas; others came on days that had never stood out as special before, but for which we now had to brace ourselves. I was astounded to find that, with one notable exception, the anticipation of those red-letter days—the elevens mostly—was worse than the day itself. I would feel a heaviness start-ing to approach as the eleventh of each month drew nearer and Lauren's death was one month farther away. But I chose to return to work on an eleven: the eleventh of June.

I had been on the air with my partner, Mike Cooper, and the rest of our wonderful morning team—producers Ian MacArthur and Gord Rennie and news host Steve Roberts—via phone a few weeks before. They'd wanted everyone to hear how I was doing, and I wished to thank them and our listeners for their incredible support for our family. In that phone conversation with Mike, I also admit-ted to something that was so ordinary that at any other time in our lives, we wouldn't have felt it noteworthy: Rob and I had laughed.

After the Ottawa memorial, we'd headed straight to our cottage to cocoon. Outside our windows, spring was settling in and making itself at home: robins built a nest on a light outside our front door and watched over its fragile blue contents, trees were dotted with buds and leaves, and our gardens were once more showing green signs of life.

Apart from daily dog walks, Rob and I hid away inside the house with a wood fire that was far more for comfort than necessity. Then, almost like clockwork every evening, we turned on the TV to watch one of two things. The first was our stockpile of both recent and ancient episodes of NBC's *Dateline*. Over time, I would come to refer to them as "grief porn" because of the show's combined number of parents and friends talking tearfully of losing a beautiful, promising, smart young woman whom they loved desperately. You'd think that our watching that parade of pain, week after week, would be not just counterintuitive but downright masochistic, and I suppose, to a small degree, it was. Sometimes, when the parallels to our own loss were too much to ignore, I'd find myself gasping to catch my breath, crying as silently as I could into my bathrobe sleeve, my hand to my cheek to camouflage the tears. But more often, we'd watch these episodes experiencing an underlying feeling of gratitude that our daughter had died in what they tell us was a painless and peaceful manner. For all of the tragedy that had befallen us, there were still always reasons to be grateful. And, just as it helped us get through the first few days after Lauren's death, that mindset helped Rob and me to keep going. To keep getting up in the morning. To keep from self-medicating.

And then, there was what's famously been called the best medicine of all: laughter.

In a 2017 interview with *Playboy*, comedian Patton Oswalt opened up about how laughter (in addition to his young daughter and new fiancée, now wife) had helped him survive the death of his wife of eleven years some sixteen months earlier. Just as our own daughter had, respected crime writer Michelle McNamara passed away suddenly in her sleep.

Asked by an interviewer, "Could anything or anybody help you punch through the despair?" Oswalt responded that watching comedy and laughing helped him to heal and feel normal again.

I highly recommend reading any of Patton Oswalt's takes on grief and depression; he has spoken about them on numerous occasions. His hard-earned wisdom is matched only by his honesty and frankness about the sheer hell he went through after losing Michelle.

Part of *our* way out of this thick fog of grief and pain came thanks to another comedian, a famous talk show host who was taking his leave of the public eye. Late-night star David Letterman was wrapping up his storied television career at the same time our world was falling down. But we had the presence of mind to set the PVR long-distance, and his final shows were waiting for us when we were ready to immerse ourselves in something other than our overwhelming misery. In the depths of our pain—and despite it, really—Rob and I found ourselves enjoying the final shows. While we were far from a time in our lives when laughter, with its wonderful accompanying burst of endorphins, would make us feel as good as it once had, we were ready for the diversion. In fact, later, Rob and I admitted to each other that we'd each felt quite self-conscious about laughing. And yet, how could we not? After all, it was Letterman!

So it was that when I spoke with my radio family on the phone that week—and was asked, "How are you, *really?*"—I told them that I thought we'd seen the first signs that we were going to be okay, and then explained that we'd laughed while watching Letterman. I added that there had been a time when I didn't know if we would ever truly laugh again, and we were comforted to know that we could. (It struck me later that, on a much larger stage, David Letterman had already played this role for all of America: in his first show after 9/11, he sat at his desk—no theme song—and just talked. He paid tribute to the fallen and the first responders; he expressed his sadness and even his quiet optimism. But most importantly, he made viewers feel as if things were going to be all right again some day—normal, even—and that we could all expect to laugh too. I'm grateful to him for helping us to realize that in 2015, just as he did for his viewing audience in 2001.)

Even over the phone, Mike and I picked up our easy partnership just where we'd left it that horrible morning during a remote broadcast in Jamaica, and it felt as natural as putting my lanyard around my neck for work again. I could sense a safety, a warmth and a certain spot where I could be vulnerable, even as I shook with nervousness over stepping back into my public life. It became clear to me during that phone call that this was where I needed to be: with Mike, our on-air team and our radio listeners. I would go back "home" again because I had a job to do: healing myself and maybe even showing what is possible with enough support and strength. Laughter was going to be a huge part of that, and Rob and I began to look at possible dates. We settled on June 11.

I wrote and posted a journal entry on my website so that CHFI listeners, and whoever else might wish to know, could understand why I chose that particular day to go back to the studio and my friends, where I was welcomed with the type of group hug usually reserved for a pitcher who's just thrown a no-hitter. Why June 11? I guess the better question, to Rob and me, was: If not that day, then when?

A dear family friend suggested I stay away from work until we'd made our way through this sea of grief and disbelief. But the truth was simple: we'd never be completely through it.

There are days, as one listener so wisely put it, that the waves of sadness threaten to take you under. But there are others on which they just gently lap at your feet. By the time I was ready to return to work, the lapping waters had outnumbered the tidal waves.

I wrote in my journal that I was also almost out of ways to express our gratitude for the support and vast kindness that readers and listeners sent our way: to Rob and me, to Phil and Colin and to our hobbled families. In direct opposition to the worst moments of that month, the outpouring of emotion that was conveyed to us all was something I never imagined possible.

And yet, when we needed it most, readers and listeners

were there for us with a gentle word (or an expression of not being able to find the words at all), a soothing card, an email, a post.

I concluded:

I don't think we would be stepping slowly into this place of peace in our hearts today if not for you.

So today I'll be back with you and with my friends at CHFI, an incredible team that has given us so much love and such heartfelt concern for our well-being. I cannot imagine working at any other place and being treated this way.

More than once, Rob and I have said that we are grateful that if this had to happen—and we still don't know why—it is at a time when we're enveloped by love and sympathy.

Don't be surprised to hear us laughing today. My soul needs this place of friendly escape and welcome distraction. Despite the fact that our world has lost so much of its meaning, there is still more to do and laughter will play a large role in the way we move on from here.

I'll say it again: we thank you from the bottom of our hearts. I hope you take these words to yours, because we will never forget the many hands that reached down to help us back to our feet. There may still be stumbles and I may reach for your hand again along the way. But knowing you are there makes every day a little easier.

Why today? It's June 11th. One month ago today,
our dear Lauren didn't wake up. On this day, her little
Coconut, our sweet Colin, turns eight months old. And
my father marks his 82nd birthday in good health and
spirits. That's why June 11th feels . . . right.
This is for Lauren. It always will be.

There were moments that first day back at the micro-phone that I teared up, my voice lacking the enthusiasm of a chipper upper range that I couldn't imagine hitting ever again. At the end of that first show and several thereafter, I felt like a scuba diver whose tanks had run out of air and who was just barely making it to the surface. Yet every day, I was able to expand my lungs a little more. To breathe and laugh and have some semblance of normalcy for just four hours a day. The sense of routine that accompanied my return to my well-worn studio chair only served to emphasize the contrast between the relative steadiness of my work life and the abso-lute tumult of life at home, where it was obvious that nothing was ever going to be the same as it was before we left on that listeners' trip in May.

Although I've done it over and over (and will again at the end of this book; I hope you'll read the acknowledgements), I can't begin to thank the closely knit team I worked with dur-ing those extremely difficult days. My partner, Mike, deftly navigated the dip-filled dance between tears and laughter as beautifully and naturally as it could possibly have been exe-cuted. Just as we had always done, we alternated between the serious and the ridiculous, and although people knew

I was hurting—as we all were in that room, and in some offices down the hall—there was also a great amount of joy and comfort going into the microphones and coming out of that studio. And, as usual, what comes from the heart goes to the heart.

The reaction from our radio audience was nothing short of incredible. With few exceptions (and, oh, there was one big, awful one, as you'll read later), people were reaching out to offer their support as I tried to climb back into my public life. Few emails touched me as deeply as this one from listener Tracey Morse, written after that first day back. It left me in tears.

Dear Erin,

I have been wanting to send an email for a month now, but simply couldn't come up with the right words or a beautiful saying to help you during your darkest hours. I would like to share with you what the passing of your beautiful daughter has taught me.

Over the past month, I have learned that you can mourn deeply for someone you never met. That you can cry endless tears and feel an amount of empathy you never thought possible. I have learned that in this busy, crazy, huge city of ours, people are kind and when one listener pulled her car over off the highway to cry when she heard of Lauren's death, strangers pulled over to ask if she was ok and cried with her when they heard the news. I have learned that the wonderful people on the radio that entertain us on our way to work are much more than that, they become an important part of our day and lives. I have learned that in a day and age when we think everyone is self-consumed, people took the time to donate blood because it was something Lauren was passionate about. I have learned that through tragedy and loss, the goodness in people comes out!

This morning, I learned that hearing a familiar voice on the radio could warm my heart and make me as happy as having a cup of coffee with an old friend.

Love to you, Rob, Phil and baby Colin,
Tracey

That beautiful email told me that coming back and simply continuing to do the show was the right thing to do, even if my scars were audible at times.

As for Rob, he was also comforted by the return to some semblance of order in our lives: walking his wife and our two little dogs to the nearby radio station at 4:45 a.m. and then, after kissing me goodbye at the door, continuing on his trek with the pups. He relished the quiet time at home to exercise, do paperwork and take care of chores that didn't involve me. But he always had the radio on, laughing along with our friends in the studio and making sure I was on solid emotional ground. I could sense his support for me in knowing that he was listening, going about his routine, just as he knew that when I got home—collapsing on the couch, exhausted from the steady and often hectic pace of putting on a normal show when everything was just so raw and new—I'd be making sure he was doing all right too.

There were the occasional moments when my voice would crack and my emotions would bubble up through the crevices to the surface. We would put listeners on the air and they would kindly take the opportunity to offer me their condolences. That was never difficult or the least bit awkward for me, and I was always grateful for their kindness. I can only hope that those messages didn't serve to bring other listeners down. After all, this was supposed to be "show business," and the purpose of my being there was to help our team wake listeners with a smile. I would hate (as would Lauren) the thought that we were anything but a source of lightness and enjoyment, even in those early days after my return. But I suppose when reality creeps in, the accompanying feelings are inevitable, no matter how hard we try to keep them at bay.

In a show that played all of the adult contemporary hits—ranging in tempo and angst from the lighter-than-air Bruno Mars and "Uptown Funk" to the bitterly broken-up Christina Perri and "Jar of Hearts"—my musical Achilles heel was most definitely Adele. It was in January of 2016, on the first listener trip that followed the fateful one the previous May, and (what else?) an early morning. I was practically propped up in my chair, doing the show after a night that was not spent sleeping; I'd suffered a bout of food poisoning and was literally "tired and emotional," a euphemism often used to describe celebrities who are drunk in public. But, oh, it was not booze but food that had taken me down, and I've no idea what it was. I'd never had any troubles in Mexico—or on any of our listener trips—from food. But as (bad) luck would have it, this time I was knocked sideways.

When I tried to talk at the end of Adele's "When We Were Young," I found my voice starting to catch, and for a moment, I could have been in the opening credits of *Mad Men*, tumbling helplessly and out of control. It felt as if I was just going to lose it completely and flat-out sob on the air— and, to make matters worse, do it right in front of a live group of listeners who had joined us for the show. I was too sick and too tired to get a grip on my emotions or my words: "I'm sorry," I choked out, "it's just . . . so awful." By *awful* I didn't mean the song; I meant losing control—the pain that the song brought out with its lyrics about the fleeting nature of youth and of life itself. Fortunately, moments like that were few. (Thanks, Adele!)

The holidays in 2015 were a particularly hard six weeks. To the delight of many (as reflected in our ratings at that time of year), we programmed wall-to-wall Christmas music at CHFI from the day of the Santa Claus Parade in mid-November, and I knew some songs would absolutely prove to be emotional triggers. Josh Groban, with whom I had a friendly relationship from his many visits to Toronto, took me down hard with his version of "I'll Be Home for Christmas." I rushed out of the studio as it played through the speakers one morning, brushing past my boss and our senior producer, and headed for an empty office to sob. And then, two minutes later . . . back into the studio, on with the show, being "on my best" once again.

I've no doubt it was hard for listeners to imagine me putting on a smile for that period of festive tunes, especially when a contest we aired every day shone a spotlight on people's hardships. For "Pay It Forward," we asked listeners to send us an email about someone they knew who needed an all-inclusive trip for two to a luxury resort. During the holiday season, we drew winners from the many submissions we received. The stories were often as heartwarming as they were heart-wrenching, with winners dealing with their own grief, serious illnesses and other life challenges. There were happy stories as well: daughters who wanted to thank their dads for always being there; sons who entered their moms in appreciation for their solo-parenting. Through the congratulatory phone calls, as nominators shared news of the win with their nominees, our participants would often take a moment to offer me condolences. It cannot have been easy for listeners to be brought back to the sad reality of my family's life, and even though I appreciated every word of kindness, I was and am sorry if it caused anyone to feel sadness for us.

In the year and a half that I continued to do mornings following Lauren's death, I learned that people were always going to hear me through certain filters. Mind you, this was not a new concept; many were the times I would be called or emailed (or even written a letter, way back when) when a listener thought they heard me say something a certain way or with a particular "tone" or, in some cases, using words I absolutely did not use. Experiences like those led me to the conclusion that "I cannot be responsible for what you hear, only what I say."

It's that kind of perception—or even projection—that would have people saying that I just sounded "sad," even on days when I was not and was, in fact, having a particularly up or light-spirited morning. For some, the concept of me actually feeling good enough to laugh and have fun on the radio was just too much to comprehend. *She just lost her child. How could she laugh?* One fellow bereaved mother told me that she tuned in when I returned to the air after my month off and thought, *Wow, just wait until the shock wears off.* But when it did, I'd like to think the cracks in my facade rarely showed. I was not being dishonest when I was enjoying those four hours on the air. They were my lifeline; our listeners were holding me up in a human chain of compassion and kindness. Any happiness people thought they heard was real; any sadness, while also real, was probably not as constant or as frequent as they might have thought.

There were a few pieces of correspondence that showed a different side to people than the generosity of spirit of which I was such a fortunate recipient. One email came from a woman I'll call Dee, who demanded that I come out and tell people the "truth." The subject was "Disappointed." That's always a great point from which to start, right? There's no word quite as laden with passive-aggression as that one, especially when it comes from a total stranger. Dee wrote that if Lauren had killed herself, we should not be ashamed, and that depression is a lousy thing. She pointed out that we must know that there's speculation out there, and that people are buzzing. (Really? They were? That honestly had never occurred to us.)

She suggested that Lauren had perhaps caught drug

addiction from a relative, and that we should not be embarrassed, as no one is perfect "on this plane." She warned me to tell listeners the truth before they lost every ounce of respect for me. She compared Lauren's death to that of Michael Jackson and said that even his passing had an explanation.

The dressing on this word salad came in the form of the twisted benediction with which she closed. Thoughts, prayers and all of that. What?

That letter not only confused me but also filled me with sadness. My entire career, including the time when I was away from the radio, had been built on transparency and honesty. As I told the *Toronto Star* reporter, had Lauren died in any way other than what we had been told—even though we weren't able to determine what caused her heart to stop—I'd have most definitely shared that with listeners and journal readers. What would I possibly have to gain by hiding or lying about what killed our daughter? Lauren herself had been all about helping others where she could and was fully invested in her radio station's annual corporate campaign to spark conversation about mental health issues. She knew the importance of using a public platform for good; watching me try to accomplish that was as much a part of the atmosphere in which she grew up as the Beatles music that played constantly on our long car trips. After a great many rewrites, here's what I finally settled on as a response:

> *She absolutely did not kill herself. I thought today's journal made that clear—so let me say it again: she did not die by suicide. That's an assumption often made*

when someone young dies suddenly. But it's wrong.

She was happy, healthy and absolutely loving her role as a mother. The coroner could have told us immediately had she killed herself. They are now examining her brain and heart to find out what happened but there are no answers.

I am shaking as I write this to you. I have been an advocate for depression awareness for some time now, as I myself have suffered it in silence for so long.

If it was suicide I would tell our listeners. If you knew me, you'd know that. Nothing about my daughter's life embarrasses me; if she'd died by suicide I'd use it as a way to spread word about it.

I'm just stunned by this email. Let people buzz and speculate. They can't touch us now. Our daughter is dead and nothing else matters—not gossip, not meanness, not anything.

As is almost always the case when someone hits Send before thinking about how their words can wound, I didn't hear back from Dee, and I was fine with that. I'd told her my truth, and besides, as anyone who has ever written an angry (but deserved) response and then deleted it knows, sometimes it feels good just to get those thoughts out there— whether or not they're ever read.

~~~~

BEING in the public eye, of course, means being judged. We live and die by ratings, for heaven's sake; what are they if not an ongoing popularity contest? I came to peace with that quite early on in my career (because I had to) when a competing radio station's sportscaster compared my face to that of some obscure old-time hockey player who was obviously not known for his good looks. You tell me what woman would enjoy being told her face resembles that of an NHL player (although any of us could do worse than resembling Sidney Crosby). It might have ended with that little shot had not a writer for a local newspaper, known for its busty beauties on page three, picked up that dig and run it two days in a row (using the second iteration of the story to correct the hockey player's name) in his gossip column on page six. To add to the absurdity of it all, I was on vacation that week and wouldn't even have known about the whole nasty thing (in those pre-internet days) had my boss at the time not thought it necessary to bring it to my attention as soon as I got back. For the life of me I couldn't—and still can't—figure out what would bring him to do that, but I guarantee he would not have done the same to my higher paid and higher profile male co-host. It was just the way things were.

That sophomoric slight brought home to me the fact that I would never be judged entirely on my career or accomplishments or failures, but on things mostly out of my control, like my appearance. My being female. My having a strong presence and the outright audacity to be more than a tittering laugh track when that was the role to which so many women in radio were relegated, especially on that sportscaster's rock station. My simple presence and success would offend some, and there was nothing I could do to change that; it was part of the dues I paid being a woman in a male-dominated business, helping to kick open doors that had formerly been locked up tight to my gender. All I could do was my best, and so I long ago put forth a concerted effort to make peace with the petty judgment and unkindness that would be out there, hopefully keeping them at arm's length (something the internet made increasingly difficult as time went on).

Years later, when that same sportscaster approached our show's producer, asking if it would be worth him applying for a position on our highly rated morning team, he was laughingly reminded of that comment. He expressed incredulity, saying, "Wow. She has a good memory."

I guess that, in his mind, I was supposed to take it "like a man," roll with it and just let it go, as he'd surely had to do about his own looks over the years. He never did apply for that job. And, yes, I recognize that my memory for slights is far too good for my own well-being. But even grown-ups need to be reminded that words hurt.

Nothing I did—no number of hours spent in therapists' offices—could prepare me for the most acidic correspondence I would receive at any time in my career. It came, as so many gentle and comforting pieces of mail did, in a rectangular white envelope. It arrived at my workplace a few months after Lauren's death. Someone had clearly been biding their time, waiting for just the right day to post a card that was so benign in appearance that I'd never suspect the verbal poison that it contained. I opened it just after 8 a.m. A song was playing on the air, and my partner, our producers and I were each working away on our own: answering emails, poring over music logs, planning the next on-air segment. To the

side of my computer keyboard sat a small stack of mail that
had been retrieved from the station's reception area that morning. My name and address appeared in neat handwriting.
Next to that, written on a slant, was the word *Personal*. There
was also a return address (which turned out to be fake)—all
in all, nothing out of the ordinary.

I tore open the envelope and pulled out a dollar-store
pink card decorated with wild roses and a butterfly. On the
outside were printed the words *With Deepest Sympathy*.
Here's what was written inside in neat, curly—and highly
legible—handwriting:

> *Dear Erin,*
> *May the enclosed words bring you peace at this time.*

Lovely enough, yes? The card seemed to echo the sentiments of the dozens of others that came our way after May
11. But it was the computer-printed letter tucked inside that
made me throw my hand to my mouth and gasp, "Oh my
God. Oh my God." I'll share the contents with you now. I
wouldn't even let my husband read this letter, so horrific were
its contents. But there's nothing like shining a light on the
darkness to overcome it, and at the risk of giving the mon-
ster who wrote this the satisfaction of knowing I read it, I'll
expose this now for the raw sewage that it is.

> *Dear Erin,*
> *Please excuse this typed letter, my handwriting is just*
> *too hard to read.*

Every day I have to listen to you on the radio—no choice at work.

Every day I am subjected to hearing all about your journal from my cubicle mate—it is easier to just nod along rather than asking her not to tell me.

Day after day I hear bout [sic] your plight with your dead daughter. Boo hoo, every day there is death.

I'm sure you must be struggling to answer the "why" question, why did she die? I bet you know the power of the universe, and here is the answer. For years you pined to be the best . . . top of the heap . . . best ratings above everyone else—and you'd do or trade anything to be at the top. All Erin, all the time. On the radio, blogging, guest speaker, never a moment without Erin. (By the way, how does it feel to think about how you told all those poor sad people to just live their best life ever after you had a lay off . . . don't your [sic] feel like such a hypocrite thinking about your "wisdom" to those people with real pain, now that you are experiencing real pain).

So the universe came calling to make you re-pay your debt. You can't ask for something big and not trade big.

Your daughter will be remembered by a handful. She wasn't a brain surgeon and she didn't change the world. She dropped out of college, married young, had a job and had a baby. She loved and she was loved. The two who deserve the sympathy are the son-in-law and the baby. They lost their future, you had enough time.

The letter goes on from there with a few more paragraphs disparaging my career and the radio station in general. When our producer Ian checked on the address—he did so in person, driving to the place from which the card and letter were supposedly sent—he determined that the street number was non-existent. We assumed then that the name was also not real. Typical, that: the meanest ones rarely give you a chance to respond.

I wish I could tell you that the thousands upon thousands of kind words that flooded our way—like the lovely, welcoming email from Tracey Morse—outweighed the few hundred vile ones, but I'm just not that evolved. The forethought and cruelty that went into writing and mailing that handwritten card and accompanying typed letter are almost unimaginable to me; only in transcribing that letter for you here have I taken the time to read each sentence. The day that it arrived I was only able to skip from one paragraph to the next, gleaning with each phrase its despicable contents.

Having read it in full now, as you just have, all I can say to whoever wrote this (and took the time to come up with a fake name and address) is: You don't know me and you most certainly don't know my family. You are wrong—dead wrong—especially about how we would move into the future. But you're most wrong about our daughter. She was not a brain surgeon, but she had a bright and promising future (the very reason she left college) and the opportunity to change lives. She made more of a difference in her twenty-four years on this planet than any poor, pitiable, anonymous troll who claims to have been exposed to me by force and third-hand while having far too much knowledge of the details of my life for that to be true.

Let's not forget the reason this person said they were typing the letter, which was that their handwriting was too hard to read. However, the writing on the card and its envelope was perfectly legible. Just maybe there were concerns that I'd recognize that handwriting, do you think?

Of course, when the name and address are fake, there's no chance to answer. But I've taken the opportunity here to do so, as is my right. I'd tell them to go to hell, but from the tone of that letter, they're already there. Imagine feeling you have to defend your love, your grief, your pain and your dead child, all because of one person's letter. That's exactly how I felt. And, of course, there was no way to respond, even if I'd somehow found the words or felt the desire to do so. Lauren died because *I* was ambitious and successful. Just try to wrap your head around what kind of mind it would take to come up with that.

I'd be lying if I said that a tiny, nasty part of me didn't feel that way right after her death, though, and that is perhaps why the letter bothered me as much as it did. I feared it might contain an element of truth. In my incoherent hours and days after Lauren's death, I kept saying to Rob, "It's 'The Monkey's Paw.' 'The Monkey's Paw.'" He hadn't studied this short story by W.W. Jacobs, but I'd never forgotten it from my high-school literature course. A horror-filled cautionary tale set against the backdrop of three wishes, it basically warns that if you mess with fate, you'll have a steep price to pay.

Rob tried to convince me again and again that Lauren's death was nothing like this. There was no punishment, no

karma. We had done nothing to bring this tragedy upon ourselves; it had just happened. Blame the lessons of catechism
from growing up or the guilt I have felt most of my life for
nearly everything beyond my control, but I somehow wondered what I had done to make this happen. The words of
that horrible letter blaming me for seeking the limelight and
paying with our daughter's life just served to underline the
inanity of my own self-incrimination. I guess what I was trying to express was my deep-seated expectation that there was
going to be a price for the blessed life I'd been given.

For so many years, I thought my own theme song echoed
that of Maria from the famous musical and film *The Sound
of Music:* I wondered what I'd done so right in my youth and
childhood to deserve the life I was living. Since marrying
Rob and having Lauren, I had always felt so very charmed.
My mother always asked me why, with the good fortune I
had, I never bought a lottery ticket. And I told her straight
out: "Mom, I have already won the lottery." I enjoyed a great
career. I had a wonderful husband (on the first try!). We'd
raised a daughter who was everything we could have hoped
for and then some. Who could ask for anything more?

So you see, I never stopped being grateful, nor did I
ever once take it for granted. Had I worked hard and sacrificed much, including, at times, my mental health? You bet
I had. Rob had sacrificed too, sometimes wondering when I
would retire and he could "have his wife" to himself. But I
wouldn't have traded any of it for the world. We were financially secure. I had risen to a place I could not have imagined,
and life was so good. So damned, unimaginably good. We

were content, having found as much balance in our lives as a workaholic and her husband could muster, and I wanted for nothing except a few more hours of sleep each night. That was all. So how could I have brought this on myself?

People will always judge how you handle something as tragic as the loss of a loved one: how much you suffer, how quickly you recover, how appropriately or inappropriately (in their opinion) you mourn. Your job is to try, try, try not to care.

You may recall that there were pages upon pages of comments devoted to the subject of how quickly Patton Oswalt rebounded when, some fifteen months after the sudden death of his wife, he began dating and was soon engaged to writer Meredith Salenger. Oswalt responded to these (mostly) anonymous critics by echoing the sentiments of a blogger who basically said that no one gets to sit in judgment of what a widow or widower does when their own partner is perched right next to them. No one who hasn't had the routine of their daily life turn into a living nightmare gets to have a say in how a survivor chooses to pick up the pieces.

In the same way that Patton Oswalt had after his wife's death, we expected Phil to quietly begin dating again after Lauren's passing. When it happened, though, we found out in an almost tragicomical way. Preparing to babysit Colin one evening, we'd done a text-connection test with Phil before he went out. A while later, Phil inadvertently texted some particularly warm and affectionate words to me—the mother-in-law! Of course, he meant to write them to the woman he was then seeing, a woman we would come to love for the companionship she provided to Phil, and the mother figure she became to his son. But at that moment? Talk about awkward—except that we didn't talk at all! Because I found out about her presence in his life in a way I know he wouldn't have chosen, we wanted to spare his feelings, and we waited until our next visit to Ottawa to bring up the subject. The last thing we wanted to do was make Phil feel bad in any way or say the wrong thing to him. After all, this would be a big adjustment—no matter how positive—for all of us.

That period also gave us the breathing space we needed in order to let this development sink in. We'd known it would only be a matter of time before Phil moved into another relationship, and although his doing so was one of the signposts showing more distance accumulating between our daughter and the present, we welcomed the relief that Phil would have, both from loneliness and heartache, and also from the heavy responsibilities that came with parenting Colin all on his own. Not only had he raised a baby to the best of any parent's abilities, but he'd also gone above and beyond, continuing with the arduous practices that Lauren had begun with such enthusiasm: making his own natural liquid laundry soap for the cloth diapers that Colin wore, and preparing and sterilizing bottle after bottle for his boy's countless batches of formula. Any parent in his position would be excused for switching to disposable diapers in a flash, or finding other ways to cut corners, but Phil did not. It was like he was keeping a promise to both his son and the boy's mother. Colin was the only thing that mattered to Phil now; we could all see that. And we were in awe of the job he was doing, even though life just kept coming at him like a wrecking ball.

Phil endured more than losing his wife; he also lost their home. It happened just one month after Lauren's death. And, as bad luck would have it, with Lauren dying in the hours after Mother's Day, disaster struck Phil on his first Father's Day. He was in western Toronto on bereavement leave from his job as a radio producer and staying at his dad's home. Back in Ottawa, an anxious dog had chewed through a neighbour's toilet plumbing line, sending water pouring into Lauren and Phil's townhouse. This diluvial development would have been damaging all on its own, but when you add to it the fact that no one from the townhouse development reached Phil until two weeks later, you have a full-on catastrophe.

There's never a good time for a flood, but this one came at a moment when Phil had gathered his strength and was preparing to move back to his home and to rebuild upon what was left of his life in Ottawa. He was ready to begin again, and then found himself set back in a way that had all of us asking, "What next?" (A psychic I later spoke with said Lauren was taking complete credit for it, having caused the flood to get Phil to move out of that house and start anew. "I did good, didn't I?" she crowed.)

Ready to pick up the pieces of his life but with nowhere to live back in the city he called "home," Phil, and Colin, were moved by their insurers into a two-bedroom downtown Ottawa hotel suite. They had lost almost all of their possessions—Lauren's too—and what hadn't been destroyed by the flood had most likely suffered water and mould damage. Months passed before the house was rebuilt, repainted, inspected and deemed ready for occupation. But that didn't mean Phil was prepared to return to the home where his wife had drawn her last breath. As his days and nights in that dark and cluttered hotel room came to an end and the move-in date finally drew near (months and months after initial projections), Phil levelled with us and said he just couldn't do it. He couldn't bring himself to go back to that house.

For us, that was all it took: we encouraged him to find another house and to make a new start. We would do anything we could to help Phil and Colin to move forward. We just love them that much, and we recognized that they had suffered for too long: Colin taking his first steps in a hotel room. A washer and dryer pushed to their limit by the number of cloth diapers that needed cleaning and drying every day. Walls spattered with uneaten puréed vegetables whose bowls had been thrown into a sink in frustration. Evenings spent trying to quiet kids who were practising their slapshots in the hallway before hockey tournaments. Nights spent alternately preparing and bottling formula while simultaneously consoling a baby who had awakened to sirens in the downtown streets. It was all too much, but, conversely, so was the prospect of moving back into that house. The light at the end of the tunnel was no light at all. So, together, we decided that, at long last, Phil deserved a break. It came in the form of a newish, larger home that offered sunshine, a guest room for grandparents' sleepovers and the hope of new beginnings.

Weeks passed between that misdirected text from Phil to me and our next visit with our son-in-law. We brought up the fact that we knew there was someone else in his life, and we gently told Phil that it was okay and that we understood: time within the vortex of grief stands still. It could have been six months since Lauren had died, or it could have been a year or five years. Everything stands still or moves at a crawl. Those on the outside who are scrolling through the calendar of a regular life simply don't get it. How can the passing of hours, days, weeks, years have any meaning when you're struggling with what your entire life and survival are about? Nothing makes sense, not even the simplest, most basic rules of our existence, including the inevitable march of time.

We were grateful—happy, even—that Phil had found someone with whom to have a close friendship and romantic relationship. He, of all people, deserved every possible shot at happiness. Even if we had not felt positively about the addition to his and Colin's lives (and we most certainly did—and do—feel it has been a positive and welcome step forward for everyone), what possible right could we have to criticize, judge or admonish him for moving on? After all, when Rob's mother died from an adverse reaction to a trial menopause drug in the early 1960s, his father remarried just over a year later. Rob was nine years old, his older siblings had left for university by then, and his dad was completely at a loss as to how to raise this boy on his own. A child can live on cheese sandwiches for only so long!

As a result of his father's remarriage to Margaret, a nurse and educator whom he'd met through church, Rob eventually helped welcome a new half-sister. Over the years, his relationship with his stepmother deepened to the point that when we were expecting Lauren in 1991, Margaret went through the steps of formally adopting Rob, just so that Lauren would be her very own grandchild. Rob and his older siblings had not stood in the way of their father's happiness and security; and where our son-in-law and his girlfriend were concerned, we wanted to take the same approach, and in doing so, look out for the well-being of the little family Lauren loved so well and left behind.

What a gift that girlfriend, Brooke, has come to be in our lives in a relatively short time. Almost daily she sends us a photo or video of Colin doing something she knows we'll find amazing (so, that's pretty much anything), and she keeps us up to date on what he's learning, how he's getting along at school and funny things he's done around the house. It's been a wonderful thing to gradually get to know this young woman who loves Colin fiercely and isn't at all afraid to stand up for him if she feels that his needs aren't being met outside their home. Brooke is a seemingly perfect fit for Phil and, like him, a caring, dedicated parent. We have nothing but praise and respect for the way she has taken over a mothering role that Phil worked so hard to make sure Colin wasn't missing. And with every day, every text and message from her and Phil, we love and appreciate Brooke more. She's allowing us to keep and strengthen our connection with our only grandson while we also build one with her. And we could not have hoped for anything more.

CHAPTER 7

Soul Survivors

Phil and Colin, summer 2017

IN THAT DARK, BLURRY HOUR AFTER WE LEARNED of our daughter's death some three thousand kilometres away, I encountered the first of many well-meaning people trying to console me with their own faith and beliefs. As Rob and I stumbled back through the hotel hallway in the pre-dawn hours, we noticed that a staff member was just about to enter our room to tidy it.

We surprised her with our return, as she had been told we'd be occupied with the broadcast until 9 a.m.; part of our arrangement with the hotel was that the radio station team would have our rooms tidied extra early, so that we could rest during the day without interruptions. We told her there had been a change of plans, and that we would be leaving later in the day: our daughter had just died at home, and we were going to fly back to be with her husband and baby son.

"Oh my," she said, shaking her head. "God is great, God is great."

I responded in a way that, for me, was uncharacteristically unfiltered (and definitely not "on my best"), but that

I simply couldn't hold in. I said evenly and in a voice thick with pain, "Well, I can't agree with you right now." Rob and I passed her to enter our room and then closed the door to hold each other, cry and begin to make those horrible calls to our loved ones. God is great, she said?

In a very short time, I put the filter back on and learned to nod and be thankful for whatever kind words people said or sent, and to be mindful that it is, truly, "the thought that counts." I know that when something as senseless as the death of a seemingly healthy person occurs—especially when it upsets the natural order of parents preceding their children to the grave—it can leave a person without the right words.

That is perfectly okay. It is all right not to have the words. And what could I expect, having blindsided this nice lady who was just doing her job in the quiet pre-dawn hours? It's not as if she had time to come up with a poem.

Most people, if they are fortunate, will never begin to fathom the pain that accompanies a loss like this. That's why the appropriate thing to say is often elusive, if not impossible. Even my own father, widowed just three years earlier, was only able to express himself to us in an email later that day.

It is with boundless sorrow that I'm writing this note to you and Rob in the loss of your only child, on my behalf, my sister Marion and brother Andy and express our sincere shock and sadness that such an extreme event could even happen in this day and age to those just out of teenage years!!

Just heard a wonderful and appropriate piece of music that brought on the cheek water, and goes thusly: "When at last my life on earth is through, I will spend eternity with you" . . . so meaningful for me (still) and now you. . . .

I smile a little picturing Phil getting the holding and feeding routine together with a little weenie that hasn't experienced anything but a 37°C degree milk supply . . . but I'm sure he will cope.

Finally, she was a darling granddaughter to me, and I'm into full "poor me" mode yet again so soon after losing Maureen. I can only give all the moral support I can. I expect to see you sooner rather than later when appropriate arrangements are made. Keep your strength up and God Bless. . . . Love, Dad.

One of the best cards I ever found, and wisely purchased in case the need for it arises, is one that says, "Sorry I wasn't in touch sooner. I didn't know what to say." How perfect is that? Whenever someone would tell me, "I don't have the words . . . ," I would respond, "That's okay—there are none." And it is the truth. We seem to feel a need to fill each void, every moment of silence, with heartfelt words or comforting sentiments when, truthfully, the whole event is so obscene that the only way to sum it up would be to open your mouth and scream until your throat is raw. There are no words. So don't feel you need to find any if you are unable. And for the love of whatever God you worship, please don't ever—and I repeat EVER—use the words "at least." Those two syllables carry such immense, debilitating power that they completely erase every good intention to which they may be attached (however tenuously).

"At least you have a grandchild."

"At least she didn't suffer."

"At least you didn't have to watch her die."

"At least you still have a husband."

"At least you had twenty-four years with her."

We heard all of these. Every "at least" minimized our grief, as though meant to remind us that it could have been worse. By the time the shock had worn off and the words that were being said actually sank in, I had to bite my tongue not to respond sharply. I just said "thank you," all the while thinking, *You have no idea.*

We knew it could have been worse—it can always be worse—but that is *our call* to make! At least we have a grandchild? Yes, and thank goodness for that, but that child will never know the amazing woman who gave birth to him. And, as delighted as we are that Colin has a new mommy who loves him fiercely, we'll never know how her son would have grown up guided by Lauren. At least she didn't suffer? That's correct—as far as we know. But her death was so sudden that none of us got to say goodbye to her. Is that fair? At least I still have a husband? Yes, I do. And I know that because he's beside me, suffering every day just as I do. At least we had twenty-four years with her? Yes—twenty-four years, one month and eighteen days. Eight thousand, eight hundred and fifteen days in all, if you count the morning on which her heart stopped. And every single year, every day, was a gift. But those days, those years together, were supposed to end when we died, not when she did. No one should die at twenty-four, when life is truly just starting to show the full payoff of all of those early years of growth and promise. So please, please, please—no "at leasts." Not ever.

Those two words are for *us* to say, and we did:

At least she wasn't driving a car when her heart stopped.

At least she wasn't carrying Colin on the stairs in their house when her life ended.

At least we had no regrets and held back nothing from her.

At least she knew how much she was loved.

We said all of those things at Lauren's memorials. When you lose a child, you are the only one who has the right to say "at least." Here are more "at leasts" we've thought of in the ensuing years. They wouldn't have been appropriate at a memorial but have certainly occurred to us:

At least she wasn't brutally murdered or killed by a drunk driver.

At least we didn't have to live with the agony of her having taken her own life.

At least we didn't suffer through years of watching her lose her health, or spend those years worrying that a disease might return and take her from us.

At least, at least, at least. But with not a small amount of guilt, I confess to you a thought that would frequently cross my mind when I heard from or met another bereaved parent. I will ask your forgiveness, and I need you to know that I am aware of just how wrong it was to have this thought—regardless of whether I actually articulated it—especially as it pertains to those two words that I have just professed to hate so much. And here it is:

"*At least* you have another child."

When Lauren died, Rob and I lost everything that mattered most to us, except each other and, at arm's length, our grandson and our own families. And even though we were still together and clinging to each other, we lost who we were as a couple: a joyful and passionately engaged pair who were starting to connect even more strongly on every level and to look forward to a promising future that held the fulfillment of dreams we'd built through nearly thirty years of marriage. Yes, "at least" we were left with a grandson. But every day, when I look at my hands, I see rings that should have one day gone to Lauren. I look around at anything material that we hold precious and ask myself which niece or nephew might care about it, or if perhaps Colin will one day. With the exception of Rob's guitars, I can come up with precious few items a young man might ever want. I ask and search and come up with few answers, eventually arriving at the conclusion that we might as well just cash it all in—not that there's a king's ransom—and divide the money before we go. The whole prospect of having your family blueprints curl up in flames is so all-encompassing that it is impossible to take in or measure. But every day there's a different little bit of reality that pokes at you and reminds you that this branch of the family tree, at least, has been cut short by a woodsman crueller than any the Brothers Grimm could have created.

So then, how do you let go of the deeply felt puzzlement and bitterness that accompany the question, "How can you possibly be suffering as much as I, when you have other children to love and watch grow?" I'll tell you: you talk openly and honestly to someone who has lost a child, that's how. If you think that it might be appropriate, you ask them about their grief instead of only dwelling upon yours. When I asked Ellen Hinkley—whose son Christopher was brutally murdered and whose story will be told more fully later in this book—if she could express how it felt to lose one child but still have another, her daughter Taryn, here is how she responded:

> *I think that this has been a tremendous burden on my daughter, as the sole surviving child . . . and couple our loss with her father leaving me . . . she felt an incredible overwhelming need to take care of me. I tried to tell her it wasn't necessary, but it was. One of her friends, when catching Taryn texting on where she was, said, "You know, you will never be able to be late or go somewhere unannounced again." I hope she doesn't still feel like that, but we are a very strong little unit now. And I just love her so much that she would be so kind.*
>
> *So yes, I have Taryn and she is more than enough, she is the best. She is the sun. She is the stars. But if I still had Christopher, my universe would be overflowing.*

I wept when I read Ellen's response and was grateful to her for taking the time to explain and not minding the question in the first place. It helped Rob and me to understand a little better.

We are fully aware that there are countless parents who are not as fortunate as Rob and I, in that we have been left a part of our child through a grandchild. We see in Colin so many of his mother's attributes, and, although the boy's eyes have changed from Lauren's blue to Phil's hazel, when our grandson smiles and they sparkle, we cannot help but see Lauren looking out at us, just a bit. She is not with him, but she is within him. And that is a thought we will hold close as we watch him grow into a man who would make her so proud.

I'm no psychologist (although I have certainly spent enough time in their offices), but I believe it is simply human nature to compare ourselves to others. The entire advertising industry has been built on that impulse, for heaven's sake! But it isn't necessarily a case of keeping up with the Joneses; we watch our children to see if they're as tall as other kids, or if they're talking at the same rate or age. When a house on the street goes up for sale, we check to see what it's worth. We wonder what people in similar jobs are making for the same work. We compare tires and airlines, resorts and wines.

But there is no comparing grief. Never, ever, ever. Grief is as unique as our fingerprints; few of us manage it in the same way or at the same time.

I once asked an acquaintance who'd suffered the loss of a dear pet six months earlier if he and his partner could ever imagine opening their hearts to another dog. His response was to snap back, "Are *you* going to have *another child*?"

I'm not sure he knew it was in that moment that our burgeoning friendship ended; perhaps it is even possible (although I find it hard to imagine) that he was as hurt and taken aback by my question as I was by his. But no matter how wounded I was by the very deliberate sharpness of his response, I learned from it. To some, perhaps the loss of a dog is perceived as the same as the loss of a child (he had none). I didn't take the time to explain that when you bring most pets into your life, you expect to outlive them, and that you don't build a whole house of dreams—like a wedding and grandchildren—around that beloved animal. I didn't think it was worth the effort. Instead, I replied, "If I could, I would. Absolutely. In a heartbeat."

I bet they get another dog.

And how I wish I had a thousand more chances to answer that question without the slack-jawed shock it invoked in me.

Never mind comparing our grief with that of others; even within ourselves, the wavelengths are longer, deeper, shorter, faster or stronger from one hour to another, from one day to the next. And so it stands to reason that no two people grieve the same—nor should we expect to. It is a huge mistake to feel that you're "doing it wrong" if you aren't through the worst of it by a certain time. I've learned through personal experience in this journey of grief that when you think you've cleared a hurdle, another one will appear as if out of nowhere, and you find yourself unprepared. It doesn't matter if you're in a crowd or lying in bed; you're never completely inured to those moments.

One of them happened to me in a theatre in a popular tourist town southwest of Toronto called Niagara-on-the-Lake. Almost exactly a year after losing Lauren, Rob and I were invited to the opening weekend of a play at the Shaw Festival, an annual tradition highlighting the best drama and musicals either by George Bernard Shaw or set in the time of his life. And so we found ourselves taking in Thornton Wilder's classic *Our Town*. (If you remember the plot of this play, you've probably just thought, *Uh-oh*.)

I'm not sure how Rob and I got to the ages we are without having seen this oft-staged Pulitzer Prize–winning drama, but when a central figure, Emily—a girl the audience has watched grow up, fall in love and then marry—dies in childbirth, we both felt ourselves sinking into our seats. (Do you know that your blood can feel as if it really *is* running cold in a moment like that?) As I began to cry, I quietly put my right hand to my eye, allowing the tears to roll down the back of my hand and my arm and off my elbow. When the play ended, Rob guided me by that same soggy arm to the sidewalk, crowded with high-spirited theatregoers. I kept my head down as he quickly ushered me to a side street in the small, mercifully dimly lit town, where I had to grab onto a lamppost to stay upright. I was gasping for air and sobbing. How could we not have known? How could we have been so blindsided?

Another year passed and Rob and I found ourselves escaping an unusually sullen early spring by flying to Las Vegas. On his birthday, I promised we could do whatever he wanted, and he chose to go to a small neighbourhood casino. As we sat there, two of about twenty people in the entire place, sipping our coffee and playing our nickel video poker, we both stopped dead when we heard what was playing over the casino sound system. It was the last few tracks from side two of the Beatles' *Abbey Road*, led off by the song Dan Clancy had sung at Lauren's Toronto memorial, "Golden Slumbers," and followed by "Carry That Weight" and "The End." The only time we've ever heard these songs together (besides when the Beatles satellite channel plays them) was on Rob's birthday in that little casino. I have no doubt that if anyone was watching the surveillance video, they'd have had a hard time figuring out why a woman with twenty dollars in a poker machine was wiping her eyes with a napkin while looking off into the distance. Then again, I suppose that, as for so many within those same walls, it was all about the loss.

I'll see a mother with a stroller and think of me, think of Lauren. I see a father playing with his daughter and my thoughts turn to Rob and Lauren; a father and son and I think of Colin and his dad. We'll never be able to watch *Toy Story* again (the third one had us dissolved in tears as we watched it in the theatre with our daughter, who was moving out to go to college, just as Andy Davis was in the movie), and we still have to be in just the right mood to listen to any Beatles at all. I struggle with Disney movie trailers, as so many of them have such strong associations. I revel in being around Lauren's cousins and their young children, and I'm gradually no longer being visited by the nagging thought that she should be here too, just as they are. I hear people complain about the demands of their children, the fatigue that they feel, and their difficulty in spending long periods of time with them and their spouses. And I just want them to stop and think of how damned lucky they are. Of course, that's not human nature: we are never quite so aware that we appreciate every single thing that is happening all of the time. I wish I knew who said it, but it is oh-so-true: "Right now someone is praying for the things you take for granted."

Not all of the moments in our lives trigger sad memories; far from it. Often, we'll see something that reminds us of our daughter and makes us laugh, because there was so very much joy in our lives. And in those moments, we strive to remember the things that made us happy and that made those twenty-four years so very full. On our second Christmas Eve without our daughter, I reached my hand down the side of a leather recliner and pulled up a small butterfly hair clip. I knew that it was Lauren's, and I held on to a fantasy that perhaps she made certain I found it to be assured that she was with us on an evening that had, for more than two decades, held so many truly wonderful moments.

We experienced the same feelings again on an anniversary of her passing, when a deer meandered sweetly up to our open car windows at the dead end of a road. Its tiny fawn ducked low in the tall grasses until only its comically over-sized ears were visible, twitching and waving our way. And nearby we saw—as if our Beatles-crazy daughter had wished it—a life-sized submarine, painted bright yellow, inexplicably parked at the end of a driveway. Okay, *what?* It felt as if our Lauren was calling out "hello!" with a belly laugh, making sure we knew she was—and is—with us.

There have been other incidents that I've chosen to believe Lauren had a hand in making happen, from the presence of a bright but rare (for us) Baltimore oriole on the first anniversary of her passing to a full rainbow on my birthday; that smell of cookies baking (when there was no one anywhere near us) and a blackbird (Beatles) fluttering in our fireplace. Dimes have appeared where there were none a moment earlier, and feathers have shown up when I've been thinking of her most strongly. All of these things can be explained or waved away, I know. But when you're grasping for a lifeline, you take whatever is offered and you make it work. Sometimes it's just enough to get through another hour of another day. And if that's magical thinking, make mine a double.

There's a certain bit of that kind of rationalizing that goes on when people are trying to find the words to console you too. But as Ronan Keating sang in the pop song (written by Paul Overstreet and Don Schlitz) featured in *Notting Hill*, sometimes "you say it best when you say nothing at all."

When people would write or say to me that God needed another angel, my immediate thought was, *What a pile of garbage! That little boy needs his mother more than any omnipotent being in the sky needs an angel.* I wasn't buying that one, but I would smile and nod, same as when people said it was part of "God's plan."

I mean, who am I—who is anyone—to say what "God's plan" is? But I do have to wonder what kind of cruel being would take a mother away from a little baby, a wife from her loving husband, a daughter from her adoring parents. I realize that true faith probably means never having to ask these questions. And I wish I had the deep foundation of beliefs that carries people through events like this. I recall seeing Marie Osmond onstage in Toronto in the year after her eighteen-year-old son, Michael, died, having jumped from an eighth-storey balcony. While the rest of her words that night have faded away, I do remember her saying, "I believe—no, I *know*—that we will be together again." Her Mormon religion gave her strength when she needed it most, and isn't that really what faith is for? To be there for the hardest times and help you to survive them? Not just to hope but to be absolutely certain that there will be light and love and forgiveness and joy again? A reunion with the one you've lost?

In a way, the community gathered around Rob, Phil and me like a congregation and gave us the same support and will to go on—that same belief that things would get better and life would one day feel worth living again. We received religious artifacts, including prayer cards and promises of masses to be said in Lauren's name in perpetuity. We also were sent three shawls that had been lovingly knitted or crocheted while their makers prayed. Each item sent our way was gratefully and humbly received, no matter what denomination. In fact, one Toronto church became directly involved in forwarding mail to us, all thanks to confusion over an address. It is a story we'll always cherish.

Even in this age of emails and texts (or, perhaps, especially because of it), Rob and I were touched to receive boxes filled with cards and letters that had been sent to the radio station in the month of my absence from the airwaves. The pieces of mail were carefully delivered to our condo and set aside for a time when we would be ready to open them and pore over the sentiments therein. But one very kind woman took it upon herself to make sure we got every piece that had been sent our way.

The secretary at a nearby church wrote to tell us that because of the similarities between their address and that of the radio station, she had received a lot of mail having to do with (she guessed) the recent death of our daughter. She took the gracious step of forwarding it to me at work. She went on to include some of her own touching words of condolence. Fortunately, I was able to phone the church, speak to this woman directly and thank her in person for her care and kindness.

Included in those boxes of correspondence were a laminated, handwritten poem, small plaques and bookmarks, angel medallions and books. Lots and lots of books. People who had come through their own darkest chapters of grief wanted to share with us the writings that had offered them the most comfort, solace and wisdom. I'll apologize now for those works that may have been lent but were never returned; so much of that time is just such a blur that it's a wonder we made it to the next calendar year. But a few stand out; they resonated with us and helped us immensely. One was *I Wasn't Ready to Say Goodbye: Surviving, Coping and Healing After the Sudden Death of a Loved One* by Brook Noel and Pamela D. Blair.

But the book that had the most impact on us—it actually turned us around 180 degrees and pointed us toward the future—was *Journey of Souls* by Dr. Michael Newton. With a doctorate in counselling psychology, Newton (who died in 2016) used hypnosis in an effort to provide counselling and therapy to patients suffering from PTSD. What he learned was that some of the trauma they'd endured had not happened in this life; he was able to regress them to previous lives. And then—stay with me here—Dr. Newton took some of his patients into the spaces between lives.

I'll pause while you shake your eyeballs so they point ahead again. I know this sounds a little like "straw grasping." I get that. But of everything we read, heard and even studied as children and adolescents (I was raised a Roman Catholic, Rob a Baptist), this resonated most loudly. *What if*, as souls before we got to this life, Lauren, Rob and I had made a pact—an agreement—that this was how this lifetime was going to be? That we were all going to experience whatever it is that we were here to learn? And *what if* that is why we took no moment for granted, why we had no bucket-list item left unchecked, and why Lauren was on such a fast track to accomplish everything that she did? Just . . . *what if*? How are our *what ifs* any different from those of organized religions?

Maybe this is just more of that magical thinking that keeps us going, that keeps us taking one step at a time and continuing to breathe. Or maybe it is more. Maybe Colin really was brought here with a special purpose; we have to wait and see and do everything we can to facilitate his development into whatever person he's meant to be. And we have to hope that somehow his mother is watching over him and guiding his soul in this journey, just as his father is doing with his son's physical presence in this lifetime. We will wait a decade or two to discover what Colin's destiny on this earth is. But for now, we're planning on using our voices and Lauren's death as a way to help others. In her "Homage to Age and Femininity," published in *O* magazine, American novelist Anne Lamott summed up our lives and our future beautifully:

You will lose someone you can't live without, and your heart will be badly broken, and the bad news is that you never completely get over the loss of your beloved. But this is also the good news. They live forever in your broken heart that doesn't seal back up. And you come through. It's like having a broken leg that never heals perfectly—that still hurts when the weather gets cold, but you learn to dance with the limp.

I suppose it's appropriate that when one has a limp, one seeks the counsel of a doctor. And it so happens that we found one who had a profound effect on our lives in those early, raw months of searching and suffering.

To paraphrase mindfulness meditation teacher Sylvia Boorstein, we didn't just do something, we sat there. A local private clinic that happened to offer weekly meditation classes reached out to me shortly after Lauren's death (the recruiter was a friend I knew through charity fundraising). What I at first thought might be a poorly timed attempt to sign me up for their executive health care program turned out to be an immense gift. We were taken under the wing of Dr. Randolph Knipping, a former coroner and emergency health doctor who was vastly experienced in a variety of areas, had opened Canada's first Cleveland Clinic and was now running a private executives' clinic in Toronto. The strongest reason for our personal connection with the compassionate and insightful doctor came every Tuesday evening: a veteran of forty years' experience in meditation practice and instruction, Dr. Knipping taught Rob and me the power of stopping, of breathing consciously and of sharing our thoughts and feelings with the other eight or so practitioners in his downtown office. It was a circle of trust and confidence, of understanding and sympathy.

Another doctor played a large role in helping Rob and me in the early months of our grieving and recovery. Psychiatrist Dr. Henry Rosenblat was there from the first moments of our bereavement; thankfully, the doctor and I already had a professional relationship. As time went on, he aided us in navigating the choppy and uncharted waters of grief, and in puzzling through how we could possibly be of help to our son-in-law. He also helped me gain some perspective and clarity in endeavouring to make a decision about the immense career and address change that would come at the end of 2016. We will always owe Dr. Rosenblat a huge debt of gratitude.

Because of him and Dr. Knipping, Rob and I are big fans of talk therapy, whether through a doctor or therapist or with a group comprising people who are also bereaved. Maybe it's an online group, and you're all there anonymously. Perhaps it's a parish priest or a favourite rabbi. But it is so important that you find someone—even if you have to pay them—who will listen to you pour out your heart. If you find yourself in a group setting, like our meditation classes were, where you go around the circle and talk about where you are in your lives or the challenges each of you faces—from the every-day to the overwhelming—you come to realize that you are never alone in your suffering. You witness that none of us has come through life unscathed. It may not be as monumental a trauma as losing a child, but almost every person you will encounter carries a weight that is often challenging enough to make you grateful for your own. Almost.

Whether it's just further proof of the old saying that misery loves company or simply a connection around a virtual version of the campfire that once drew our ancestors, talk therapy is a chance to share and to hear of pain other than your own. It is a reminder that you are not alone. For fellow bereaved mother Ellen Hinkley, the idea of therapy, of paying to have someone listen, didn't resonate. Instead, she turned to a friend who'd also lost a child, as well as a circle of bereaved moms who would knit and talk. I can think of no more tribal way for women to join hands and hearts symbolically—sharing and healing while creating something beautiful in so very many ways—can you?

Life is filled with dichotomies and ironies that seem to become clearer when the less important details melt away. Even though it leaves you so often enveloped in fog, being shaken to your raw core by the loss of someone you don't want to live without tends to put things in perspective: you learn who your friends are and who is no longer worth whatever precious energy you have left. You start to prioritize things according to what has to be done and what you want to do, instead of what you feel you should do, or what someone else might want you to do.

You strip away the extraneous activities and former obligations because—guess what?—you have an excuse no one can question. You will never need more nurturing than you do when you're in the depths of grief. And it is in that moment that you'll find one of the most ironic truths of all: there is strength—true power—in vulnerability.

I truly believe that, if we're lucky, people want to help us when we are suffering, and we should not miss out on a chance to be held or comforted when it is offered. After all, we need only look at survivors of natural disasters to see how fast the news wheel turns. Our pain becomes a part of recent—and then ancient—history in a very short period of time. The world moves on. But we don't have to—not until we're ready. And I say *to hell* with anyone who feels that our timeline doesn't suit theirs. Sometimes, those little "get over it" nudges come from the most well-meaning people.

I remember about a month after Lauren's passing, my father remarked to one of my sisters that he'd had a phone chat with me and that I "seemed to be over the worst of it." My younger sister, who would soon go on to experience her own hobbling grief, lost it on him. "Dad," she said, "she hasn't even begun to get through this, never mind over it!"

My dad's reasoning came from a lifetime of Armed Forces stoicism and ingrained prairie practicality and toughness. At one point, I had to ask him to *please* stop reminding me that both of my grandmothers had lost children in infancy. I pointed out that this was in the 1930s, when infant mortality was at a far higher rate than it is today, plus they all went on to have more children, which was not going to be an option for me. I love my dad and knew his heart was in the right place, but once again, the perils of comparing grief or loss were clearly on display. We'd all lost my mother three years earlier, and he dealt with the passing of his wife of fifty-five years with great grace and strength, but losing a parent (and, to some extent, the death of a spouse) is something we are all preparing for, in some way or another, from the moment we're old enough to grasp the concept of mortality. As for the death of a child, how can there be guidelines on surviving something that is never, ever supposed to happen?

One of the most common reactions I heard from people who'd also suffered the loss of someone dear was their own surprise that the world kept turning so blissfully unaware in the aftermath of their own searing tragedy. In the early days of our darkness, I felt as if I wanted to dye my hair white or tear my clothes or wear a black armband; somehow, I reasoned, the world should see how everything inside me had been carved out and that nothing was ever going to be the same. I did none of those things. Instead, after stumbling and falling in a parking lot during our first trip home from Ottawa following Lauren's death, I carelessly (rather than deliberately) wore a black dress that showed the raw, scabby wound on my knee at her Ottawa memorial. When I realized that my knee's ugly red and brown patch would show beneath the risen hemline as I sat facing the group of mourners at the gathering in Lauren's memory, I didn't care. I wasn't going to bother covering it up with pantyhose; I'd let everyone see how her death had taken me down.

In time, of course, the scab disappeared, and now there's just the faintest of scars. It would take far longer for our hearts to begin to mend, as every day some new memory, some fresh pain would open the wound again.

That's not to say that Rob was physically unscathed by the sudden loss of his dear daughter. In the days of May between her first memorial in Ottawa and the second in Toronto, it was as though I was watching a physical transformation in my handsome husband. Rob is a man who has always prided himself

ERIN DAVIS

on staying fit—fit enough into his sixties to play in goal twice weekly against hockey players who were much younger (and stopping their shots with success more often than not). But as we walked through a grocery store parking lot, I noticed how this profound loss was weighing on him like a lead yoke. His shoulders had become rounded and slumped, his pace slowed, and the pronounced lines in his face—carved by a lifetime of laughter—were now mirroring the deep, fresh crevices in his heart. I remarked to him that I was seeing this change and urged him, urged us, not to let this age us. We promised ourselves and each other that death was not going to claim us the way it had our young, vibrant daughter; death was not going to leach the life out of us or make us give up on our attempts to defy the inevitability of time. Eventually we would find a way to smile that showed a return of the sparkle in our eyes; we'd find a way to reignite our souls' pilot lights after they were so cruelly extinguished that May morning.

As time goes on and your own healing begins and continues, the immense pain of loss dissipates among those who knew your loved one. As much as it hurts to witness this, I suppose it truly is the way life is meant to go: the suffering shouldn't be endless, and everyone must have the opportunity to embrace hope and joy once more. But as the one who experienced the greatest deprivation, you'll probably find it increasingly hard to find anyone who will listen to you or who will be generous enough of spirit to bring up the name of the person whose absence has made your life so difficult. For some, this is because they don't want to cause you upset when it appears you're doing so well. For others, it could be a matter of wanting to move forward and thinking that by not bringing up the deceased, they're helping you to heal.

Nothing could be further from the truth. Yes, having our daughter's sweet name brought up by strangers in airports, shopping malls and emails was sometimes a reminder of our loss (in that rare instance that it wasn't already at the front of our minds). But that momentary jolt was always replaced by a sense of gratitude that people were thinking of her. As long as she remained in their thoughts, she hadn't yet disappeared completely, right? I wonder about people like Marie Osmond—mothers whose loss played out for all the world to see, making headlines in newspapers and tabloids, and who will always be greeted by caring people with (at best) sad eyes, tilted heads and words of condolence, or (at worst) inappropriate questions or comments.

For those of us not in that white-hot spotlight, the passage of time means fewer mentions, and there comes a day when you don't bring up your loved one's name for fear of making others feel awkward. At least, that's how it's been for Rob and for me. Family who knew and loved her don't talk about her much anymore (even though she's all we want to talk about). We want to laugh; we want to celebrate her zaniness and the hugeness of her heart and her life! But to everyone else, I suppose, it is time to move on. As one numerologist put it to me, people around us are thinking: *Why aren't you over it yet? Change your thinking, change your life!* As though a saying on a coffee mug or a poster depicting an imperilled kitten will somehow help everything to make sense. Please! When I am drowning and need a lifesaver, don't throw me a candy with a hole in it. Throw me something to keep my head above water, just this one day. Say her name. Tell me your memory of her. Remind me of the time something she did touched your heart. Perhaps it was a thank-you card or a kind gesture. Or maybe she made you laugh. God, how she made people laugh.

If you're like us, the days that will be harder than any are the anniversaries. Some call it their child's "angel day"; we don't. May 11 is a tremendously hard day in our lives, although I have found, personally, that the days leading up to it are more emotionally gruelling than the actual day itself. The entire month of May is pretty miserable, given that Mother's Day comes within a few days of the anniversary of our daughter's passing. And, of course, there is always the echo of the sad fact that it was her first and last celebration of that special occasion.

So you'll understand why it is difficult for me to get my head around the thought process that some well-meaning people go through when they wish me a Happy Mother's Day or send virtual flowers via social media, emails and so on. Yes, I am—or was—a mother, but am I still? My only child, our daughter, is gone. I have no one to mother. No one calls me "Mom" (or, in moments of exasperation, "Muh-thurrrrr"). Conjuring happy memories of that day can only bring pain, as I know from going through every card she wrote a note in or made for me by hand in honour of the holiday. It will never ever again be happy. So then, why, I wonder? Why are people who know about Lauren's death still wishing me a good Mother's Day?

One year, when I was feeling especially raw, a little message showed up on a public Facebook page. I didn't know the sender, but she included a little animation with the words "I Nominate You for Best Mom Ever!" with flowers and little sparkles. It sat there for a few days before I screwed up my courage and wrote to this nice lady and asked her to please take it down. I told her that it was just too hard for me to see, and that I didn't feel I was a mom at all now. I didn't mean to make her feel bad, but I just had to say something to someone. She apologized profusely and said she'd just wanted to do something nice for me. You can probably never understand unless you've gone through it, and I pray you don't. I guess I'm asking a lot for people to try to take that extra step to imagine how things like the "mom" stuff can hurt.

As you can easily imagine, the first year is, by far, the hardest. If you're lucky, like we were, you have a thin shell of shock to provide protection from so many of the harsh realities of what has happened to your life. But still, the Big Days carry an awful weight.

Leading up to the first anniversary of Lauren's death, I thought I was going to be all right. Boy, did I get that one wrong! My plans to soldier through it all on sheer willpower from my comfort (and comforting) zone on the radio were derailed starting on Mother's Day, which fell upon May 8 that year. Rob and I had agreed to go to brunch with a dear friend and his elderly mother, but when I awoke that morning, I found I couldn't even get out of bed. I had never experienced a migraine before, but everything I'd ever heard or read about them seemed to be happening to me: blinding pain, nausea and an inability to move or even speak more than a few words. So much for the brunch plans!

Knowing that the other emotional shoe was soon to drop right on me, I didn't go to work the following three days. We lay low at the cottage, going out on May 11 to a park about an hour's drive from us. There, we visited a tree that had been planted by a wonderfully thoughtful radio listener in our daughter's memory, near to the one in memory of her own son. We left a small dragonfly keychain on it—a symbol of the afterlife that was handmade by a fellow bereaved mother—as well as a personalized guitar pick from Lauren and Phil's wedding. We also left a small bouquet, its stems held in a white silk bag, accompanied by a blackbird feather we'd found on our dog walk that morning. Always on the lookout for signs from Lauren (including that oriole we spotted), we felt she was with us through that awful first anniversary day.

Experts suggest that some of the feelings we may notice on special days include confusion, sadness, longing, irritability, worry and frustration. But they also remind us that mourning takes a lot of time, and grief never entirely dissipates. We have to be patient, as do those around us who wonder why we're not dressing in bright colours yet or why we aren't diving back into our lives.

The heaviness of the loss of our child returns on her wedding day, although more so for me than for Rob. I invested a lot of emotional energy into planning Lauren's wedding, putting on the event that I wished I'd had. On somewhat of a shoestring budget, Rob and I had thrown a wedding in 1988 that I'd always wanted a chance to improve upon. In 2013, with Lauren, we got that chance. After a small country-church wedding (so small that, because of space constraints, a string quartet had to be whittled down to a duo that played—of course—Beatles selections), the reception was held at a local historic inn. The decor was gorgeous (thanks to our good friend Allan Bell) and the dinner carefully planned, and the event went off without a hitch. Even with sweltering June heat and the threat of rain, the day could not have been more perfect.

Lauren invited both Rob and me to accompany her down the aisle, an honour I cherish as much now as the day she asked us. But rather than choose the professional emcee (that would be me), Lauren and Phil requested that their fathers share the duties at the reception, which worked out beautifully. And how could I possibly be offended? Too often in our lives, Lauren had sat on the sidelines while I was in the spotlight. There was no way on earth I wanted to share even a sliver of it on that day. Despite the Beatles-soaked sweetness of the wedding ceremony and a beautiful list of heartfelt speeches from friends and family alike, the emotional highlight of the day and evening for Rob and me was the daddy/daughter dance. We had been planning for that moment for almost her entire life.

Lauren's favourite song as a toddler was "Itsy Bitsy Spider" from the Carly Simon album *Coming Around Again*. Carly and her children sang a version of "Spider" that ran seamlessly into and around her hit song that shared the album's title. In 1992, I ran the video recorder after Lauren requested and then, in her daddy's arms, danced to that song. And when the camera stopped, I said to Rob, "We're going to play that at her wedding." And we did. Rob put together an amazing audio-visual presentation that began with the old video of the two of them dancing and went into a series of photos of Lauren growing up. It was projected onto a screen behind the father and bride as they danced together to that same wonderful song. Far away from the centre of attention, I stood tucked into an alcove by the kitchen door of that rural hotel ballroom and wept. It was truly the moment we'd planned for her whole life, and I promise you, although I was crying harder, there were very few dry eyes at the reception at that moment. It was pure magic.

Beginning to end—from the sleepover with our girl and her bridesmaids the night before to preparing her hair and makeup in our little naturally lit boathouse on the lake—it was all so wonderful. And that's why the day holds such great sadness for me. It was supposed to be the beginning of her new life. But not even two years later, that life—so filled with happiness with her handsome new groom and the promise of their lives together—would be over.

Other days that carry heaviness are, of course, all of our birthdays (especially hers), and Mother's and Father's Day: all of those events where we'd shared special memories. Rob doesn't want a card or acknowledgement or anything other than quiet on Father's Day. I know I said that I was grateful that her passing came in the spring rather than the sad season of fall, but it makes for a very hard March through June. Perhaps the weight of those dates, those months, will lessen with time. That is our hope, our aim.

And then there's Christmas. How lucky we were as a family to have shared her last Christmas together. Even my elderly father and one of my sisters and her husband had come in from across the country. We were joined by her cousin Meaghan, who was close to Lauren and had recently had a baby as well. What a joyful, boisterous gathering it was! The tree was fourteen feet tall, we took the time to pose and shoot special family pictures together, and I will cherish that memory forever. I'm glad that what I consider to be our last family Christmas—the last holiday not coloured by sadness and regret—was just as special as it could have been.

During the first holiday season we spent without our daughter, we quite literally ran away from home again. Through my hairdresser (where all of the best information is shared), I found a fellow Canadian who rented out his house on the island of Sint Maarten in the Caribbean. We booked it and stayed for two weeks.

We spent Christmas Eve 2015 watching episodes of *Homeland* that we had downloaded onto our computer. Christmas Day we went to a nearby hotel and had massages; we did our best to avoid anything the least bit forced or festive. New Year's Eve was shared with Benedict Cumberbatch and Martin Freeman as we immersed ourselves in episodes of *Sherlock*. Our days were spent outside watching hummingbirds build a nest far too close to the ground but that afforded us the rare luxury of spying on the two Tic Tac–sized eggs therein. We did our best to pull ourselves out of our deep blue mood by playing the silly app game Heads Up. We'd start our day in a sad state and end up laughing at our own stupidity while trying to guess, give or act out clues for this charades/Password-type game. We did whatever we could to get ourselves through that awful, awful season.

Which brings us to our next perspective check and something that is, like the "at leasts," only ours to say out loud: someone always has it worse. Although we have confessed to wondering (albeit unfairly) how anyone could suffer as much as we have, when many bereaved parents have other children on whom they can focus their hopes and dreams and futures, we acknowledge that we have a grandson. And that we lost only one child.

In 2016, I was called upon to emcee a gala in honour of the incredible Malala Yousafzai, the youngest Nobel Prize Laureate, who was shot by a Taliban gunman. Malala's father and mother were in attendance at the Toronto event, staged as a fundraiser for the Daughters for Life Foundation. This foundation was started by Dr. Izzeldin Abuelaish, a Palestinian obstetrician and gynecologist who lost three of his daughters and a niece in one horrific moment, when an Israeli tank launched several shells at his apartment during the Gaza War of 2008 and 2009. His call for peace has resonated across many continents, even from his new home in Canada. And I was humbled not only to be in the presence of Malala's parents, but also to witness for myself the incredible power of forgiveness and the strength that comes with a message of peace.

Dr. Abuelaish is an associate professor of global health at the University of Toronto. He has written the remarkable book *I Shall Not Hate: A Gaza Doctor's Journey on the Road to Peace and Human Dignity*, which was effective in reminding Rob and me of the suffering that goes on around the world, far beyond our borders, our walls, our own hearts. In meeting

Dr. Abuelaish and his family and hearing their story, we were witnesses to the power that comes from accepting what fate has offered and then making the very best of what has been given to you. We have never lost sight of the fact that we are extremely blessed to live in a country so bountiful and beautiful, almost completely untouched by fear and unrest. Although I go to sleep each night saying a silent prayer that our daughter will visit me in my dreams, I am always aware of the fact that I am on soft sheets in a warm bed, under a strong roof and in a peaceful country. So many of our fellow travellers in this journey have lives that are filled with such misery that they have little hope for security or even the simplest joys. We will never take for granted what has been left for us. Still, in the words of a friend's mother who lost sight in one eye and was told to be grateful she wasn't rendered completely blind: "It's bad enough."

Until you are in a situation where you suddenly find yourself (or already are) childless, you probably don't realize how often the question "So, do you have any kids?" arises. It is an ice-breaker, a conversation starter, a nice way to get to know someone on a bit of a personal level without going, you know, too deep. That is, 9,999 times out of 10,000, when the answer is a simple *yes* or *no*. Except when it is, "Well . . . we *had* a daughter. . . ."

When I blogged about "the question," one woman wrote to tell me of her sister-in-law, a nun, who begins almost every exchange with someone she meets with the words, "Do you have a family?" Even though my correspondent found the query mortifying, perhaps for the friendly nun it's a trusty ice-breaker. And she's certainly not alone in using an other-wise innocent question about kids as a conversation starter.

The quandary is when to be honest and when to tell a white lie. In the split second between the FAQ and the answer, there's a list of questions we ask ourselves: Will we ever see this person again and, if not, is there any reason to share our painful story? If we *do* tell them about our daughter's death, who is it for—this public declaration of grief and loss—us or them? And once we've told our awful truth, then what? As you can well imagine, that litany of questions means a lot of filters to run though in a split second—an *explanation espresso*, if you will. In time, you learn to see the question coming and prepare your response, but early on in the grieving process, you can get blindsided.

Sometimes, if you let your guard down, you can even blindside yourself.

Right after Lauren died, Rob and I were at an airport. We'd just gone through security, and while I was awaiting Rob's possessions on the conveyor belt, I struck up a conversation with a woman who appeared to be Lauren's age carrying a baby Colin's age and size. For reasons I still cannot fathom, I blurted, "He's so beautiful. Our daughter died when her son was his age." The harried mother, whose circles under her eyes matched her dark ponytailed hair, looked at me—this woman who'd started a conversation at the airport security line—in what I can only imagine was disbelief. She offered her condolences and asked unobtrusive questions about our daughter's passing, but I've kicked myself a hundred times since that inexplicable breach of discretion and wondered:

Did I intentionally want to scare this woman into appreciating every moment with her baby (as if that's even possible), or was I simply comparing her to my own beloved, exhausted daughter and wishing she was there in that lineup with me? I don't know. But I've wished more times than I can count that I hadn't seemingly grabbed that passerby's ankle when I was sinking in my quicksand of grief that day.

Someone said that "manners mean not making others feel uncomfortable," and I've always been someone who appreciates them (that airport exchange notwithstanding)—and no more so than when the subject of whether we have children arises. Sometimes my husband and I will obfuscate: "Our daughter's family lives in Ottawa." That's vague enough. But the trick is finding a way to word one's answer so that it doesn't invite a follow-up, of which there are plenty. Is she in radio like you? How often do you get to see her? Does she come and visit regularly? The follow-ups are where we find ourselves having to stammer through a white lie (I've more tells than a dog's tail at a poker game) or do our best White House press secretary imitation. The alternative is just to find a way to say "she died . . ." without making the person who asked such an innocent question in the first place want to sink into the floor. Even as a professional communicator, that's been a challenge.

We've come up with a near-Twitter-length version that succinctly tells the story of Lauren's death: "Our daughter died in 2015 after her heart stopped in her sleep, leaving behind a husband and a seven-month-old son." That statement is usually met by a bit of silence: a moment of remembrance, perhaps, for the light-hearted chat that has just come to a sudden end. We usually thank them for asking, relieving them of the need to say more. We're not always successful in terminating the conversation—and, to be clear, sometimes we don't want to—but just as carefully as we choose our words, we also need to choose the setting for our openness.

For example, if there's alcohol around, we're likely to start seeing eyes well up with tears (which is sweet), or mouths outrunning brains (which can be laughable, if you just take it the right way). One woman we met at a cocktail reception, having overheard us talking to another couple, said, "Well, at least she went quickly." Full stop. That's where a waiter should've dropped a tray, the music should have ceased playing and everyone should have turned with open mouths to look at this woman. Of course, that sitcom kind of reaction happened only in our heads. In real life, we just agreed with her and changed the subject. What else can you do, really, besides pointing out that right there on those shoulders of hers is a head that could use a really good shaking? Nah, not worth it. As my husband is fond of saying, "Don't confuse thoughtlessness with malice." (He really did come up with that. I try to live by those words. Mostly.)

For reasons exemplified by the well-intentioned woman at the bar, we are judicious with whom we share our parental status—which is, to borrow from the performers' union to which I peripherally belong, "membership withdrawn in good standing." People who have entered our lives in the third act, the one after childhood/adolescence and marriage/parenthood, may not be aware of our loss. As much as we feel as if we're missing a limb or have a face tattoo, our grief doesn't show. They enter our house and see pictures of a smiling teen holding her cello, a sparkling bride flanked by her beaming parents, or a painting of our daughter embracing her sleeping baby. The obvious conclusion is that we have a child and a grandchild, and they ask about them.

About two years after losing Lauren, we met new neighbours who had no idea about our family's story. They came to our home and asked if we had children, and immediately the "filter questions" clicked into place. Were we going to see these people again? If we told them the Ottawa Little White Lie ("Yes; she has a family in Ottawa"), would they talk with other neighbours who know the story and wonder why we weren't truthful?

For people like my sister Leslie, it is probably easier to be *almost* truthful and say, "I have two children." Yes, she had four, but unless she wants to disclose the facts, she doesn't have to. Someone we spoke with said they say they have "two children here and one in heaven." I'll never play the "heaven" card, so that's out. But it works for her and that is truly the most important thing. Leslie would even have to say, "I have two here and two in heaven," given that she suffered the loss of her first baby during pregnancy and then lost an adult son as well. Just how honest do we have to be here, anyway? Is it a case of people asking how you are and not really wanting to know? Because that happens a lot too. There are so many things to consider when deciding how open to be about something as enormous as the loss of a loved one.

A few months after moving to British Columbia to begin the next chapter of our lives, we were invited to what we learned was an annual barbecue at a neighbour's house. As this was our first time meeting many of the people on our street (except for a friendly wave while we passed their homes on our dog walk), we weren't sure who knew "our story." I'd come from a life where it seemed everyone was aware of the loss of our adult child. So you can forgive us for having the feeling that people would know; it's just how we had lived for so many years. But in this new life, there were very few people who knew the reason we'd left our previous lives in search of new ones in a new city and province. So we wondered: *Would we be asked "the question"?*

If people did know, they didn't say, "Oh, you're the new folks whose daughter died. Welcome!" or anything at all, really. There were two nearby neighbours who may not have been kept abreast of the talk of the street—if there was any to begin with. Reality check: why would there be? As we waited in line for burgers and salad, I struck up a conversation with the woman, who had at her side a lovely young girl. I asked the girl's name and we were introduced. Then the girl's mother asked if my husband and I had any children. I was very pleased with the response that emerged, since I'm never quite sure what's going to come out. I have no pat answer; it all depends on the circumstances, the mood I'm in or how surprised I am by the timing of the question. But this time I was ready.

As parents of a "limited edition," saying we don't have children is not an option. Early on in our search for ways to make a conversation easier for those asking, I thought perhaps I'd just say no. But even considering that response felt like such a massive betrayal of our daughter—as if some-where around us she was saying, "Are you kidding me?" and wondering how we could erase twenty-four years of her mak-ing our lives so rich.

It is an unfortunate thing: If you lose a husband, you're a widow, and if you lose your wife, you become a widower. When your father dies you're fatherless; when both parents die, you become an orphan. So why isn't there a word for par-ents who have lost a child? Come on, Germany, I'm counting on you! You invented a word for weight gained from eating when you're sad (*kummerspeck*, or "griefbacon"), so don't tell me you haven't got one for parents who have lost their child!

My friend Nancy consulted Latin and English dictio-naries and then headed to the internet as she attempted to bestow a name upon this horrible state. She came up with *liberiloss* (Latin for "children" and English for "loss"), *puer-perde* (Latin for "child" and French for "loss") and, finally, *puerloss* (Latin for "child," English for "loss"). Sorry, but they all felt like lose-lose scenarios.

But China, known for its mandated one-child fam-ilies, does have a special word for this kind of loss: *shidu*. Wikipedia explains: "Shidu is a phenomenon denoting the loss of a parent's only child. The parents who have lost their only child are known as *shidu fumu* in China."

It only just now occurred to me how many parents in China must find themselves in the same shoes we wear. And sadly, as useful as it is to have a term to describe us, I hope that the word is never needed enough to become a widely used part of the lexicon outside of its country of origin.

Someone suggested recently I try the term *kidow*. While I get why that might be fitting, it sounds too much like *kiddo*, a cheery term of endearment (and one I still get as a grown woman from my dad), and comes off as a little too flippant for such a debilitating condition—enduring the death of a child. I'll pass, thanks.

I did come across a piece on the internet about things the writer had learned since her child died, and she used the term *loss parent*. Try rolling that around: "Oh, we are loss parents." I suppose it's fitting enough, despite its *Peter Pan* similarities (are these where lost boys come from?), but until the term becomes widely used, we would just end up explaining it anyway. So we're no further along, are we?

Until then, somewhere between spilling our hearts' darkest contents and denying the existence of an amazing human being lies the middle ground. Not a happy medium, in any way, but a place where no one needs to hurt. There has already been enough of that.

I answered what should have been just polite conversation filler at the street party in a mostly honest way and then deflected. "We have a daughter in Ottawa. And how old is this young lady?"

In that moment, I felt inordinately proud of myself: I'd stolen home plate while the pitcher was looking somewhere in the outfield.

Sandy Sanderson, a wise and deeply funny boss of mine in radio, once passed along this sage advice: "You would be astounded how little people talk about you." He wasn't being callous; he was just reminding those of us in the meeting that people are much more wrapped up in their own lives than we realize. We're just bit players. As don Miguel Ruiz says in my favourite chapter from *The Four Agreements*, "Don't take anything personally." Remembering that it is "their movie"—and we are barely in even the shortest of scenes—has come in handy more times than I can count in both my personal and professional lives.

What is sad but true is that our own movie's second act shifted from family film (a romantic comedy, even) to horror flick. Of course, we aren't alone in either the real world or that of the arts; we found that even the most popular literary, stage and film classics took a turn for the deeply dark side. Again, I wish we had been familiar with the play *Our Town*, for there is no way at all we could have foretold the deeply sad plot twist.

It is ironic, really: as a parent, part of raising a child is letting your mind jump ahead three moves to the worst thing that could possibly happen—Watch her on those stairs! Don't let her do somersaults or she'll break her neck! Don't let her sleep with a stuffed toy or on her back . . . or front . . . or side . . . whatever is going to take her in her sleep! And then your job is to prevent it. I was always told to relax and was chided for gasping when our toddler got near the edge of a deck or too close to a swimming pool, or wobbled her bicycle while riding safely at the side of the road. But I swear to you, I was always in that mindset of "what is going to happen to her?" and trying to prevent it. I'm sure most, if not all, parents are like that.

What I find sadly funny about it all now, though, is that

it was not a hot dog that went down the wrong way or a fall from a bunk bed or a toboggan careening into a tree that took our daughter from us. It was a heart that stopped beating. Losing Lauren was everything I feared but nothing I could have prevented. And if I dwell on that for anything longer than a fleeting instance, I could lose my mind.

And so our job is to keep going. To remember and hold close our hope that our souls will be together again one day and to reflect with joy and love and laughter on the times we had here, the three of us, in those golden twenty-four years. To be grateful that we have no regrets and can say we were the best parents we could be (with room for improvement, of course), that we raised an amazing human being and that we have to go forward in a way that honours her spirit and her memory.

Part of the way we are doing that is by helping those who are, if not bereaved themselves (and I hear from many through my website email), then close to someone who has lost a loved one. We do it by sharing with them information like favourite books or readily available information found in brochures from our local hospice. We do so by constantly reminding anyone who will listen that someone who is suffering needs to talk and repeat their story. It helps us to process our thoughts and feelings. You need to accept that you cannot take away our pain and that trying to cheer up someone who is suffering in the aftermath of losing a loved one is like trying to will a wound to heal simply by saying that it must. Although it is not easy to witness or engage in, you have to allow us to express our feelings of anger, sadness, guilt or sorrow without judgment and without a Cher-like slap to the face and a "snap out of it!" admonition. Even if it is a little more subtle than that fabulous *Moonstruck* moment, your calls for a stiff upper lip won't help a broken heart. There is no getting over it, just getting through it—remember?

Grief takes time. Be patient. There may be guidelines or road signs, but there is no hard timeline. For some, sadly, it will take forever. Just remember that.

Please do not forget us when the shock and pain that you felt upon hearing of our dear one's parting have faded. For us, those feelings are still there times a hundred, or a thousand, and we feel them every morning the moment we open our eyes and realize that nothing is the same as it was such a short time ago. If you think of it once in a while, maybe send a text on the day of the month that she died—or any day at all! Post a heart in an email and we will know we are in your thoughts. Telling us that you are thinking of us down the road doesn't tear off a scab; it is more like kissing a scar. It just shows us that someone still cares and that we are not suffering alone. And as overused as the words "thoughts and prayers" may be, they still mean something when they're said in sincerity and meant to ease our pain.

And then, if there comes a time when the person who has lost a huge piece of her past, her present and her future all in one tragic moment feels as if she might be ready to pick herself up off the floor, you might consider being there to guide her gently back to life. Perhaps include her in new activities or help encourage her own growing independence. Add her to your social circle or keep asking her to join you until you get a positive response (or a convincing reason why not—maybe she just doesn't like your friends or, worse yet, you). And please, please, please keep talking about the person who died.

Yes, we realize that they are gone—we haven't lost our minds, at least not entirely—but you have to know that they are still very much alive in our hearts. We dream about them. We cry for them. We ache with a longing that can never be fulfilled. We fantasize that they'll come to the front door to surprise us one more time. We hear a ping on our phone and think: *Oh, it's a text from her!* (I had to change my text notification sound effect, as every time I heard those five little percolator notes, I thought of Lauren and that she might be texting.) The phone rings and our dearest one is the first whose name comes to mind. That person will never truly be dead to us—don't you see? In our case, this person, our child, came from our bodies, and she is a part of us forever. Where, for a time, you may see something that seems like an amputation, we see a leg that suddenly isn't working right, and it doesn't make any sense. *"It was fine yesterday. . . ."* She was our child and she always will be. We will always hold in our hearts not only the memories of our time together (from the moment we first laid eyes on this sweet baby with the long fingers) but, equally palpably, the hopes that we held for her that will never be fulfilled. All of those are swirling together: the mental snapshots, the raucously bright watercolour dreams, the strains of her music and the joy of her laughter. They will not fade, and just because you do not see or hear them does not mean they have faded for us.

I wrote this on October 11, 2015, after baby Colin's first birthday party at which Lauren was not toasted or mentioned. I wanted to scream it but dared not open a barely healing wound in her husband and father. So, after the paper plates and banners were disposed of, I sat and penned this plea:

LAUREN DAWN

Speak her name, please . . . for our sakes, speak her name.
We know that she's gone. That our lives aren't the same.

We cannot ache more than we already do,
So, remembering her is a kindness. It's true.

We sense you tread softly, as you skirt the abyss
But it helps us, you see, when you do reminisce.

Do you worry of adding to our pain and our strife
By reminding us that she is gone from our life?

Our daughter has died. This is now who we are.
But memories prevent her from drifting too far.

Your silence—it adds to the rumbling pain
When we long to know she's in your thoughts once again.

Let your words paint a picture of laughter and joy:
Of her music, her childhood, her husband and boy.

Speak of her wedding, how she laughed and showed grace
And the love and pure joy on that beautiful face!

Tell us something she said that will always ring true
And simply remind us what she meant to you.

Keep her alive in your heart with words spoken
That ours will stay whole—just a little less broken.

Oh, speak her name, please, that her life will go on.
As this love will forever—for our Lauren Dawn.

When you recognize that—how alive she still is to us—
you help our souls to survive. And keeping our beloved one's
memory alive means more to us than anything. *Anything.*

Chapter 8

Surviving the Worst That Could Happen

Erin's final broadcast, at Casa Loma, December 15, 2016

ONE OF THE MOST UNEXPECTED OUTCOMES OF the tragedy of losing our beloved Lauren was the strength that I—and, by association, Rob—was given by the response and support of the people who listened every morning and corresponded by email. I had always felt a closeness to our listening audience, or more aptly, to the individual people who made up our listening audience, but I'd never imagined that after all of the years that I'd tried to make their mornings a little happier, a little gentler, they would one day be there for me. But that is exactly what happened.

Back in the radio studio, as the weeks passed, listeners began to awaken not only to the music and voices on our radio station but also to something happening on its airwaves in those dark, early hours. It seemed that simply by showing up and turning on the microphone every day, I was inadvertently becoming proof of life after death (at least in this way).

I knew in my heart that this is exactly what Lauren would have wanted me to do: what I loved and what she loved. Radio. In fact, one of the four or five psychics I spent time with in the first year after her passing said exactly that. "It's not about you, Mom," was Lauren's message. "This is about *them* now—just as it always has been. You have to be there for them."

Yes, I talked with psychics or mediums. With one of them, fresh off the Jersey Shore, I experienced a truly meaningful "passing over" ceremony in Sedona, Arizona, during which Lauren seemingly explained her death to us by means of a reading. Interestingly enough (lest you think they are all charlatans out to take advantage of a bereaved mother), although I was also in touch with three or four others during those early months after Lauren died, I was actually warned off it by the second-last woman I consulted, who gave me an intense hands-on kind of reading. She cautioned that I would be messing with my own strengths and energies (auras, if you will) if I continued to seek readings more than once a year. I took her advice to heart and laid off on my efforts to communicate with Lauren through someone else.

There was one encounter, though, that was truly noteworthy for the circumstances under which it came to be, as well as the results it yielded.

I met with a medium and author who would only do readings for other parents who had suffered the loss of a child; she herself had lost a daughter in a car accident when a driver crossed into her daughter's lane. This woman's depths of depression led her to learn that she had psychic abilities and was actually able to communicate with the other side. She came highly recommended by no fewer than thirty listeners who reached out to me in the early days after Lauren's death. We were lucky to book an appointment with her some six weeks after making initial contact; she has since stopped doing readings altogether. Family health challenges played a role in this decision, but I have no doubt that the kind of work she did with her clientele was extremely draining. She sounded somewhat defeated when I spoke to her over the phone for the final time. She had given so much comfort to so many, and I only hope she found some for herself along the way.

Our time with this woman (who asked that I not mention her name here lest she be contacted by other parents seeking her abilities) assured us that Lauren is with us every day and that she wants us to move forward and to encourage her husband to do so in any way we can. Without going into a lot of details about how I knew this medium was "the real deal," I can tell you that she brought up names, dates and significant other elements of our families' and our own lives too frequently to be coincidental.

I like to think I'm not naive; I believe there's a fine line between being a believer and being a sucker when it comes to trying to communicate with the so-called other side, but I also think there are far too many mysteries in the universe for us to close our minds and hearts completely to the possibilities. Besides, if it provides hope and peace and isn't hurting anyone, where is the harm? Of course, there are those who prey upon the vulnerable; I know that and am in no way encouraging people to seek out psychics or mediums for answers. It was just something that worked for me, and even for my more skeptical husband.

Recently, I looked back on a reading I got from a friend of a friend, named Cyndi Tryon, just before Lauren gave birth. She made reference to a Caesarean section (but said it probably wouldn't happen), and then she said that my own mother showed up and said she'd be there with Lauren and showed an eleven on her watch. Was that eleven the day Lauren was to give birth, or the same day seven months later that she died? I don't know. But it doesn't bother me to think that my mother was with her dear granddaughter on either—or even both—of those days.

Whether I signed up for it or not, the message I was getting across the board was that it would be my job now to follow my own little family's motto and "be on my best." I'd have to keep going and show that you can survive anything. It might get a little messy at times, but I had a job to do, and that was to offer up hope that life could, indeed, go on. It would never be the same, and the sun might not ever shine with the same bright intensity, but it would still come up every day nonetheless, and I'd be there calling play-by-play on each sunrise.

Someone expressed concern to me at one point just after my return to the radio that by doing this show, by seeming to heal so quickly and before their ears, I might be doing a disservice to others dealing with their own grief. How could I be there laughing and carrying on with my life when they couldn't get out of bed in the morning?

I considered my response very carefully. It hadn't occurred to me that just surviving as best I could, and in so public a way, might be causing harm to someone walking the same path. My answer to that is: all I can do is *me*. As much as I tried for decades to reflect the feelings and experiences of our listeners, an effortless kind of empathy that had always served me well in my radio career, I came to realize that I can't be responsible for the thoughts or the healing processes of others who've been dealt a blow like we were; I can only do the best I can.

Really, that is what survival after a catastrophic loss is all about: doing your best (without harsh judgment from others or from within), being open to and willing to seek help and realizing there is no set timeline; there are no rules. I have heard from and read about enough people who share this washed-out road to know that some who've suffered this kind of trauma can't get out of bed for weeks, months, even longer. There are some who barely keep going, and others who simply don't. One bereaved mom, who writes to me regularly, visits her young child's grave daily and has done so for the past thirty years, and on the dates surrounding his birth and his death, she tells me she routinely takes far more painkillers than are prescribed to her in hopes of overdosing. The pain is palpable in this woman's anger-laden emails, which are so often barely legible because of the prescription drugs she is taking for pain (of all kinds), and, honestly, I wonder how she makes it through each day. I wonder, too, just how many more days she has left to suffer. I have tried to tell her that she has more strength than she knows, but my words fall on deaf ears. She's been on this road for so long.

On the other side of the shroud is the remarkable story of strength and hope that is Ellen Hinkley. I say remarkable because, as public as our ordeal in losing our child was—partly of our own choosing—Ellen and her family had the unbearable burden of waiting several excruciating years to see her child's killer come to trial. Then she had to live through the further publicity of a court procedure.

In a story that many Torontonians and possibly an equal number of people across Canada remember to this day for its exceptional cruelty, the inference of a crime sparked by homophobia, and the duration it took to come to a conclusion, Christopher Skinner was brutally murdered in 2009. The twenty-seven-year-old, who was said to be following in his father's footsteps toward a career in law, was on his way home from younger sister Taryn's birthday celebrations in Toronto's Entertainment District. In the wee hours of that morning, a fight broke out between Christopher and the driver and passengers of a vehicle on whose windows he is said to have pounded after being denied a ride home. Christopher was punched and kicked by as many as five men and then run over by the escaping SUV. While, mercifully, Christopher's suffering ended when he later succumbed to his injuries in hospital, the pain of his parents, family and friends would go on for years, as everyone was left suspended in a jagged limbo of not knowing if the killer or killers of this charismatic and promising young man would ever be apprehended.

It took four long years for the first big break in the case to come: an ex-girlfriend of one of the vehicle's passengers tipped off the police, who were able to build a case by wiretapping the phones of the suspected driver. Lauren's death led Christopher's mother to reach out and offer her condolences and empathy. Eventually, she would also provide a perspective for me—and you—that I hope you'll find as invaluable as I have, from her unfathomable position as the mother of a murdered child.

Ellen's husband and daughter faced the media during the course of the trial that led the evening TV news for weeks. Christopher's case had captured the city's attention not only because of Toronto's low crime rate but also because this homicide was particularly brutal. Many wondered if it was a hate crime because Christopher was gay, although the police later determined that this was not the case. Ellen herself says that while her now ex-husband and daughter answered questions and made statements, she would mostly stand by and cry. She describes that time in her family's life in one word: "surreal."

> At a time when you are trying to process the fact that your child has gone and will never return (and that means all the things he will never, ever do with you again, like Christmas, celebrate birthdays or the birth of his nephews, just hang around), now we were dealing with interviews with police, media, press conferences, updates from police or, at times, long silences from the police. [We were] always wondering if the suspect was caught, would that make it better?

Once a suspect was apprehended and brought to trial, Ellen displayed incredible bravery and honesty and was completely dedicated to honouring the memory of her dear

Christopher. In one harrowing, unforgettable chapter of this trial, the bereaved mother took the microphone to share how losing her son had affected her life:

Victim. Impact. Statement. A horrible, despicable thing to write. Something I never expected to have to write when looking down at my newborn son, 34 years ago. I hate to think of myself as a victim—I have been doing everything in my power NOT to be a victim since Christopher was murdered on October 18. But I am. I am just as much a victim as Christopher John Andrew Skinner.

How? Financially, my business foundered as I was not able to devote my full attention to the running and managing of an entrepreneurial business. People came into my shop to see the poor mother of the boy who was murdered, not to purchase wool. I became the latest entry in that infamous club no one wants to join: the club of mothers who have lost a child. I had to take time away from the shop.

Relationships have foundered and been lost because folks did not know how to "handle" the news about my son's murder. They were afraid to say Christopher's name, they were afraid to say the wrong thing. So they left.

But more importantly, how did this affect me, emotionally? I do know that I will never again have daily interactions via social media or telephone with Christopher—almost every morning when I opened my computer at work there was a cheery note, and lively interaction throughout the day. I will never again know the magnificence and strength of my boy's hugs, or feel his care and concern for his mom. I will never again have heart-searing talks with Christopher when he wanted my advice. I will never be able to watch Christopher's pure joy when with his extended family. And his family will never know pure joy again. I have been told I was a soft place for Christopher to land after a tough week of city life. And of that, I am proud.

I felt that my role became caregiver, to take care of my remaining family; my husband and my daughter. In fact, my ailing 78-year-old mother told me that on October 18, she lost not only her beloved grandson, she lost her daughter. Why? Because I could not provide the emotional support she required, and also care for my nuclear family. My mother, Nanny-Junne, has now passed away, and this horrible incident contributed in no small way. Christopher was her life.

Places that brought me pleasure were no longer places I wanted to visit. Family vacation spots became difficult to go to. I have spent almost 6 years trying to establish new Christmas traditions that would bring us joy, while still trying to maintain and cherish the memories of past Christmases.

I will never understand how one person's carelessness, cowardice and arrogance can take my life, my sunshine.

This is my life now. This will never change. My loss is always with me and always will be. Always living with the essence of Christopher and a sense of what

if . . . what kind of family man would he have been?
What kind of uncle would he have been to his unborn
nephew? What kind of son would he be towards me in
my old age? I will never know. I will never feel his love
towards me again.

I try and find ways to cope. I try and find moments
of joy. And with the help of my wonderful daughter,
and good friends and family, I am occasionally able to
do that.

But please, let there be no doubt. I am a Victim.
Just as Christopher was. Thank you for listening.

Can you even imagine having to share how broken-hearted you are with strangers and media alike? I mean, Rob and I chose to open our hearts to people about the sadness and the tragedy of our daughter's death. How Ellen managed to put her loss and pain into words and then deliver them to her son's killer and everyone else in that courtroom is beyond me.

Ellen lives in Uxbridge, a township about a fifty-five-minute drive from Toronto. I asked her how hard it was to be part of such a big story in such a small town, something she touched on in her statement when she mentioned selling wool and being somewhat on display. She said that many women came to tell her that they, too, had lost a son. But some just wanted to chat or gossip. She would have none of it.

One huge idiot I will never forget came in and leaned
on the counter and said, "So how's it going with your
son's case?" I didn't know her, she never shopped at

*my shop and I've never seen her since. I did kick some
people out of my shop because all they wanted to do
was talk about the case and Christopher. My response
was to put my hands up in front of me and say, "I'm
sorry, I don't discuss that here. If you wish to purchase
some wool, I would be happy to help you; otherwise you
have to leave."*

Eventually, Ellen says, her tough approach worked. Like
so many in the early stages of grief, returning to a job—just
putting one foot ahead of the other and concentrating on
something, anything, besides the pain—was a great help, as it
helped bring a semblance of her past "normal" life back to her.

What Ellen's wool shop in Uxbridge was for her, my place
behind the microphone was for me: it wrapped me in the
normalcy of radio (a form of media whose participants are
rarely called "normal," myself included). The fact that I had
something into which I could immerse myself gave me the
illusion that I was living the life we had before the needle
was pulled off of our sweet, sweet record. Every day I had
to put on my face (both with cosmetics and a smile), "be on
my best" and put on a show. It's not unlike the belief that if
you curl your mouth upward, even when you don't feel like
smiling, you'll fool yourself into thinking you're happy. We
would do that occasionally in our yoga or meditation classes:
eyes closed, smiling while we inhale. Somehow the brain
translates that physical act of smiling into some form of happiness. It doesn't always work, but it's effective often enough
to keep me trying. What do we have to lose?

Ellen Hinkley's version of community support and fellow-ship came in the form of a shared passion. She found it odd, but comforting, that at one time she had five bereaved moms in her knitting group. She hadn't advertised it, but people came and found a safe place to listen and be heard. She says that when it was only the bereaved moms, they could talk freely about their children's passing and how they were feeling that day. Ellen adds that there was a bit of gallows humour, too, as you can only share that with someone who's been there.

Few people can understand the pain of losing a child; one bereaved mom described it to me like being an alien on Earth—you know when you meet another of your kind, because you speak a different language on a completely dif-ferent level from everyone else. Fewer still could begin to grasp the unique set of trials and reverberations Christopher's death and its aftermath would bring to Ellen and her family.

Anger is something Rob and I were fortunate not to have had to deal with in overwhelming amounts. Yes, we were angry at the senselessness of being robbed of our daughter, of our future together and of all of the dreams that we held for that bright and happy future (especially if it had anything to do with taking a drug to aid breastfeeding as it was prescribed), but our overwhelming emotions surrounding Lauren's death, and the loss of her in our lives, were gutting sadness, bewil-derment and depression. And as with numerous subjects of Dr. Elisabeth Kübler-Ross's groundbreaking work surround-ing the five stages of grief in *On Death and Dying*, we also dealt with denial and acceptance. But we came to under-stand that those stages do not appear or manifest themselves in any particular order, are not experienced in equal amounts, and do not apply in all cases. For example, we did no bargaining: Lauren was gone in the same flash with which she'd arrived. We didn't have a chance to beg the gods to "take me!" No bargaining here whatsoever; it was way too late for that.

I asked Ellen if the anger she felt in any way mitigated her grief or provided a distraction from the enormity of losing her only son.

> *Having the suspect caught changed my focus. . . . I no longer could be distracted by the police search (and remember, I was hoping that his capture would make me feel better). In some ways, I could now begin being really angry at a group of people. But right from the beginning, I always said, "What about his mother? What about his family?" I never thought we were talking about a monster here; we were talking about someone who had a mom and dad. How were they managing knowing that their child could commit such a monstrous act?*
>
> *Before you think I was angelic in worrying about other people, a great deal of the time I was so angry that his selfish behaviour could take away my son. And I really hope he is suffering in jail. There, my angel wings are gone.*

Have I told you how much I honour and admire Ellen's honesty? She also shared this perspective, which I found to be most helpful.

*My very good friend, who had also lost a child, rec-
ommended this: think of a window shade in your
mind. When you are strong and calm you can pull it
up and look at all the circumstances that surrounded
Christopher's death: the fact that he was beaten, run
over and left to die on the side of the road. But when
that is too much to bear, pull that window blind down,
take a deep breath and wait for another day.*

*There were press conferences where all I could do
was cry in front of the media and the police force. There
were court appearances where cruel harsh details were
bickered over by lawyers [and] made me lose my breath.
In fact, I didn't even know what the accused looked
like; he had to be pointed out to me. I think I deliberately did not want to know. There were friends who
discussed the case and analyzed it, in front of me. All
I could think was "THIS WAS CHRISTOPHER! You
are talking about Christopher!" I just sat and cried and
screamed inside.*

In 2013, the man who beat and then drove over
Christopher Skinner pleaded guilty to manslaughter and was
sentenced to eight and a half years in prison, two of which
had already been served at the time of sentencing.

Since enduring the horrific ordeal of losing her son and
a lengthy and public trial, though, another chapter has been
written in Ellen Hinkley's life story, and it has all of the hall-
marks of being the beginning of a happy ending. As Ellen
puts it, "I think that if there were cracks in the marriage to

begin with, they become chasms with the burden of grief."

Thankfully, though, that chasm became an opening for happiness to emerge once again into Ellen's life. In 2016, she met someone whom she describes as "the light of my life."

It happened seven years after Christopher died and two years after my marriage died. I know I needed time to recover from both deaths.

I thought, "How can I date someone, as a bereaved parent?" Well, I met the right person, who will listen to me talk. He just gets sad when I do. A moment of victory: walking through a shop that specialized in Scottish stuff and I heard "Amazing Grace." Not only did I not cry, I sang along. And poor Mark had his eye on me, trying to figure out how to get me the heck out of there. He was pleased when he saw I wasn't upset.

Small victories. Small achievements. They all count.

Ellen and Mark were married in 2018, opening the window shade to a new morning: one filled with promise. I raised a glass to the happy couple, hoping that even though it was sparkling fruit juice and not real champagne, my wishes for only good things in their lives together would come true.

CHAPTER 9

I'll Drink to That: My Own Personal Rock Bottom

Grand Marshal Erin, Toronto, St. Patrick's Day, 2006

I F THERE IS AN UNDERLYING FEELING OR ATTITUDE
we have adopted in the months and years since Lauren
left us, it has to be that of gratitude. It's the same senti-
ment I expressed at Lauren's two memorials. But after the
guest books and leftover programmes had been delivered to
us in boxes and the flowers had long lost their petals, the
thankfulness, on many fronts, remained. However, there are
few things for which I am more grateful than the fact that
going into this horrible tragedy, I had already logged several
years of sobriety. I was going to need all the clarity I could
muster just to survive losing Lauren, never mind achieve my
goal of getting back on the radio and putting on a happy face
(or, more importantly, voice).

I remember when I started to use alcohol as a painkiller
instead of simply a social lubricant, as "normal" people do.
At twenty-two, when women my age went out at night to
meet each other (and perhaps Mr. or Ms. Right), I was home
alone. A 4 a.m. alarm isn't exactly conducive to being part
of a vibrant social network, nor (somewhat surprisingly) is

working in a primarily male industry. I'd had my flings, but basically, I had no close friends of either gender. And I felt isolated and alone.

I dreaded going home to the emptiness of my modern two-bedroom apartment. It was situated above a downtown subway stop and shopping mall, and I recognized keenly the irony of being so close to throngs of people but feeling such solitude. With no prospects for a date on the Friday horizon (despite taking the unusual and expensive and somewhat humiliating step of signing up with a matchmaking service), my solution would be to climb into bed in the midafternoon with a gin martini in a big brandy snifter and sip myself to sleep. Drinking alone: How could that possibly turn into a problem? Besides, I thought I was smarter than that. I would only drink my evenings away until I found someone with whom to share my life and its many little triumphs and frustrations. I would be just fine, thank you.

Lasting love should have saved me in 1986 when I had my first date with Robert Whitehead. Nine years my senior, he was also my boss at an all-news radio station, where I spent four years co-hosting mornings with four different partners. It was a revolving door of "work husbands," all of whom felt vastly superior to the young woman sitting across from—and often carrying the show for—them. Rob tells me he was my biggest fan from his first day at the Toronto flagship station of the CKO network, where he'd worked his way up the corporate ladder to a position in management, a job he'd come to despise. A producer and creator at heart, he found himself trapped in the workplace drudgery of pencil pushing, number crunching and dealing with inflexible unions and disgruntled employees.

Although it began quickly and looked for all the world like something out of a Nora Ephron–penned movie, our courtship was fraught with complications and drama. I'd invited Rob out to dinner with me one night when I had been offered a free meal in return for doing a restaurant's commercials. We followed dinner with the Second City Toronto improv show *Not Based on Anything by Stephen King*, and it was late that evening that two amazing things happened: first, I was up past ten o'clock on a "school night"; second, as we reached for our wine glasses, we both felt a blast of static. Not a shock, exactly, but something that would look like a tiny lightning bolt, if I were to illustrate it. It's not an exaggeration to say that the sparks had begun to fly and neither of us wanted the night to end. As for that little lightning bolt, I've experienced that shot of electricity only four times in my life: that night with Rob, the time I heard the man who would become my college professor talk about Loyalist's radio broadcasting program, the moment Lauren was born, and the day I first heard my radio mentor Valerie Geller speak. All four moments would have life-changing implications for me.

Try not to gasp in envy when I tell you that Rob drove me home in his brand new Chrysler Magic Wagon! In retrospect, that probably seemed like an unusual choice of vehicle for a single man in his thirties (unless his planned next move was to start buying little stick-figure wife and children decals to put in the back window). If I'd thought to ask him about it, Rob would have explained that the Magic Wagon allowed plenty of room for him to transport his cumbersome hockey and musical equipment. But I didn't ask: I had more on my mind than why he was driving a minivan—because, to be honest, I wasn't just enamoured, I was confused. I dated lawyers and stock traders. This motorcycle-riding guy—who was more Doobie Brothers than Brooks Brothers, who wore wide, crocheted ties (including a memorable one in light pink), and who sported a beard—was so not my type. What was going on with me?

It wasn't until much later that I stumbled upon a reading a psychic had given me when she was a guest on our radio show two years earlier (I had stuffed it into a photo album and forgotten about it). The woman, who'd called in from Los Angeles to do the segment, said I would marry a man named Robert. I'd been doodling on a desk calendar while she talked to me on the phone, and there it was in big block letters: ROBERT. I never dated another Bob or Rob, and I certainly didn't go out of my way looking for anyone by that name. Interesting, though, isn't it?

Back to 1986: after what was far too late a night already, I invited Rob up to my apartment for a drink and we proceeded to make beautiful music together. Okay, that's not a cliché (at least, not in this case). He picked up my guitar, I sat at my electric piano, and we played Beatles music long past midnight. But when he played a little-known song called "The French Waltz" by Nicolette Larson (written by Scottish-born Canadian Adam Mitchell) that happened to be my very favourite, I knew this guy was really special. He was so special, in fact, that when my 4 a.m. alarm went off for work a few hours later, I'd had all of ten minutes' sleep. And I didn't care. I was floating on air!

He took me to breakfast later that same groggy morning, when what I'm sure was a bumpy show ended, and told me that this couldn't possibly work. Endeavouring to hold on to a smattering of pride, I agreed and told him I'd figured as much, which was an outright lie. Turns out I was right. Try as we (okay, *he*) might to squelch them, the sparks flew again, and just three weeks later, in a state of feeling absolutely no pain after a radio industry awards event, we weaved our way home on foot. Passing through a sprawling downtown mall bustling with holiday shoppers, we paused outside a jewellery store. There, Rob carefully balanced himself on one knee and asked me to marry him. I said, "Yes!" put my hands on his face, kissed him firmly and then helped him up so we could run inside and choose a ring. And it was a beauty!

When I tell people that we were engaged after just a three-week courtship, I usually skip over the next part, the awful part: the part where I thought my heart would actually stop from all of the pain I was going through. When Rob and I went to dinner and Second City that night—November 12, 1986—it was most definitely not a date: he was available only because his girlfriend was away. Engaged-to-be-engaged, his almost-fiancée (a much-loved woman who freelanced in our workplace) was on a trip to Europe, during which she was trying to decide if marriage was the next step she wanted to take, and if Rob was the guy she would take it with. When he told her that he'd begun seeing me, she cut off her lengthy trip to come home, seemingly having decided that she did indeed want to become the second Mrs. Whitehead (a title that, ironically, I never opted to take). And that's when Rob realized he couldn't follow his heart and be with me. He was no longer in love with her, but he had to do what was right and that was to honour his commitment. She had offered support and encouragement when his first wife left him after ten years with a huge pile of debt and an even bigger sense of relief. His new fiancée was—and remains—a wonderful person, with whom I'd go on to have a warm relationship at work many years later at a different radio station, when I pushed very hard to have her hired full-time on our show. But at that time, she was the reason my heart had been broken, just as I was the reason hers had been too.

I gave Rob back the diamond ring we'd chosen together that booze-soaked evening in the mall (against the advice of my three furious sisters, who insisted I should teach him a lesson by keeping it) because I didn't give up hope. I never hated him. I just hurt so badly because I knew in my soul this was the man I was supposed to spend my life with. There were sparks, for heaven's sake! We sang and played "The French Waltz" together! We both loved root beer schnapps! (Okay, so not all of it makes sense.)

After seeking counsel from a psychiatrist, as well as from a monk who'd been recommended by one of the few co-workers who was in Rob's corner when he split up with his fiancée, Rob decided he would follow his heart after all and return to me. We picked up our courtship where we'd left off, and despite the cautious vulnerability that our earlier drama opened in me, I proposed to Rob in the summer of 1987. And although we were married in February of 1988, it took me at least a decade to heal from that breakup. Not letting go, it turns out, is my superpower.

In addition to a new and wonderful marital status, 1988 also brought a fresh career challenge: I was offered a position on the morning show of one of the top radio stations in Toronto, CHFI. Rob and I had both had enough of the all-news grind on CKO (the station and its network actually folded one year later, so we were prescient to take our leave when we did), and I had actively sought work on a music station. Soon enough, I was phased out of my newscaster role and moved into a high-profile co-host position with a well-known personality, Don Daynard, a man thirty years my senior who bore a physical resemblance to the comedian George Carlin blended over time with the actor Wilford Brimley, and who idolized John Wayne. Ironically, when we began together, the two of us provided bookends to the demographic our station was seeking: I was twenty-five; he was fifty-four.

Despite our age difference, Don and I had tremendous chemistry and moments of great affection that were evident to listeners: the show and the radio station quickly rose to number one, a position we proudly clung to for a decade. We were advertised in extensive TV campaigns; people knew our faces as well as our voices, and any sense of radio anonymity quickly disappeared. We'd moved to another level of popularity, and these were heady, wonderful times—outside the studio. The four hours we spent together, however, were often an uneven mixture of laughter, tension and anxiety.

Don seemed to resent the fact that my job was to bring in the younger end of the audience, eschewing conversations about movie actors from the black-and-white era in favour of, say, the latest on the Spice Girls. I brought a young mother's perspective to the show, and my partner quite often could not have cared less and wasn't interested in pretending otherwise. I felt unwelcome on the show I had come to share and had been so thrilled to be a part of. It was frustrating to me and deeply hurtful. And I took those feelings home with me every day, ready to drown them at the first opportunity.

The rear-view mirror perspective of time has taught me that I readily made myself vulnerable to much of the pain I experienced by expecting or hoping for too much from my partner. What I wanted and felt I'd earned—respect, appreciation and genuine affection—were things he was perhaps not so much unwilling as simply unable to give. Maybe it was because he was born in 1934 and was a product of his time. My dad was born one year earlier, and I could certainly draw similarities: when Dad (also named Don), a former airline pilot, referred to flight attendants as his "girls," I'd gently correct him, all the while hoping he didn't use that terminology with them. But I knew he said those words not out of malice but simply because he'd neglected to notice—or care about—a change in the times and terms. I transferred that understanding of my dad (and a lot of other feelings, as it turned out) from my father Don to my partner Don, but it didn't make things any easier. In the highly male-centric business that radio was at the time, not upsetting the apple cart was as much a part of my job description as doing news, reading entertainment or cheerfully bantering with my co-host, our producer and our sharp-witted airborne traffic reporters.

Don retired in 1999 at the age of sixty-five, and as ready as he was to go, I was genuinely sad to have him disappear from my life, because there were good moments and even good days. I never lost my perspective about what he did for me. I learned so much from him, and although not all of the lessons were ones I wanted, they served me well in the years to come.

Sadly, sixteen years after our last show together, we reconnected in the shared role of grieving parents: in 1991, the year my daughter was born, his only son took his life at age thirty-three. Don Daynard's kindness in reaching out to me when he heard of Lauren's passing reminded me of and rekindled the warmth I'd felt for this man, despite our vast differences. I have also come to wonder how it is that he kept going, kept performing, when he wasn't happy at work, and especially in light of the immense grief he was suffering after having lost his son. Of course, we didn't talk about it at the time; remember, this was a man who idolized John Wayne. You wouldn't find Duke sharing his feelings over a camomile tea, would you?

I say "tea" like it was an option; it wasn't. There were two choices for me in those days: coffee and whatever was filling my wine glass or tumbler every evening. You see, for many years, the dull thrum of a hangover was easier to bear at six in the morning than the unpredictability of the atmosphere in the studio. And so, between bouts of therapy and prescriptions for depression, I drank.

I sipped Japanese sake, heated up in sixteen-ounce measuring cups in the microwave (just as ancient tradition would dictate, I'm sure). I gulped wine, always cold and always an oaky Aussie Chardonnay, and later a Pinot Gris or Grigio. But my poison of choice remained the same straight-liquor concoction that had helped numb my pain during those first years in the city: martinis. I savoured the icy thickness of gin from the freezer and the tang of giant olives on a toothpick. I preferred my martinis like my jokes—salty and dirty—and would add half an ounce of olive juice to the gin and vermouth mixture. The brandy snifter had long ago been replaced by a fine crystal martini glass that was as joyful to my senses of touch and sight as the syrupy clear potion it so elegantly held. (Fun tip: A travel coffee mug makes a great martini shaker. Freezes well too! *Just don't actually travel with it.*)

I will say at this point that not once did the issue of my increasing self-medication come to the attention of listeners. I'm not in denial (well, at least not about this); at no time during the 1990s did I endanger my career or give less than what was perceived to be 100 percent. The term *high functioning* could have described me perfectly. Was I as sharp with a comeback or a quip as I would have been had I not imbibed the night before? No. But on the occasions when I was wise to let someone else have the punchline (remembering my place, after all), that dull edge served me well. Perhaps because of the level of alcohol consumption among many radio people, mine escaped the notice of my co-workers, too, until much later on. Did I get drunk at company gatherings? Of course I did—we all did! In fact, it was the person who wasn't constantly refilling his or her glass who stood out, just as did the non-smokers among us. I wouldn't be the only one to indulge in a cigar at a ratings party; many were the mornings I was reminded that the cheerful idea to have a cigar is God's way of saying, "Put down the stogie and the Errol Flynn and go home." If only I'd ever listened to that voice. It had long been silenced, rendered as useless as the on/off switch that I'm told people without a drinking problem actually have and really do use. What a concept! (Fun tip #2: Mixing Grand Marnier and Courvoisier gives you a drink called an Errol Flynn. A one-time Hollywood heartthrob, Flynn died at fifty, cirrhotic and no longer handsome, but probably with one of those mixtures on his bedside table. "I am what I drink. Cheers!")

Of course, weekends—without the restrictions of a 4 a.m. alarm and the feelings of remorse, headache and unquenchable thirst that accompanied drinking through the week—were the real time to let my hair down and get my drink on. After all, I deserved it! Whether I was celebrating a great week of radio or refilling the martini or wine glass to forget something or someone who had hurt me, Friday and Saturday evenings all took on a consistent fog; Saturday and Sunday mornings were spent lazily recovering on the couch, often in front of a cottage fireplace.

One therapist I saw, an Austrian native, said that in Canada, cottages were "a place where Canadians go to drink." She wasn't wrong. We'd plan our water skiing outings so that I would get the last drive in for whomever wanted to ski before we began serving salt-rimmed margaritas or tart gin and tonics on the lakeside deck. A winter afternoon staple (before wine or martinis) was the Bloody Caesar: a delicious Canadian invention utilizing clam and tomato juice that makes for a far superior version of the more mundane Bloody Mary. A small meal in their own right, our Caesars were constructed with care and perfection, from the celery salt–rimmed glass right down to the pickled bean or celery stalk that adorned each vodka-based drink.

Just as, at age eight, I'd enjoyed rolling my grandfather's cigarettes and not blinked a judgmental eye, Lauren took great pride in her ability to "build" a perfect Caesar, with a bartender-worthy rimmed glass and just the right amount of Tabasco, Worcestershire, lemon juice and cracked pepper. Lauren's Caesar could stand up against any professional's. It's pretty telling that I never really taught her how to bake or even how to cook (I never did the former and rarely did the latter), but she could build a drink. Fortunately, since I never won Mother of the Year, I won't have to give it back for telling you this. What do they say about confession being good for the soul? Ugh.

Eventually, my morning-after regrets and remorse started to outweigh the welcome, comfortable numbness of the night before. I got tired of feeling even more fatigued than normal for someone who gets up at "the crack of stupid" (we also called it "the butt crack of dawn," among many other euphemisms for the hours at which morning radio people rise), and of not having the energy to work out and main-tain a healthy weight. Even though alcohol made me feel more comfortable in social situations, as well as wonderfully blissed out during my time at home, it didn't take a rocket scientist to realize that words were coming to mind a little more sluggishly than they should have during the show, when everything was live and immediate. I risked hurting a brain that had served me well and rarely failed me, and I recognized that fact. At home during sober hours, I'd started saying "umbrella" when I meant "elevator," "dishwasher" when I meant "microwave." I chalked it up to fatigue and my brain not being on duty, but the truth is, my wires were getting crossed. My husband was starting to notice it too.

What was happening to the woman for whom "be on your best" could have been a forehead tattoo? Well, until anyone other than Rob took notice, I felt I was safe. Maybelline concealer could hide the dark circles under my eyes, and besides, who wouldn't have eye baggage worthy of Samsonite, working the hours I did?

Did Lauren take notice of my addiction? Mostly no, she told me years later. The only time we talked about my drinking was when she was eleven years old and I told her that "Mommy's going to quit." In the evangelical openness some addicts feel when they're looking at freedom from their habits (and seeking someone to whom I'd have to answer if I didn't meet my goals), I expressed to her my remorse if she felt that my illness had had any kind of bad effect on her. She said it hadn't and she was unaware that I had a problem. Lauren did admit to wondering, however, why I was so tired every weekend and just wanted to lie on the couch. Later, I was able to warn her about the dangers of drinking, especially as a child of someone who didn't have an off switch. As a result, she drank very rarely and, when she did, it was lightly. She had neither the constitution nor the need for alcohol. But that doesn't mean she didn't have strong feelings about it.

Rob has told me about one of the very few heated exchanges that he had with our daughter when she was a teen, aware of drinking among her schoolmates. In no uncertain terms, she expressed anger at his enabling me: his inability or unwillingness to "make" me stop. The conversation came in the year before I decided to quit, and I didn't learn of it until very shortly before you did. Of course she knew; she noticed everything. Don't forget that this is the child who made pocket change and earned toys by repeating the colourful words she'd heard at home. (This is me giving back that imaginary Mother of the Year award—again.)

In 2002, I quit drinking altogether, but I had help. First, I sought out a doctor who was a friend of my family doctor and happened to be an addictionologist. After having blood taken to make sure there was no liver damage (there wasn't), I was prescribed something I'd read about and requested: a drug called Antabuse (disulfiram) that blocks an enzyme involved in metabolizing alcohol intake. Whenever I felt that I might be in a situation where it would be hard to say no to a drink, I would take a tiny quarter of a tablet of this drug, which was designed to make the user really nauseated if she ingested any alcohol. I never tested its efficacy; I was taking it as an insurance policy because I had simply put my mind to it and I was quitting. Just like that.

I also had the assistance of a book that came into my

life quite by accident. At work, there's a table in the cafeteria where people leave things that have been sent in from companies hoping for publicity. On any given day in the "shark tank" you'll find coffee mugs, CDs by artists you've never heard of and, occasionally, books. One day, while filling my coffee cup, I looked down at the cluttered table and spotted a book that was meant for me: *The Thinking Person's Guide to Sobriety*. I won't go so far as to say it was the nudge I needed to quit drinking at that time, but I felt Bert Pluymen's story was my story. When he wanted to quit and expressed his desire aloud, his friends, family and co-workers all tried to tell him he didn't have a problem, so why was he quitting? But they didn't live in his body, feeling the way he did after a night where he'd tied one on and then promised he'd never do it again, before . . . you guessed it . . . doing it again. Pluymen also said that he'd quit for periods of a week or a month—sometimes even three months—which gave him the false notion that he could quit anytime. He subsequently learned that this was an on-and-off disorder, and that half of all addicts aren't drinking in any given month.

He adds that he had a big case of the "yets" when he got sober: not *yet* having been arrested, losing a job, drinking in the morning or noticing tremors in his hands. So what made it obvious to Bert Pluymen that he had to quit? It was how often he found himself trying to control how much he drank. Something I didn't know is that only people with drinking problems have to moderate how much they drink; folks without them control the amount without thinking twice.

I've noticed over the years just how true that is. How someone can stop at one or two glasses of wine, where I would be going until the bottle was empty (mostly at home, of course, where no one could see) and then following that up with a few ounces of vodka or gin. No off switch. But this book made a light go on.

I read and reread it. The words of this former rock-star lawyer, who had successfully argued a case before the United States Supreme Court at age twenty-eight, resonated so clearly that I took them to heart. His book illustrated to me that everyone's elevator goes down to a different "bottom." I didn't have to wait until I lost my marriage or my career before quitting drinking. I could do it now and my life would be better. I believed that. And so I quit.

For a while.

After eight months of sobriety, on June 14, 2003, I'd get some news that would send me practically running to the cupboard above the fridge. That's where we kept a fully stocked bar, which hadn't been a temptation to me during my months of new sobriety. I had convinced myself I wasn't going to drink, and besides, I had those tiny quartered tablets awaiting me if ever I thought I might slip. Plus, it was a cottage! Who would come to visit if we didn't have a bar at the ready and a well-used ice maker? And so, there they were: an azure-blue bottle of gin and its partner vermouth in green glass, just waiting to cool my searing pain on a breezy June afternoon.

The radio station I'd called home had started to slide in the ratings. My long-time partner had retired four years earlier, and his replacement and I weren't delivering the same chemistry or numbers. Left floundering without direction, we were soon to be put out to sea as another ship came toward our slip. Unbeknownst to most of us, the plug was about to be pulled on our sister radio station, leaving a younger, hipper morning team without a home. So it was decided that my partner and I would be taken off the show and it would be given to them. My contract had a "mornings only" clause, and so I found myself fired from the job I'd had—and loved—for fifteen years.

If this wasn't a damned good reason to drink again, what was? Right?

My sudden departure made the newspapers, internet and evening television news; I felt a sickening combination of failure and embarrassment to see my picture in the paper the very next day as I waited in an airport lounge for the flight to British Columbia to cocoon with my parents, who by this time had moved to the west coast of Canada to retire. I needed to get away from the fishbowl, the intense curiosity and the speculation as to why I'd been let go. I felt humiliated. Unwanted. Done. Old. Lost.

The trauma of losing the job I loved at age forty, after holding such a high-profile position for so long, didn't hit only me; it was a shock to our entire little family unit.

While Lauren was feeling the effects of our sudden unsteadiness, the stalwart *yin* to our spinning *yang*, husband and father Rob was as steady as ever. Once I'd returned home from my escape with my parents, we started to look at our options, which included listing our house and cottage for sale and pulling up stakes. I didn't think I could live in or around Toronto if I wasn't in the business I loved.

In the meantime, what I didn't know was that Lauren had shared her anxious questions with her father, and later she wrote about the experience in a chapter in her seventh-grade school project. Quoting a lyric in Joni Mitchell's "Big Yellow Taxi," she called the chapter "You Don't Know What You've Got 'Til It's Gone."

In June of 2003, though I didn't know it, my life was about to change drastically. On June 14th, my mom was let go of her 15-year-long job at the Toronto Radio Station CHFI, to bring in a new morning show.

Well, when big things happen in our lives, we tend to retaliate. So my mom's first solution, since she was born and raised in Western Canada, was to move to Osoyoos, British Columbia. After reviewing many brochures and websites, I thought that it might not be such a bad thing.

Then the reality of it hit me. Just months before, I had been informed that I had been accepted in Spectrum Alternative School. Plus, I was going to lose my best friend, my wonderful cottage, not to mention all of the family's friends that I've known since before I can remember. I went through a really emotional time after that.

It didn't help our daughter's confidence that, between my martini-fuelled crying jags, I also half-joked about pitching it all, leaving the big city and opening a yarn barn in the mountains of my native Alberta (even though I'm not a knitter and my crocheting is, let's say, "holier" than thou). I was ready to give up the career that I loved, so devastated and humiliated was I by this gutting turn of events. I felt that even though I believed I was not done with radio, my beloved medium must certainly be done with me!

And then, as things have tended to do in my semi-charmed life, a few little miracles happened. An interview I gave to the *Toronto Star* that resulted in an article entitled "Fans Soothe Jilted Davis" drew attention to the outcry that my firing had elicited among the radio station's many loyal listeners. While the comment section on the station's website was overflowing with anger and bewilderment, the inbox at my own website was filling up faster than I could answer. (It would take me a full six months to respond to every one of the four-thousand-plus letters of support and disappointment; I held onto those email addresses so I could update now-former listeners as to my whereabouts.)

That newspaper article, featuring a picture of me sitting on the bow of a tour boat heading down Ottawa's famous Rideau Canal, led to three amazing events. First, thousands of readers learned of my relatively new website, erindavis.com, which had been set up only three months earlier as a place to blog daily (which I still do). Second, a renowned theatre producer in Toronto, Ross Petty, contacted me and asked if I'd be willing to audition for the role of Fairy Godmother in his wickedly silly Christmas musical comedy *Cinderella*. (It's actually a panto, a British-based form of interactive theatre featuring a villain in drag—that would be Ross himself, in this case—and lots of family-friendly double entendres.) And that same week, I was contacted by a representative of the Ford Talent Agency, who asked if I'd be interested in hosting a daily nationwide TV talk show. What was happening?

I said yes to the offers and landed the role in *Cinderella*. Lauren was elated. As she wrote about that tumultuous time in that same school project:

> *I was extremely emotional and I spent a lot of time crying in my bedroom for weeks on end. Finally, my mom was presented many job offers, including being invited to audition in Ross Petty's production of* Cinderella *for the role of Fairy Godmother. She got it, and we're staying in Ontario for the time being. I guess the Fairy Godmother really did make my wishes come true.*

Even though the TV show coincided (collided?) with rehearsals and performances of *Cinderella*, I managed to pull off both. Truthfully, it all took a toll: by the end of 2003, I was diagnosed with bronchitis, pleurisy and pneumonia, but I didn't miss a show, on stage or on the W Network. And still, I drank just about as hard as I worked for that four-month period. Martinis after rehearsals and performances every night, then to bed before the next day's TV show. I think I might have mentioned the term *high functioning* already in this chapter?

No matter how late the night before, I'd set my alarm for 4 a.m. That's when I'd prop myself up in bed with a cool cloth over my eyes to hide any signs of drinking the previous night.

Then I'd get up at 6:30 for an 8 a.m. pickup to take me to the TV studio. (I realize as I write this how much like Joan Crawford I'm sounding here. How many more of us are there, I wonder?)

Once the curtain dropped for the last time on *Cinderella*, I returned to just one job: hosting *W Live with Erin Davis*. A live national one-hour talk show, it aired every weekday on one of Canada's second-tier cable channels. Had social media existed (or any promotion at all), I might have been able to draw in some viewers from other provinces, but as it was, the ratings were too meagre to merit a second season of what I felt was an engaging hour of quality live television. So I "bowed out" and surrendered the 11 a.m. time slot to another morning talk show newcomer who also happened to share my initials: Ellen DeGeneres. I couldn't have lost to a better person—not that we were competitors in any real sense of the word. Still, in my soggier moments, I wondered how many jobs a person could lose in one year. I had more time on my hands than I'd ever had in my adult life, so Rob, Lauren and I took advantage of the spring and summer by travelling to Europe. By the fall, I'd found work as a fill-in on the morning show at a station that was a direct competitor to my former radio employer. And then things started to click all over again.

A man I was aware of in the radio market, but with whom I'd never worked, became my new morning wake-up show partner. Right away, we both knew there was something going on here. A blue-collar guy with a blue-ribbon heart, Mike Cooper was pretty much a legend in our radio market: while working for the number-one pop music station in the 1970s, he'd ridden a Ferris wheel for weeks, right into the record books. He had a voice as big and deep as anyone in radio, and I figured someone with "pipes" like that must have an enormous ego to match and a brain inversely sized. How wrong I was! His heart matched his voice, our senses of humour and wits were perfectly paired and the two of us hit it off beautifully. Radio magic—that indefinable lightning called "chemistry"—was happening again right before listeners' ears. We soon enjoyed number-one ratings.

Meantime, the station that had let me go in June 2003—which had been on a downward slide ever since, largely because former listeners could not get past the way they felt I had been treated—was beginning to take notice of what was happening at the competition.

Mike was not only a perfect radio partner but a convivial and willing drinking partner as well. He is one of the few people I've known who say they can hold their liquor and then actually do—which makes it ironic (but true) that he was eventually instrumental in my decision to quit for good. But that would come later, when it appeared I might be putting both of our careers at risk.

For now, I was soaking up the days of wine and rising ratings. I was happy and secure in my job; our family was breathing a collective sigh of relief. Radio wasn't done with me yet, and we would be staying put.

Then, six months after my pairing with Mike Cooper, a dream I'd literally thrown into the fire rose from the ashes. You see, back on New Year's Eve 2004, in a gin-soaked ceremony of symbolism, I took that year's calendar off the wall and tossed it into the flames of our cottage fireplace. Despite all of my wishing and hoping, the station I'd called home for so many years hadn't called to invite me back. Clearly, it was time for me to embrace the change and move into a new year and new dreams. But in the spring of 2005, something amazing happened: the boss who'd let me go in June of 2003 called and asked if I'd be willing to discuss returning to the CHFI morning show. My response was cautiously positive, and we met for coffee a few days later. Julie Adam began with a heartfelt apology. I think we were both nervous (I know I was), but our initial coffee went well, and we began to talk more often. And once I'd been assured that Mike Cooper could come with me, the wheels were in motion for my move back "home."

It was a triumphant return. I was able to come back with a new sense of confidence, appreciation and respect, although deep down there were still voices in my head asking: *If I was too old for the job two years ago, how can I be right for it now?* The hours of therapy I'd paid for (and would for years to come) helped assuage those concerns and, in the fall of 2005, a major advertising campaign announcing my return to CHFI—and pairing with Mike Cooper—was launched.

Did I stop drinking then? Oh, heck no! Why would I? There was too much to celebrate; too many dinners with good friends and fine wine. I had no intention of slowing down. *Besides*, I thought, *I've got this.*

Of course, as anyone who has a dependency on alcohol will tell you, there comes a time when, if you're lucky, you realize that the control is actually not in your corner at all: it's the booze that's in the driver's seat. I believe that I still didn't let it affect my job performance, and I'd defy you to find a listener, even on our group trips to all-inclusive resorts, who could tell you I had a problem saying "No, thanks" when the server was refilling wine glasses. I like to think that I did a solid job of hiding my weakness. Of course, I could be wrong. Alcohol tricks you into believing all kinds of untruths.

So what was the tippling "tipping point?"

It came on St. Patrick's Day 2006—or in the wee hours of the morning that followed. My comeback had made waves significant enough that I was asked to be the grand marshal of the annual St. Patrick's Day Parade, and with a name like "Erin" (plus a dog named Molly Malone and an Irish king somewhere way back in the family tree) you can be sure it was a huge honour. I gratefully accepted, taking part in luncheons and gatherings that led up to the big day. I only wish I'd had something to eat before or after the parade. On an uncharacteristically chilly March day, I sat atop the back of a convertible and, bundled up in a green wool cape and soft yellow leather gloves, waved at the festive crowds shivering along Canada's longest street. It should have been a triumphant day—the icing on my comeback cake. Instead, I let my celebrating get out of control. I was not "on my best," to put it mildly, despite the vow I'd made to myself the night before not to let anything smear the memories of this great honour.

Rob insists that I was told by many of the organizers of the week-long series of events that I was the best grand marshal they'd ever had. Perhaps it was the Guinness talking, or a bit o' the blarney, but doggone it, what else was I to do but drink right along with my hosts—many of whom had put their abstinence promise for Lent on hold for this very occasion. After the parade wound up, we found ourselves at one of the city's many Irish bars. This one, with close ties to parade organizers, had a private lounge upstairs where the special smooth and aged whiskey was poured freely for the big day's VIPs. I didn't realize just how freely until I attempted to leave my perch atop a dark wooden stool: as I tried to stand, I fell to my knees, to the laughter of everyone, including me. At least three people ran to my aid and, brushing off my satin grand marshal sash and gathering what was left of my dignity, I got to my feet. That is the last I remember of that night. How I managed to negotiate the narrow, steep stairway that took Rob and me down to a waiting cab, I have absolutely no idea. Nor do I have any memory of the trip home or how I got into bed.

What I do know is that about four hours later, I slept through my alarm clocks. Rob heard them and tried to rouse me, with little success. When he finally did, I was able to call in to our producer at the radio station and tell him I had no voice from shouting during the parade and wouldn't be able to do the show. I could hear Mike in the background, angrily saying, "That's just grrrrrreat!"

I'd let my partner down.

I went back to sleep, having assured myself that my excuse was valid: it's true that I had no voice, but I was also still drunk. There's no way I could have faked my way through a four-hour live radio show. Apparently, though, I did think I could fake my way through ninety minutes;

ashamed, I walked across the street and went in to the station at 7:30 a.m. and finished the show. (To be truthful, I don't remember that either, but Rob does.)

I can't recall how the meeting was set up, or who called whom, but Mike, Rob and I met up later that same day at a local wing joint. Mike was not happy with me—justifiably so—and told me I'd let down the show. I wish I remembered more about the conversation, but I think that my shame over what had happened—how I'd seemingly deliberately sabotaged what should have been a high point in my life—managed to submerge a lot about the aftermath of that night of bingeing. A night that probably should have ended in a hospital, not on an elevator floor with my husband struggling to drag me to our apartment door. Pretty "grand," huh? I couldn't figure out why my arms hurt so badly and why I was limping in the days immediately following the parade debacle; reluctantly, Rob told me what he'd had to do to get me home. I was mortified.

I wish I could tell you that the pain and shame with which I remember the fog of those two days in my life were enough to scare me sober. They weren't. But one morning a few months later, I awoke and said I'd finally had enough. I was tired of waking up feeling like "death warmed over," as my mother would say, and I decided then and there to quit. Once again, with the help of Antabuse and Bert Pluymen's book, I quit drinking. It was July 4, 2006: my own "Independence Day."

Having tried unsuccessfully to stop drinking a few times in the past—my record was several months—I knew how to go about doing it. I didn't do anything as drastic as pour the contents of all of the bottles in our condo and cottage down the drain; we'd need them for visitors. I also didn't forbid Rob to drink, and when he felt sheepish over wanting a Manhattan when I was sipping a diet Dr Pepper, I reminded him that it wasn't his fault I didn't have an off switch. Besides, I'd also tell him, living with me would be enough to make you want to drink, right? He'd laugh. We did have an arrangement we both adhered to: if he was going to drink, there would be no hanky and definitely no panky. We both agreed that it wouldn't be fair if he had alcohol on his breath and we were, um, embracing. That's part of how it worked for us. I didn't try to make him quit, and we had just a few ground rules.

There were challenges on listener trips when everyone was getting pretty well-lubricated with all of the free libations around the pool, at the welcome parties and so on. But I remembered previous trips during my drinking days, when we'd done a clothed conga line right into the swimming pool, or I'd spent countless hours in the hot tub while the Errol Flynns flowed. For someone who was so protective of her image and so careful not to be the topic of gossip, at times I'd been careless enough to let down my guard. In fairness, a good number of those folks partying with me wouldn't have noticed any particular loosening up on my part, but still . . . I was being needlessly reckless. So it came as somewhat of a relief to be sober on those trips, if only to make the 4 or 5 a.m. show starts (depending on the time zones) a little easier to take. But come on—did they have to put whole bottles of booze in the rooms? Talk about waving it under my nose!

We would tuck those bottles into the closet as soon as we checked in. Out of sight and all of that.

You may wonder why I sought the wisdom of a book rather than Alcoholics Anonymous and its Big Book. I'll tell you straight out: pride. That oh-so-dangerous deadly sin. Very early on, when I was online exploring the possibility of sobriety, I told a chat room that I had a high-profile position and was very worried about being outed for my dependence on alcohol. A few less-than-kind posters called me out on my ego (probably justifiably) and were anything but understanding and supportive. Now, of course, the cold and often cowardly anonymity of a chat room or website does not at all compare with the heart-to-heart compassion that can come out of a real-life support group, and I should not have let that experience sour me or scare me away from an AA meeting. I have not yet closed the door on the possibility of attending a meeting, as I know how very successful the program has been for so many. And in this life, I think we need all the help we can get.

During the time immediately following Lauren's death, I thanked my higher powers more times than I can count for the strength it took to persevere and achieve sobriety, starting that day. Lauren's death, which occurred just a couple of months short of my ninth anniversary of putting away the martini shaker, tested my resolve in a way that made losing a job seem as trivial as breaking a fingernail. Still, somehow, my sobriety held through the ordeal of losing and saying goodbye to our daughter.

~~~~

THIS is where I should stop writing and let you move on to the next chapter, but that would be taking the easy way out. This book is about being honest and sharing the travels and travails that have brought Rob and me to where we are today. So I have to tell you the truth: the week I announced I was leaving Toronto radio in late 2016, I began drinking again.

It happened innocently enough, and it wasn't the first time this challenge had been put in my path: Rob and I were flying off to spend a few weeks together in the sun, and I asked our flight attendant for a virgin Caesar (no vodka). I got one. When I requested another, he forgot the "virgin" part. I tasted the vodka immediately, said to myself, *Why not?* and down it went. My blessed life as I knew it was over in so many ways, a man I detested with every fibre of my being had been elected to the highest office in the land just south of us, and I was, to tone down the vernacular, all out of damns to give.

I leaned across to where Rob was seated and told him right away that there was vodka in my Caesar. He didn't protest or try to talk me out of it: he hoped that after over ten years of sobriety, I'd find my off switch and, in return, give him a wife who could have cocktails with him and just roll with the idea of feeling no pain after being tortured by so much of it. Caesars were followed by wine with dinner and a nice port to top things off. This was going to be a great vacation!

When we got home from that booze-soaked trip (so much for the off switch), I managed to control my intake— one glass of wine after dinner, and never in front of anyone but Rob—right up until the day, one month later, that we said goodbye to Ontario and boarded a flight to our new life. Then I could imbibe all of the martinis and white wine I wanted! I felt I could freely numb the pain of the litany of horrendous losses we had suffered in the previous months: our child, proximity to our grandchild (because of our choice to move), my entire radio life and the identity I'd spent my career building up. Who was I now? Where was I? We knew a total of six people in the area to which we were moving, after thirty years of being in a city where I was surrounded by friendly and welcoming faces at almost every turn. Suddenly, every insecurity I'd had since childhood came back with a vengeance: I was that new kid in school again, the misfit stranger. The kid who would decide with every meeting: introvert or extrovert? I hadn't realized until I arrived in our new province just how weird it would be to know barely a soul and not to worry about putting on makeup (which I still did for months, even for a neighbourhood dog walk) in case I was recognized or someone wanted to share a selfie.

Rob and I both experienced the extreme loneliness that comes with uprooting and having to find everything from a doctor and dentist to a hairdresser and dry cleaner. We came to see our new home, with its breathtaking ocean and mountain views, as a nice, new place in which to be sad.

For the first three or four months, as we settled in, I found myself sinking into a hole of remorse and regret. How much of that came from the aftermath of imbibing again, I'm not sure; I only know that enveloping myself in the days surrounding Lauren's death, as I did (and Rob did, too) for this book, pulled me down further than I'd been since the actual event. Do not think that I regret for a second agreeing to write and share these experiences with you! But the process of doing so definitely did have a toll, and it was a cost that until now I have disclosed to only those who shared a bottle of wine with me during those months of 2017.

As I watched the numbers on my bathroom scale rise, the darkness under my eyes deepen and my ambition to stay active dwindle to nothing, I continued to indulge in unhealthy doses of both self-medication and self-loathing. Rob and I both were in a deep state of mourning for the lives we'd left behind, and this was how we dealt with it, together.

You might be asking the same question we asked ourselves: How is it that I survived the loss of our daughter but began drinking a year and a half later? I have a few theories: after decades of answering to others (including three pre-dawn alarms), I had no one for whom I needed to behave responsibly in this new post-radio life. No early mornings, no show to carry or to which to contribute; there was no one to disappoint or disgust with my weakness, or to turn to for help, for that matter.

We were rudderless with no horizon in sight, floundering aimlessly with only the mission of writing this book to tether us to any kind of duty or feeling of purpose.

But suddenly (and not for the first time), radio came to my rescue: in May 2017, I was approached to fill in on the midday show at our local Rogers radio station, Ocean 98.5, in Victoria. Without hesitation, I said yes, and with that, I had a reason to get up each day and find things to talk about in a concise (and hopefully interesting) manner. And I had to answer to someone besides my bosses: listeners. Of course, my daily online blog had continued, but in this case, radio was much more of an immediate demand. And I wasn't going to let anyone down.

So I started to find some purpose, once again. And eventually I decided that, since I did not have the ability to say "no thanks" after one or two drinks like most "normal" drinkers, it was time to stop poisoning my body (especially the brain I had always relied on to serve up just the right words at the right time) and to take this problem by the reins. I sought help from our family doctor, who agreed that an antidepressant might be what I needed, embraced physical activity again and have now been sober since the beginning of the second year of our new life here.

Although it was easy to use Lauren's death and the upheaval in our lives as the best excuses possible to indulge in a habit I knew was doing me physical harm (and who was it hurting but me, this time around?), I recognized how angry she would be with me—and with her daddy—for letting this happen again. I had marked ten years' sobriety in July 2016, for God's sake. How could I have let all of that go?

It was easy. No one could really blame me. But it wasn't the right thing to do. If Rob and I were to live the lives that Lauren would want us to, until we can be with our daughter again, then changes had to be made. And they were. This time, the date I chose was Groundhog Day, February 2. I had seen my shadow and it foretold a world of hurt. So before I fell back into that hole, it was time to stop.

I take nothing for granted about each day without drinking as it comes. I am grateful for each one. Yes, although they do get easier, the evenings can be hard, but the mornings—and their clarity—are so much better. I hope that, soon, embracing sobriety will feel as natural a part of me as it did for those ten years. I know that I can do this, and I will. One day at a time.

CHAPTER 10

Purposeful Mourning

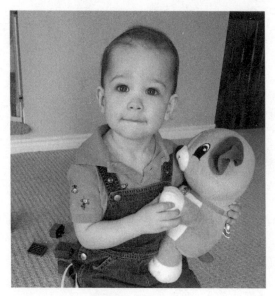

Colin, summer 2016

S TRENGTH COMES IN SO MANY DIFFERENT INCAR-
nations. Much of the time—perhaps most of the
time—we come by it because there's simply no
alternative. Someone wise once said that you don't know
what you're capable of until it's the only thing left to do, and
it's so true. I have lost count of the number of people who
have said they don't know how they would survive in my
shoes, or that they can't imagine how they'd keep going, or
just how strong I must be. But to them, all I say is that I'm
not doing anything different from what they would probably
do. I just happen to be doing it on a stage, of sorts. Whether
on the radio or through my blog, I've just lived out loud. But
I've kept living, and that's the key—just as it has been for
countless parents before us who have also faced devastation
and gotten up to fight another day.

The strength of women like Ellen Hinkley—who manage
to dig their way out of the darkness to happiness after having been immersed in so many levels of pain that every day
must have felt like a new circle of hell—is something that my

own family and siblings are going to have to draw upon. You see, almost exactly two years after we lost our daughter, my youngest sister's son died—the victim of a suspected murder. Almost unbelievably, this is the second child that she has had to bury. Twenty-five years earlier, when Leslie told our mother that her baby would be stillborn, Mom responded in sadness and incredulity, "This kind of thing *doesn't happen* to our family." She was right.

Until baby Katrina's death, we'd enjoyed what most people would probably casually observe as an enviable life: happily married parents, four ambitious and achieving daughters and a comfortable and sometimes adventurous middle-class existence. There were challenges, to be sure, as there are in every family: divorce, disease and dissent. But nothing like the heartbreak Leslie suffered when she endured the still-birth of her first child.

It could be argued—my self-imposed ban on comparisons aside—that nowhere is the loss of a child so amplified by the pain of broken and still limitless dreams as when a baby is lost before or during birth. No matter how much time a mother has had to bond with that baby before its arrival in the world, whether two months or full term, there comes with losing that child an inevitable, piercing pain—a realization of the unfairness of such a helpless human being not even having had a chance to take a breath.

Whether we know it or not, someone close to us has probably suffered a miscarriage. It's estimated that, although statistics are incomplete, some 15 to 20 percent of all pregnancies end in miscarriage. In my own family, it happened to two of my three sisters, as well as my dear niece and my own mother (during the pregnancy before my arrival). The feelings of sadness that accompany this kind of loss are coupled with the hormonal changes the body experiences during pregnancy, only adding to the expected feelings of depression and other immense emotional distress.

In addition to shock, anger and depression, a grieving mother-to-be often experiences sensations of guilt. A woman whose pregnancy has ended with the death of a baby (called a "stillbirth" after twenty weeks of gestation) may wonder if she should have known there was something wrong, or what she did to have brought about her unborn child's death. Certainly this was the case when my younger sister lost her daughter in 1993.

Leslie was pregnant with her first child and had seemingly sailed through seven months. A busy phone book advertising sales executive, she looked like she was managing it all. But late one evening as she was helping to meet a huge deadline at work, a fellow ad rep pointed to Leslie's belly and said, "What are you doing here? You should be at home taking care of that baby!"

Those words would haunt Leslie for months—even years—as she asked herself repeatedly, "What did I do wrong? Did I bring this on?" Because the very next day, she was on her back, sick with a cold for which, in good conscience, she could take no medication. On day two of cold-induced bed rest, she noticed a lack of movement in her belly.

At first, she wondered if her sickness had laid the baby low, and whether it was just taking it easy, like Mommy. But worry set in, and she and her husband bundled up against the January cold and made their way to the hospital, where a barrage of tests was done during a long and anxious day. To make matters worse, nurse after nurse refused to give them any information. One, however, tried to assuage their concerns by lightheartedly saying that there must have been something wrong with one of the ultrasound machines. If only.

After waiting nine hours for word—any word at all—Leslie and Peter were now really fearing the worst and wondering why no one would give them any information, good or bad. They left that hospital, which was the one nearest their home, and made a silent drive to another one half an hour away, the hospital she had visited regularly during her prenatal doctor's appointments. It was there that their fears were confirmed. In the small and lonely hours of the next morning, her doctor showed up and, tears in his dark brown eyes, asked softly, "Leslie, what happened?"

Of course, no one knew. That would be a question that several tests on a little girl who would soon be named Katrina would fail to answer. But first came what I, as an outsider, perceived to be the next hardest part: waiting for the baby to arrive naturally.

When Leslie called me in a hotel room many miles away to tell me her tragic news, I asked when she would be giving birth. She relayed the doctor's recommendations that nature be allowed to take its course: the baby would wait in utero until Leslie went into labour. Next to the news of her unsuccessful pregnancy, I thought this was the saddest, sickest thing I had ever heard. But her doctor was firm in his belief that this pregnancy should be as physically non-disruptive as possible for Leslie so that she would be in good shape for her next one.

I could not imagine having to keep a dead baby inside me, my "baby bump" a constant reminder of the dreams that were never to come true. It's no wonder some women choose to be induced immediately upon hearing of a baby's prenatal death. But Leslie decided to listen to her doctor's advice and wait until her baby emerged in her own time and, in so doing, proved completely wrong my assumption that it would be a torturous period.

Understandably devastated, Leslie and Peter left the hospital and went home, where my sister did what she hadn't done in seven months: poured herself a stiff drink and lit one of her husband's cigarettes. And then she cried for hours. She told me she had never known a pain like this and feared her heart would burst in her chest over the tragedy of it all.

But then something happened that startled not only Leslie but also the rest of her concerned family. Because of the ultrasounds, she had learned the baby's gender. So, the would-be parents named the child, and Leslie began to bond with her in the precious time they had left together. She says she talked to Katrina, listened to and sang Queen and Bon Jovi ("The Show Must Go On" and "Bed of Roses" were her greatest hits, she says) and got a chance to say her goodbyes before they even really "met" in person. The ten days between Leslie's learning that the baby would not survive and her going into natural labour gave her a chance to come to grips with what was happening and to prepare for the baby's arrival.

ERIN DAVIS

Although every mother in this sad situation may have a different opinion, Leslie calls her doctor's instructions to let the pregnancy and nature take their course the best advice she received during that tumultuous time. She feels that, had she gone into the hospital for tests and come home the next day with no baby, it would have been too much of a shock, and she really would have been, in her words, "screwed up." Of course, the option of waiting out the birth of a child who has died is not always realistic; after or even during a two-week window (sometimes immediately upon discovery of the baby's death), there can be concern about infections, blood clots or other possible complications. For my little sister, however, waiting was the best course of action. She related her situation to me, saying, "You would carry your dead child as long as you could—that's what a mother does." And I certainly get that. If I could have, I'd have never left that Ottawa funeral home sitting room. I would have sat at Lauren's side for as long as they would let me, no question.

And so it was, on a frigid January night, in the same hospital where her mother and father had been given the worst news expectant parents can receive, Katrina made her arrival into the world, weighing just over two pounds. Leslie was taken to a private room, where the speakers that carried regular announcements reminding mothers that it was time to feed their babies, and so on, were mercifully turned off. A gentle and kind female Salvation Army officer, who came in at four o'clock in the morning, cleaned and dressed the little grey baby and took pictures of her for her parents, which, along with those clothes, would later be given to them as keepsakes to look at whenever they felt they were ready. (In some cases, a midwife or volunteer will describe the baby to the parents, if they're reluctant to lay eyes on the child.) Although it was an option, now, twenty-five years later, Leslie has expressed second thoughts about the way she handled the short time between her baby's stillbirth and when the child was taken away to prepare for burial.

Leslie says she regrets having chosen not to hold Katrina in her arms. Her reason at the time for not doing so? "I couldn't," she says. "I just couldn't. I gave birth naturally; I still had to dilate and go through contractions, and although the pushing wasn't that hard, I still had to endure all that, even though she was smaller. The whole birthing was exactly like the next three that I had," she says.

"But now I wish I had held her, because I didn't feel I was a good mother by choosing not to do that." Her husband didn't hold the baby either, but he did see her in the Salvation Army officer's arms. Tiny Katrina was buried in a little white lace coffin in a plot near her paternal grandmother. As is the case with most stillbirths, I'm told, the funeral home did not charge for the infant's coffin.

There was no definitive cause given for the death; in a case of what she termed, coincidentally, "chicken and egg," Leslie says it was undetermined whether the placenta shut down, causing the baby's death, or, because of the baby's death, the placenta shut down, no longer needed to nourish the child.

Words of sympathy to parents of children who did not survive gestation or birth must be as carefully chosen as those delivered to other grieving parents. In this case, there are a few extra phrases to avoid, including "there must have been something wrong with her," "at least you didn't give birth to a child with deformities," "God needed another angel," or "it's all for the best." Once again, if people can't think of anything to say that they're 100 percent sure is going to be of comfort, it's best just to offer a hug, a meal or quiet support. A loss is a loss is a loss. Whether it comes after seven months (in or outside of the uterus), seven years or seven decades, the death of a loved one with whom you've bonded is sure to cause heartache. I would hope that no one would ever consider that a tiny baby takes up any less space in a parent's heart, or its loss—no matter how far along—causes any less pain.

One of the most important things that those who love and support mothers of miscarried and stillborn children must remember is never to suggest that the mother is somehow at fault. Avoid the dreaded "at leasts" and, as with any grieving parent, don't hide from their pain or make them feel they should conceal it. Talk about their baby and their loss, but only when they want to. Realize that being around other infants or children could easily trigger their sadness, and the mere sight of a stroller can be enough to cause tears. Don't assign what you feel is a reasonable amount of time to their healing process. For some, the loss of a baby is something they never "get over." No amount of telling them they have an angel in heaven, or that they'll be able to have more children, will take away the pain of their loss. As is the case when an older child dies, it's the sudden end of the dreams—so achingly close to becoming reality—that hurts the most. The future has suddenly been erased; the road you were most surely going to be taking has disappeared.

My sister recalls returning to work after a relatively short time at home, taking her doctor's advice to get back to some sense of a normal life and eschewing the maternity leave to which she was entitled. A few days into her return, she paid a visit to a weary co-worker in a nearby cubicle. When Leslie asked her what was wrong, the friend said that her baby had been up all night, and she was exhausted. Leslie responded, "I would do anything to hear a baby crying at night." The woman was mortified at having said something that, while honest, was inadvertently insensitive to Leslie's loss. To this day, that same (now former) co-worker says she has never forgotten their conversation, which, thankfully, did not diminish their closeness.

Happily, Leslie would soon be kept awake in the night by a baby's cries too. In May of the same year that Katrina was born and lost, Leslie became pregnant with her second child. A son, Michael, arrived safely in February 1994, but not before Leslie went through worry and anxiety as she approached and then passed the twenty-eight-week mark of her second pregnancy. For this, and the two that followed, she was treated as high risk. And all three births went beautifully.

Just thirteen months after the death of so many dreams, a happier chapter began when Leslie and her then-husband became parents to a fair-haired, blue-eyed, healthy baby boy who was the spitting image of his Danish-blooded father. That boy turned twenty-three on February 11, 2017.

It was to be his last birthday.

Just two and a half months later, a raging house fire in the seemingly bucolic BC city of Kelowna appeared to have claimed Michael's life. It took several months to obtain DNA confirmation of what both the RCMP and our family knew would be the sad truth: for reasons suspected, but as yet unconfirmed, Michael may have been the victim of a homicide. He may even have been killed before the fire was set.

As of this writing, there are many details that have yet to come out in the investigation, and it would be wrong to go much further into the sad story of Michael's association with the darkest elements of society, in a city that has become known for its rampant drug use and fatalities. Those of us who know the circumstances of his life and death believe Michael was targeted once he'd made the decision to get away from the people with whom he'd associated and to find a better life: he'd landed a job; was, by one account, cleaned up and no longer using drugs; and was seeking to become not only a good provider but also a positive role model for the young son who bears a jaw-dropping resemblance to his adoring dad. There are some lifestyles that are easy to slip into, with their promises of fast financial and material rewards, but desperately difficult to get out of. It appears that Michael found himself trapped in one of them.

As the investigation into Michael's death slowly moved forward, our hearts ached for my sister and her family. I find myself in a position of such unlikely kinship, knowing far too well how Leslie feels to have lost an adult child.

Like me, my younger sister has a grandson who will be a living link to the child who's gone. And now, living in the same province, they see each other with delightful regularity. Unlike me, Leslie has other children: a teenaged son and daughter who mourn their half-brother in their deal-with-it-later teenage kind of way, while giving Leslie and their father strength to go forward. I feel her pain in a way I wish I did not, but I am grateful at the very least to know the words to say (and sometimes, more importantly, not to say) to try to bring comfort and to make some sense of the unfathomable. Although the circumstances of our children's deaths could not be more dissimilar, the hole caused by their leaving is a shared, literally familiar pain between two sisters.

Because Leslie is in the unusual and awful place of having lost two children, I posed a question that goes against one of the primary lessons I've learned in the grieving process: don't compare one death to another. But I knew my sister would give me a pass and let me, so I asked Leslie if there were any differences or similarities in the grief she experienced as a mother twenty-four years apart.

She felt that Katrina's death hardened her in a way that ensured her heart could not break again the same way it did when she found out her child had died in utero in 1993. Michael's death was, of course, a world apart in circumstances. Baby Katrina had died completely innocently, while Michael—who certainly did not deserve a death sentence—had participated in a lifestyle that put him at a higher risk of dying than had he worked at a tire store (which he had, just a year earlier). Leslie said that with her first child's death, she felt no anger, just overwhelming sadness; with Michael's, there was a surplus of anger that eventually made way for sadness as well. In neither case was Leslie to blame but, of course, each child's passing was accompanied by a long list of questions and more guilt than one person should ever bring to bear upon her own shoulders. I wish her every bit of the strength she'll need for the future, which hopefully will bring if not closure (a word that comes up often in courtrooms on *Dateline*), then justice.

Through the years since our own child's passing, I've been in awe of the many parents who find ways to channel their grief into pursuits that honour their children and their abbreviated lives. One woman, who came into our world after Lauren's passing, shared with us her belief—one that turns out to be quite widespread—in the significance of dragonflies as they pertain to the afterlife. She had delved into the spiritual symbolism of these insects when searching for a way to try to ease the pain of a dear, close niece who had lost her husband just ten months after they wed. Little did Barbara Cassells know that, four years after giving her niece some dragonfly jewellery, her own belief in and connection to the power of these insects would be tested one hundredfold. Her heart heavier than ever, she found herself moved to craft thousands of the bugs—using colourful beads and parachute cord—to help herself, even as she endeavoured to lessen the suffering of others.

In 2014, the Cassells family had to say goodbye to their twenty-four-year-old son. Like our Lauren (also twenty-four when she left us, also born on the twenty-fourth day of the month), Nathan lived in Ottawa, where he attended university.

In January, while home with his family in Pickering, Ontario (he was due to return to university that very week), Nathan suffered a massive heart attack. It turns out that he had an undiagnosed enlarged heart. Because of his youth and strength, paramedics were able to revive him and get his heart started again, but he had been down too long. Barbara writes:

He was brain dead. The pain is still stabbing as I type this. He was rushed to the hospital. I followed in a police car. I will never ever forget that drive in rush-hour traffic, sirens blaring, tearing down the shoulder of the 401 [highway], watching the ambulance carrying my son speeding to the hospital, pulling into the ambulance bay and seeing them straddling my son, pounding his chest to keep his heart beating. Things no mother should ever see and can never be forgotten. They rushed him in and I was rushed into a private waiting room. Once he was stabilized, I was taken to see him. I saw the doctor checking his pupils, his reflexes, shaking his head. I knew. Only machines and drugs were keeping him alive.

He was taken to ICU. I sat with him most of the night. They told us it was only a matter of hours as he was bleeding out [hemorrhaging]. His [vital] numbers were dropping. I sang to him, lullabies I sang to him as a small child; I held his hand, told him over and over I loved him. His dad brought his sisters back first thing in the morning. His numbers continued to drop. It was literally a matter of a couple hours. I did the last thing I could for my boy. We said our goodbyes and I asked that the machines and drugs be turned off. I held my son in my arms and he was free.

He thanked me for that, you know. I saw a medium who knew of the brain death, of the tubes in his throat. Nathan said he did not like those and thanked me for letting him go.

The pain is as fresh as yesterday. . . . Do you sometimes look at what you have written in disbelief and wonder how this possibly could be true? It does take a toll. . . .

Yes, yes, yes. I cannot believe any of what's happening in our lives either, Barbara.

She went on to tell me that it was when she was taken to her knees in grief at Nathan's grave that a dragonfly visited her three times; Barbara notes that there was no body of water nearby. She says that's when she remembered the story of the dragonfly and knew Nathan was telling her he was okay.

On the second anniversary of her son's passing, Barbara began to make simple but significant key chains from beads, rings and the parachute cord that she feels evokes such an image of both strength and trust. In the first year of making them, Barbara gave away more than twelve hundred free of charge, many of them through bereaved family groups. She continues to do so to this day.

Barbara encloses each one in a tiny clear bag, accompanied by a printed story about the dragonfly (derived from an old fable, perhaps most famously adapted in Doris Stickney's *Water Bugs and Dragonflies: Explaining Death to Young Children*). Barbara very kindly made some for us, personalized in memory of our Lauren, and I tailored some later for Leslie and Michael. In a lovely homonym that resonated with our lives, it's the story of a beetle. The water beetle turns into a dragonfly and discovers a world more beautiful than she could ever have imagined! (It's really worth looking up.)

Not unlike the dragonfly of that sweet story, the promise inherent in Nathan's life was to be saluted in a couple of different ways after his passing too. Barbara shared with me that at his funeral she was able to place a diploma confirming his degree from the University of Ottawa on his casket, along with a mortarboard. "This, my son," said Barbara, "is your convocation." The entire church stood and applauded Nathan's determination to graduate and make his mother even prouder than she already was. In June 2014, the university, which had hastily approved Nathan's degree and made sure Barbara had it in time for the funeral, invited the family to their late son's actual convocation.

We were seated in the very front row. As his name was called, his sisters went forward to receive his diploma. The entire hall of over 2,000 people rose as one and gave my boy the longest, loudest standing ovation I have heard in my entire life.

Oh, just imagine.

A mother's grief is intertwined with pride and the feeling of so much promise unfulfilled; it is the horrendously deep and endless chest into which we daily fold and carefully lay our dreams and sorrows for the loss of so much brightness, so much hope. Oh, so much loss.

Arguably, Canada's highest-profile bereaved mother is Margaret Trudeau. Not only does she have the distinction of being the wife of one of the country's most famous prime ministers, Pierre Elliott Trudeau (Canada's fifteenth), but she is also mother to its twenty-third prime minister, Justin Trudeau. Now in her early seventies, she is the author of four books in which, with consistency and disarming frankness, she details her battle with mental illness.

In 1971, twenty-two-year-old Margaret Sinclair became the young, pot-smoking flower-child bride to an older, intellectual and charismatic politician: a fifty-one-year-old man who gave a nation with all the personality of a bolt of red-plaid flannel a sexier, more worldly makeover. As a couple, the Trudeaus captured the imagination of the masses: some watched this intergenerational marriage with curiosity or skepticism; others viewed them as worthy successors in the world spotlight to the previous decade's Kennedys (who'd been replaced by the staid and standard Johnsons and Nixons). Margaret drew large audiences—and even votes for her husband—as she occasionally campaigned with him. She tells of her idea for Pierre to toss aside his long-winded speeches, and of him suggesting she take the podium herself—which she did!

Margaret bore Pierre three sons, and the fact that two of them arrived on Christmas Day (two years apart) became a source of great God-complex humour aimed in a mostly good-natured manner at Monsieur Trudeau and his bride. Unbeknownst to most, behind the walls and doors of 24 Sussex Drive (which Mrs. Trudeau calls "the crown jewel in the federal penitentiary system"), this young mother was waging a battle against the demons of undiagnosed addiction and illness.

After six years of marriage, the couple separated, although Margaret continued to live in an attic suite at the prime minister's official residence. In 1984, their divorce was finalized. Margaret, who is convinced she'd have had better care—and likely been diagnosed properly, sooner—had her name not been Trudeau, sought and seems to have found the treatment she needed to regain her health and her equilibrium. In time, she remarried—this time to a real estate developer, someone out of the political spotlight—and had another son and (at long last) a daughter. She also continued to write and would embark upon a career as a television host.

For a time, all seemed well, and it appeared that Margaret Sinclair Trudeau's tumultuous life had finally found a measure of balance and tranquility. And then tragedy struck: in 1998, Michel, her twenty-three-year-old son with Pierre, was struck by an avalanche while skiing in a British Columbia provincial park. He was swept into a lake and drowned, causing much of a nation to mourn alongside the Trudeaus. After all, many of us had grown up right along with Justin, Alexandre ("Sacha," as he was known) and Michel (nicknamed "Miche" by Cuban dictator Fidel Castro). How could this be?

At a speech she gave in Ottawa in 2017, I watched as Mrs. Trudeau's otherwise lively, sparkling eyes filled with tears when she told the gut-wrenching story of the passing of her "Miche." For her, that loss brought on a spiral of depression so deep and long-lasting that it threatened her own life.

Only one year after Michel's death, Margaret divorced from businessman Fried Kemper. Then, just the following year, prostate cancer claimed her first ex-husband, the former prime minister, at age eighty. In the traumatic aftermath of both the passing of her son and her first husband (she claimed that even though the marriage had ended, the love had not), Margaret's health continued to decline. In fact, doctors warned her she was possibly subconsciously emulating Pierre Trudeau's refusal, in his final days, to take nourishment.

In an interview that appeared in the October 8, 2010, issue of *Maclean's* magazine, Margaret describes her state of mind at that time:

> "I didn't want to breathe. I had to remind myself to breathe," she says, tearfully. "I felt I had to go with Michel. I couldn't see any other way. I couldn't have him alone." She pauses. "Maybe I should put it another way: I didn't want to be alone. In my grief I was so focused on the loss of my boy that I forgot that I had a full life and lots of people who love me very much who are alive and well and here."

It was a family intervention and a complete breakdown that finally led Margaret to get the professional help and medication she needed in order to survive the loss of her son, her marriage and her ex-husband in such quick succession. Today, she travels across North America, an honorary patron of the Canadian Mental Health Association and a popular public speaker, advocating for openness about mental health issues like her own bipolar disorder and manic depression, the same ones she writes about in her book *Changing My Mind*.

Not one just to talk the talk, she tries to make a point of meeting with all those who line up to speak with her after an engagement, regardless of whether they're holding a copy of her book in their hands or simply want to clasp hers. Margaret Trudeau's need to connect and to help seems entirely genuine, and it is touching and reaffirming to behold.

Another high-profile bereaved mother is Susan Bro. You may not remember her name, but you'll remember the circumstances under which the spotlight was turned toward her. Susan endeavoured to turn the death of her daughter, Heather Heyer, during the protest of a 2017 white supremacist rally in Charlottesville, Virginia, into something positive; in her words, to "help make Heather's death count." She founded a non-profit anti-hate organization to provide scholarships and help others join her daughter's fight, and announced its formation at the MTV Video Music Awards just two weeks after Heather was run down by a speeding car during the protest.

Like Susan Bro, a great many parents use the grief that follows the death of their children as a catalyst for change.

Whether it's those who raise their voices for tougher gun laws or lobby City Hall for a crosswalk where there was none, these parents often, like Heather Heyer's mother, feel a deep desire to make their child's death matter. One day, Rob and I may become two of them, but in our case, it's not clear what caused our daughter's death. Do we suspect that the drug she took to help her to lactate may have contributed to the stopping of her heart? Yes, we do. But was Lauren one of the estimated ten thousand Canadians who die every year as a result of taking prescription drugs exactly as prescribed? We just don't know. And as parents who suspect a prescription took their child, we most certainly are not alone.

Nancy and Shaun McCartney have tried—often in vain—to bring the attention of Canadians to the potential dangers of a drug their son was taking after being given a sample at the doctor's office. The Bolton, Ontario, family lost their dear son, Brennan, at age eighteen, after he went to the doctor for symptoms of a chest cold. Sounds innocent enough, right? Asked about his spirits, the usually outgoing Brennan admitted to feeling low about a breakup and was given a sample of an antidepressant called Cipralex. Four days later, after having left the house the day before and not returning, he was found dead in a park near his home. Brennan had hanged himself. Nancy and Shaun McCartney became proactive in their search for a link between their son's death and the selective serotonin reuptake inhibitor (SSRI) he had been taking.

The McCartneys didn't seek media attention. Instead, *it* came to *them* through an investigation into a possible link between SSRIs and suicide. Their motivation is not a long, drawn-out and costly lawsuit.

When I asked Nancy McCartney, who was an elementary school principal at the time of Brennan's death, how long it took after losing her son for her grief to turn into anger and action, she responded:

> We were not immediately angry. We were seeking to understand and seeking answers as nothing made sense; there were no red flags. We [Nancy and husband Shaun] were going for individual counselling with Dr. Leslie Balmer, and I remember saying to her, "I can't help but wonder if the medication had something to do with Brennan's death." Leslie had been wondering the same thing.

It was at that time that they learned from the coroner that no toxicology testing had been done because of the manner in which Brennan died. Nancy says that's when the anger began.

> We felt that the Coroner was not interested in determining the cause of death as they knew "he had died from hanging." They had no interest in examining any mitigating factors. We knew that many people died from suicide and we naively thought that the Coroner's Office and Health Canada would want to know why. We thought they were in place to protect the citizens of Canada.

The McCartneys have been motivated to find another way to make a difference. Their mission is to inform Canadians in general—but especially youth—about the dangers not only of this particular drug but also of taking any prescription without reading the fine print. The biggest challenge they have faced is maintaining the energy needed to sustain advocacy, as well as balancing their battle with their need for healing and personal wellness.

> *We did not want anger to consume us. We did not want to be bitter, angry people. We both felt that Brennan would want us to feel joy. I also have the personal belief that I will meet Brennan again and he will ask me, "So, Mom, what did you do with your life?"*

Today, in addition to their work trying to bring attention to the possible deadly side effects of Cipralex, the family honours Brennan's memory as a fighter for the underdog with the ARK Award for "acts of random kindness" at his high school. Nancy is also endeavouring to open people's eyes and minds to suicide and the role medication can play.

> *I find the platitudes to be very draining. . . . People are very skeptical when you speak of medication and suicide. I keep going because I keep hearing about other people losing their children in similar ways. I reach out to bereaved parents if it feels right (hence my contacts with you). Being a bereaved parent is a very lonely experience.*

Thank you, Nancy, for teaching me that we don't say "committing suicide." Rather, it's "completing suicide," or saying instead that someone "died by suicide." "Committing" implies some sort of a crime, like larceny or perjury. And that is not the way that parents whose children died by suicide want their family stories to be told. Give them that small and tender mercy, for God's sake.

There's a quote I absolutely love, and Nancy and Shaun are another example of the feeling that Antoine de Saint-Exupéry wrote about when he said, "Love does not consist of gazing at each other, but in looking outward together in the same direction." But what happens when your world is so blown apart by the loss of a precious child—a person that you and your loved one brought into the world together—that there's no horizon, no hope of normalcy or anything good ahead even to imagine?

Of course, we all evolve during the course of a marriage (given enough time), but nothing could be as huge a change as suddenly losing a child. It's a doorway you enter through knowing there's no going back. So do you move ahead together, or take separate paths?

Fortunately, Rob and I have always been "the other half of the sky" to each other, to quote a well-known saying. And so it was that when those skies turned black for weeks and months on end, we found ourselves holding tight, trying to keep our quicksand-thick grief from taking us both under at the same time.

How did we survive when so many other couples succumb? There is really no answer, except that perhaps we were and are at a point in our relationship where there has never been more steadiness or strength. Had we lost our child earlier in our marriage and in her life, however, I am almost certain the outcome would not have been the same.

I remember telling Rob, when Lauren was in single-digit years, that if anything happened to her, we wouldn't survive as a couple: we'd feel so much guilt, blame, anger and sadness that there would be no room for us to function individually, never mind together. Part of the certainty of my pessimism stemmed from knowing that I would probably climb into a bottle and never come out. A lengthy lifespan would definitely not be in the cards for me, not that I would have wanted one without the daughter whose light illuminated our entire existence.

The fact was, we had said our goodbyes to Lauren as our "child" when she moved away from our home and city. When she died, we didn't have to endure the torture that so many parents do: having to pass a nursery that was not going to be used, or a child's or teen's bedroom that was suddenly empty and unnaturally still, bereft of joy and the noise of life. I had only the slightest taste of that sort of loss when she moved away: after we had packed up a U-Haul to help Lauren settle into a townhouse in Ottawa so that she could begin college, I cried every day for a solid week. I ached from missing her joyful voice, her cheery presence and just the contentment that came with knowing she was around. Rob took it differently: he'd already said his goodbyes to the preteen child with whom he'd been so very tight. As a stay-at-home dad, Rob had had an unusually close relationship with his daughter.

Lauren wrote about it this way in a grade-school project:

> *Our family doesn't exactly fit the stereotype. My mom is the provider and my dad is the caregiver. That's where I head into talking about how close my dad and I are. Dad's at all of the practices, recitals, lessons, games, you name it and he's already there. He's truly more than I could ever ask for.*
>
> *In theory, I'm close to both of my parents. But naturally, since my mom worked in the morning and wasn't home for most of the day, I'd grown to know my dad a little better. I'm just about as close to my mom as any girl my age, sure, I like to go to the mall every once in a while for a girls' day, shopping for shoes or going to the weekly yoga class to loosen up, but I'm probably more close to my dad than the average 12-year-old girl.*

In the years that passed after that oh-so-honest portion of her "Who I Am" school project was written, I felt blessed to be given a chance to grow closer and forge stronger ties with our daughter as an adult woman. So you see, losing Lauren wasn't the challenge to our relationship that I'd once feared it would be. Lauren had grown to become a wife to someone and mother to someone else, which meant that this young person had already left us in one way.

Perhaps that is why, when she came home for a visit, I would be filled with an anticipatory joy I could only compare to those Christmas mornings of my childhood. As I emerged from the warm fog of sleep, I'd realize that Lauren was in the house, and I could hardly contain my excitement. At what I thought she would deem a decent hour, I'd knock on her door, a cup of tea in my other hand, and call out with all of the subtlety of an ambulance siren, "Little Dee . . . !" (another one of the many nicknames we had for her). Lauren would always indulge me with a half-smile and a groan, as we both knew I was crazy. Crazy for her. I never hid how truly overjoyed I was when she was with us, no matter how often I ran the risk of Lauren's eyes rolling so far back in her head that they stayed that way.

One of my fondest memories will always be the day of my fiftieth birthday. The three of us had spent my fortieth in New York City, dining at the iconic Rainbow Room in Rockefeller Center on a rare night that there were tables open to the public, dancing to a live orchestra and enjoying one of the finest views and meals we would ever have, but it was the home-made surprise she gave me a decade later that will always be at the very top of my life's-favourite-moments list.

Rob and I had planned a small get-together with our friends from our years with a rock tribute band (I sang and played keyboards and sax; Rob played bass). About twenty of us in all were going to gather at our cottage north of the city to enjoy a casual dinner and birthday cake and to make some music. In the late afternoon, with an hour to go before the first guests were to arrive, the doorbell rang. I immediately went into panic mode. A towel on my head, I'd been finishing up some last-minute kitchen chores, so I hadn't dried my hair and was definitely not ready for company.

I went to the door, Rob right behind me, and when I opened it, I couldn't believe my eyes: it was Lauren, who had come all the way from Ottawa! She and her dad had planned it all. She'd taken a small commuter plane to the downtown Toronto waterfront, took a cab several blocks to our condo, got the car key that awaited her at the front desk and then drove our car an hour up to the cottage to surprise me.

I stood there at the front door, and as if in a scene out of *I Love Lucy*, I just bawled. In fact, yes, I'm quite sure "WAAAaaaah . . ." was the sound that came out. Ugly cry and all, it was simply the best surprise, the best birthday ever. She stayed just that one night and sang and made music with our friends who had known her since she was a baby, when she'd sleep peacefully in a playpen in an adjoining bedroom as we worked out the harmonies and chords on rock hits for a few hours each week. Growing up around them, she forged close ties with our Generations bandmates, and even got an extra grandmother out of the deal. As delighted as everyone was with this surprise visit, I still regard it as a gift I'll always cherish. It was also the last of my birthdays we marked together. If it had to be the last, I'm grateful it truly was the best.

And you know, perhaps that is what has saved us: that perspective and gratitude we try so hard to let envelop us, even when the unfairness of it all threatens to sink in. That's not to say Rob and I are always on the same page at any given time or on any given day; people do grieve differently, and when a couple has seemed so "in sync" in every other way, the strange language of sadness can hamper efforts at communication. There are instances when we're reluctant to share with each other our true feelings, so afraid are we both of pulling the other down in case they're having a "good" day.

One night in a teary exchange, Rob shouted that he was so tired of me being angry at him.

"I can't help it, I can't help it!" I shouted back. "I'm not angry *at you*, I'm just so angry!"

Not that I often needed one, but that rare loud exchange was a timely reminder that I wasn't the only one suffering; Rob was just better at keeping his emotions and pain inside, so I didn't minister to him or offer a soft word as often as he did to me.

Often, it is just an unfortunate fact that, as the old tune goes, "we only hurt the ones we love." They're always within figurative swinging distance of our pent-up emotions and—if we're lucky—are most likely to forgive us when we treat them unfairly. It's not right, but it's the way it is . . . until it isn't. Walking away from the anger, the sadness, the unbearable darkness that comes day after day is, I'm sure, not just to be expected but a form of self-preservation. After all, other parents and siblings are suffering too. Sometimes that act of walking away turns into another loss: that person never coming back.

Instead, when we lost Lauren so finally, so entirely, on that dark Monday morning, Rob and I grew closer, which is something that after (then) twenty-seven years of marriage, we didn't think would be possible. It's as if we were holding each other up: one helping the other when he or she stumbled, and pulling each other from the depths of depression and sadness whenever one of us descended. We count ourselves extremely fortunate to have been able to weather our loss, as we know that some couples cannot bear the weight of the pressure and hardship that accompany the death of a child. Couples like Ellen Hinkley and her ex-husband.

As parents and survivors, all we can do is just keep going, trying to find any bit of joy in each day. We mine the memories for ones that make us smile more than they make us melancholy, and find it gets a little easier with each passing year. We try to live in ways that honour our children or we feel would make them proud of us.

For Ellen Hinkley and her family, this attempt to honour comes via the Christopher Skinner Memorial Foundation, whose annual golf tournament supports several local charities with an emphasis on kids, since Ellen says Christopher was "a big kid at heart." For Barbara Cassells, it's the joy of sharing the hope that comes with each dragonfly keychain she makes and gives away. For Susan Bro, it's spreading a message against the kind of hate that resulted in her daughter's death. For the McCartneys, it's the award given out at their son's school saluting random acts of kindness. For Margaret Trudeau, it's spreading a message of hope for those who suffer mental illness; each, in its own way, is an effort to be a living example of proof that we can survive even the worst tragedy if we seek and get the proper help.

For us, it's telling the story of Lauren's death, and the anguish of not knowing if it could have been prevented. It's living out loud after losing Lauren; seeking and finding happiness wherever we can and not denying ourselves the pleasures that may lie within each new day. We love to travel and are now finding the time to do more of it, even hosting cruises. And my ties with radio were not quite cut: that fill-in gig on the midday shift at our new local radio station lasted for nine months. As I've already mentioned, the opportunity was serendipitous, coming when I was beginning to feel untethered and unsure about our move away from Ontario, where Rob and I had lived for more than thirty years. Once again, it seemed that radio was a lifesaver after this latest big loss, the one we'd imposed on ourselves when we left our friends, our grandson and his family, and our lives behind to try to start anew, knowing few people and precious little about the area we were now calling "home." But gradually, with time and the patience and kindness of friends and family here on Vancouver Island, we have begun to feel grounded as our roots start to take hold: Rob is playing hockey a few times a week, and I am looking forward to more emceeing and public speaking across the country. After all that we have endured, Rob and I are intent on proving that there is, indeed, life after death.

Chapter 11

Dreaming a Little Dream

Lauren in Mexico on our first family March Break vacation, 2004

T HERE ARE THOSE SWEET MOMENTS OF MERCY, the ones where I'm immersed in the frothed-milk softness just before waking from gentle dreams of Lauren, when we're together and happy and all is right with our gauzy, sepia-toned world. She's still with us and we're still with her; those are the fleeting seconds that keep me wrapped in the fleecy warmth of how things used to be.

Of course, the alarm clock or daylight and the reality of where we find ourselves now come back in a whoosh that lands squarely on my chest and sits there with heaviness until I sit up, rub my face and shake it off. Sometimes, I let the tears start to leak from my sleepy eyes as I lie on my pillow, willing myself back to that place of contentment. But the years since Lauren left us have shown me that there are little ways to cope with the waking hours. Joy can be ours again, and although it will never feel as complete as it once did, it is our right to feel happiness. That's what Rob and I have kept telling each other, even through the changes that have brought us to a new life, pushing ourselves forward through the thick, dark curtain of loss.

I want to begin this final chapter by saying thank you. If there is a word more weighty than *mourning*—even if it has broken—I'm not sure what it is, but I do know that it took a certain strength and sympathy (even empathy) for you to decide to spend this time with me, with my husband and our family, and I am grateful to you for coming along. Also, sorry for using the word *grateful* so often. But I am. We are. So, thank you again.

Since we're here and you know who I am, let me tell you who I think you are. You are one or more of three kinds of people: you have lost someone close to you (like us); there is someone dear in your life who has suffered a catastrophic loss; or you have never gone through the loss of someone and felt the extreme pain that accompanies that experience. If you fall into that last, fortunate group, it is with not even a hint of bitterness that I say, "Lucky you."

I believe you can belong to that group and still know how it feels to lose someone or something that meant a great deal to you: someone with whom you shared a special closeness. Until we lost Lauren, I would have counted myself among that group. When my mother died in 2012, I mourned her loss. I still miss her and know that I always will. But I have become certain that the brain aneurysm she suffered—and which basically killed her on the spot, even though she was kept on life support until three of her four daughters could come to her side—was the way Mom would have wanted to leave this life. She suffered very briefly, but was pretty much

brain dead before the ambulance arrived at the small bunga-
low my parents rented in California to escape the Canadian
winter. One moment, she was sitting with Dad, eating off a
TV tray and watching a rerun of $M^*A^*S^*H$, and the next,
she was complaining of an awful headache and how hot it
suddenly was. Then she was gone.

Throughout her life, Mom always made it clear that when
the time came, she didn't want to linger or be a bother to anyone. She would rather have gone as quickly as she did—even
possibly without being aware of the goodbyes and kisses we
gave her before the tubes were taken out at the hospital—
than to stay alive living anything less than the happy life she
had come to enjoy in her senior years. Antidepressants had
been a friend to my mom during the last third of her life,
and she was painting gorgeous landscapes and watercolour
florals, golfing, playing pickle ball and joining neighbours—
fellow Canadian snowbirds and American residents alike—
in embracing every day. The aneurysm ended a life that had
been as happy in its final chapter as it was at any time. And
for that, we were all grateful. (That word again!)

The day before what would have been my mother's
seventy-ninth birthday, and after a lunch in a crowded
California café where we dealt with the shock of what was
happening by teasing my father about the older ladies possibly eyeing him (there's that humour, saving the day again),
my sisters, my dad and I headed off to the hospital where we
would be faced with the heavy task of saying our final farewells to our mother. As big band music and a few Josh Groban
selections my eldest sister had chosen played through a small

speaker, we said soft words and laid six red roses—one for each of her four daughters, her husband and herself—in her still but warm hands. After an hour, the time came for us to leave the room as the nurses removed the tubes that were keeping her alive. We returned to her room from a quiet family lounge a few minutes later.

The mechanical clicking that had accompanied her aided breathing had stopped, and all we heard above our sniffles and quiet words to our mother were the slowing beeps as the numbers on a machine registering her heartbeat continued to drop. Aware that the staff was waiting to come in and prepare the private room for another patient, we steeled ourselves for the final goodbyes. Down, down, down the numbers dropped: 98 . . . 82 . . . 60 . . .

When the numbers had gotten down near the teens, my sisters began to gather up their jackets, the speakers, their purses. I sat at the bedside and rubbed Mom's arm, speaking softly to her all the while. As the beeping pattern changed, I looked up.

52 . . . 60 . . . 72 . . . 88 . . . the numbers began to climb! What was this—some kind of miracle? "She's not quite ready to go yet," I said hopefully. But when I stopped rubbing her arm, the numbers and her heart rate slowly began to drop again. Was Mom sending a signal that she knew we were there—that she wasn't going to be leaving us all?

As lovely as that would have been to believe, I suspect the truth is that she really did go on her way when she fell to the floor in her bathrobe at home. What we were witnessing was some kind of static-electric reaction to me rubbing her skin. Of course that was it . . . wasn't it?

After another fifteen minutes, we knew the end was near, and I said to my mother what I am sure would have made her laugh (she laughed so easily in the last decade or so of her life): "Well, Mom, you know how much they charge for hospital parking, so we'd better get going . . . ," and with that, we stroked her hair, kissed her forehead one more time—my sisters, my dad and I—and we left that quiet hospital room. When I turned and went back for one last moment, the nurses were already there. It was over.

As we walked out of the hospital, I seemed to leave my body and look down at our sad, broken family. I could see myself falling to my knees, and indeed, it did cross my mind briefly to crumple to the sidewalk and just stay there. But instead, we all calmly walked to the car, and I never let on to anyone we passed on the way that the woman who had meant more to me than any other human for the first half of my life was gone.

We would hold a memorial the following year, the evening before Lauren's wedding, when family from across the country had gathered for a happy celebration the next day. We sent Mom off with a beautiful service filled with music interwoven with visual presentations and shared memories by her husband, children and grandchildren at what we called a "Momorial." Later that evening, we all joined in a big party at a local pub in celebration of her life and Lauren's upcoming nuptials. Mom would have just loved it all, especially when her daughters and granddaughter took the stage to make music with the band (all friends of the family). I've always thought how generous of spirit it was for Lauren and Phil to share part of their wedding weekend with Lauren's grandmother, even though it meant tears of sadness were intermingled with tears of joy in the span of just a few hours. But oh how we partied that evening!

As time passed, there was a peace in knowing that Mom's death was how things were meant to be, and all of us—Dad and my three sisters and our families—came to accept my mother's absence, no matter how big a void was left when we could no longer hear her voice, share in laughter and listen to her advice (whether it was appreciated at the time or not). Of course, in a few short years, we would come to be grateful for my mother's passing for another reason: she would not have to endure the pain of losing not only her dear granddaughter Lauren but also, just two years later, her first grandson, Michael.

Through the passage of time and a gentle easing of pain that the changing of every calendar is meant to bring, my sisters and I were able, thankfully, to bear witness to the fact that there is always hope for happiness: in 2016, my father found companionship and joy with the "girl next door," a woman three years his senior who literally lives in an adjacent suite in the retirement home he entered two years after Mom's passing. In his way, as he always has, Dad showed us that life does indeed go on. And all of his daughters are quite honestly thrilled for him. After all, who doesn't deserve happiness, especially after the enormous loss of his lifelong partner, the girl he'd known since she was a child accused of stealing his xylophone? (A charge she always denied, by the way.)

So you see what I mean when I said earlier that I was fortunate for so long to be in that group of those who had never gone through a loss and pain that forever scars you. My grandparents and my own dear mother had gone before, and we had cried over the loss of special pets, of course, as nearly everyone who enters adulthood has. But again, these were the kinds of losses that one can come to terms with, the kind that are expected and prepared for and endured.

Let me make myself very clear here: I am not for a moment saying that there's something wrong with you if you lost a parent and didn't recover from it in a year or two or even ten. We all deal with loss and grief so very differently, and no two people handle it the same. Frequently in the time since Lauren's passing, Rob and I have wondered how we are doing and whether we might even be living with something that's been named "complicated grief." Fortunately, there's a scale that exists—a test, if you will—that allows people to get a sense of whether what they're going through is to be expected at this point in their recovery from the loss of a loved one. Having answered the Weill Cornell questionnaire (easily found online by searching "grief intensity scale") about longing for the loved one, inability to function in daily chores and so on, Rob and I were both somewhat relieved to see affirmation of what we both believed: we were—and are—coming through our grieving at a healthy pace. I took some comfort in feeling that we're moving along, Rob and I, in the right direction. So far.

There was a scene in a TV show we saw last year that summed up how we feel about our lives now. There had been an awful car wreck in which a long piece of metal rebar came loose from the load of a truck when it rear-ended the car ahead of it. That rebar became a potentially deadly projectile, shooting forward and piercing the headrest, as well as the driver's skull, from back to front. As a paramedic, a friend of the hapless victim, calmed him before transporting him to the hospital, he exclaimed that the man—having survived what should have been a deadly crash but with this horrific injury of having a bar through his head—was the "luckiest unlucky son of a bitch" he'd ever met. That's kind of how Rob and I feel every day: we're blessed in so very many ways and are trying to live happy and fulfilled lives. But there's no escaping that, every day, we're just lucky to have survived our wounds.

Because of the outpouring of kindness and support from radio station listeners, and the same compassion that still shows up on Facebook or in emails in reaction to my daily journal, I have always felt the arms of a virtual community around our little family as we move forward. But those same social media outlets that helped save Rob and me are having a surprising effect on others who walk in our shoes.

It's a dichotomy, really: today, we openly mourn people we've never met, a phenomenon that truly became part of the modern grieving conversation with the death of Diana, Princess of Wales, when people cried openly for days and left fields of flowers and a sea of plush toys at the gates of Buckingham Palace. But at the same time, our social media platforms, especially Facebook and Instagram, are expected to reflect a sunny and optimistic outlook. It's why so many experts claim that the cheery veneer of posts—so many of which seem only to show life at its happiest—just serve to make those who aren't sharing that same warmth feel as though they're missing out, that their real lives simply don't measure up to those of the people they follow, regardless of whether they are celebrity strangers or the girl next door. It would seem that in an age where everything is on display, few things—especially feelings—are what they would appear. And yet, that's what is expected of us. The tune from *Bye Bye Birdie*, "Put on a Happy Face," could not be more fitting for the twenty-first century, and those of us grieving do not escape the unrealistic expectation that we should grit our teeth and say that everything is just fine, no matter how *not fine* things really are.

We are expected to pick up and move on—because, face it, our social media friends certainly have. Nowhere have I seen this situation more poignantly articulated than in a post emailed to me by the website What's Your Grief. This post cracked my heart wide open.

Laura Abbruzzese lost her partner of four years in 2016. In a blog entitled "Trust Me As I Grieve," she writes with piercing honesty about the admonitions and unsolicited advice she's received from well-meaning friends about openly sharing her grief on social media. Boy, you sure feel her pain here, and I admire her for such a stunning piece of honesty (and thank her for letting me share this with you):

> *I recently passed the 14-month mark of losing the man that I love. I feel very strongly that I have done well*

and have made the best choices that I could during this time. I am proud of my resiliency. I have made a strong effort to live my life and stay positive. This essay is about the misunderstanding of grief by people who have not experienced this kind of significant loss, yet offer advice about moving on with life after death.

I know it is done with love and the desire to see me live out the rest of my life without this heavy burden of loss and tragedy. I already know that this burden will always be with me—nothing will ever change that. But I have to tell you something else. Something important. Here it is: you cannot create a road map to a place you have never traveled. There is no road map for my journey and I am figuring it out as I go. All I ask is that the people in my life trust that I am doing everything I can to live my life and go forward without my favorite person.

If you have never experienced the sudden and tragic loss of someone you love, I am afraid it is not your place to tell me when it's time to move on. A little more than a year after his death, being told by some of my dearest friends that it is time to stop grieving nearly destroyed me with anger and sadness. They asked, "When are you going to take his belongings out of the apartment?" They said, "Stop posting memories about him on social media!" They said other things like, "don't let it define you," "you are not getting any younger," and "maybe it's time to stop being sad." Okay, point taken. However, one thing I have learned through trial and error is that it is not possible to just stop the grieving process. Still, as a favor to my friends, I can continue to travel this road alone inside my head where you cannot see it or feel the discomfort it may bring. I understand how you may not be ready to appreciate the window of experience I am offering you.

I guess you are right, not everyone needs to know how much it sucked last weekend to go through the closet and put his most worn clothing into a plastic bag for donation. And I still have more closets and storage spaces to go though. I cried for every shirt and every pair of jeans I folded and placed into a bag. I smelled each shirt to see if it still had his scent. I found one that had a faint scent of his cologne. I kept that shirt along with all my favorites and put them in a storage bag to keep. I labored over which ones to keep and which ones to donate. But point taken, I will no longer share this kind of experience publicly so as not to make anyone else uncomfortable.

In my own social media life, I've pulled way back from blogging or posting on Twitter or Facebook about the immensity of pain that some days bring. I will generally only open up about what's tugging at my heart on the days that have significant weight in our lives; days where people might forgive me for, as one (later apologetic) journal reader called it, "wallowing" in the memories. Imagine using my own blog on my own website to express my raw emotions at any given time! It's all I've ever wanted to do, really, despite the fear it strikes in my heart that someone like that reader would rap my knuckles for being so honest.

For me, the most powerful way of dealing with my feelings has always been to put them into words, whether through the sappy verses I wrote about unrequited love in my teens (and that was just about the only love there was) or the pages upon pages I have filled in diaries since I was twelve years old. I continued to journal as I grew into adulthood; the online journal I began in 2003 has more lines than the little five-year diary I dutifully filled out every night back then. I have been fortunate to have the online journal, a place where I can peel back the layer of composure a bit and share the maelstrom of feelings with people who care enough to come by and visit.

Within my first year of having left Toronto, when I was feeling sad, lonely and disconnected, I was admonished following one post for being "depressing." It came from a woman who had lost her husband a few months earlier and would turn to my journal for uplifting content. She felt it necessary to point out that "at least you still have your husband." *Disappointed* was also in the subject line of that one, I believe. Never a good sign. After all, what right did I have to express myself on my own website? Sigh. As I say, it's not easy putting it all out there. Even in these pages you've read here (and thank you for that), I've feared being *too* open about how difficult it has been to try to put our lives back together after they were so close to perfect.

And so, there's one bit of writing I haven't shared until now, something I penned on a rainy day in our little boathouse on Lake Simcoe. I'd gone down there to light some candles, burn a bit of sage and listen to a collection of meditation pieces. As my tears mirrored the water streaming steadily down the boathouse windows, I tapped this out on my laptop.

It is June 30th. Soon another month will be displayed on the calendar and we will no longer be able to say, "Our daughter, Lauren, died last month." Time is passing and we will be expected . . . to heal . . . to get on with life . . . as though, through some alchemy of time, our tears can magically be turned into pleasant memories. No longer should we be "dwelling" on the unconscionable tragedy that has befallen us in losing you. But we will not forget. We cannot let you go. You were everything to us and now you are gone.

Our hearts tear afresh daily, the edges pulling away from where they began to mend just a day before. Every dawn brings new hope and misery, renewed faith and fresh desperation. Every night brings quiet darkness, the silence fertile ground for questions and sorrows, emptiness and loneliness.

We mourn together; we mourn alone. No one person, no army of loving hearts can hold us in their arms and fill the space that belongs only to you: that cherished holy ground, mossy and green in its freshness and promise. We weep at the stinging, ever-growing awareness of the vast emptiness of our lives without you: the sunshine of your spirit, the garden of loveliness, the beauty of your being.

Our lives will never be the same. Nevermore will we know the "bubble" of perfection in which—with full awareness—we found ourselves: proud, loving parents of a beautiful human being, and grandparents to a perfect, happy little boy. We looked toward the future, our eyes squinting at the brightness of the mid-morning sun. We wondered how we could be so blessed. We wondered when it would end.

It ended on May 11, 2015. It ended with a heart that stopped and like a clock that keeps time for the universe, the waves of change and sorrow stopped the earth.

I would tell anyone who asked how to move forward to find themselves a space where they can share their feelings, even if, when they're done, instead of a circle of people quietly whispering "thank you," or a doctor's receptionist making your next appointment, they click Save and those emotions go wherever our documents hide until we search them out again. Maybe simply by writing the words or recording them into a smartphone, those feelings will be set free into the ether, and the healing can continue. I can imagine going back from the future to check in on where you were then, as compared to where you are now, and, hopefully, feeling a sense of accomplishment and healing. I know we do.

You might wonder, *What if I'm not directly bereaved, but I'm concerned about someone who is?* That is where Rob and I found ourselves ten years ago when a very dear friend passed away in his late seventies from rapid-onset brain cancer. A week after we said our goodbyes to Carl, his wife of fifty years was hospitalized, having suffered what was medically diagnosed as a heart attack, but what we all suspected was actually the very real possibility of a broken heart. To our great relief, Helen decided that she wasn't going to leave her children with another funeral to plan. This woman of extraordinary strength seemingly willed herself back to great health and has spent the years since volunteering and helping others who found themselves in similar conditions in their process of recuperation and healing. But not everyone who has suffered such a huge loss can be like Helen, bouncing back with such determination and success.

Feelings are, as we well know, neither good nor bad, right nor wrong. They are just feelings, and they're a necessary part of grief and sorrow. But as with nearly everything else we are forced to navigate in our lives, there are road maps. We were fortunate to find free advice in the form of printed materials through our local health system. Victoria Hospice (VH) is a non-profit society that has been established to enhance quality of life for those facing death: whether as patients, in a role of support or as someone who grieves. Hospice support is available either at the click of a mouse (search for "hospice" in your area) or via a phone call. All you need to do is ask.

The advice from VH includes honouring your sadness: accepting it as a natural and unavoidable part of having loved someone and recognizing that it is a part of your life right now.

If you can, share your experiences and your sadness with friends, family or members of a grief support group—anyone who will listen when you talk, when you cry, when you laugh and reminisce. And it doesn't even have to be face-to-face. Victoria Hospice suggests we can use the internet or take up a project or an activity that allows us to maintain a greater sense of privacy. But whatever we do, it's impossible to overemphasize how important it is to express our sorrow. Maybe it's a regular time and place that we go to feel sad and to cry, whether during our morning shower or at a graveside. Perhaps we'll take up meditation or find time to walk with nature to be with our loved one's memory, or take those extra few moments in the milk froth of early-morning sleepiness. However, experts advise us to avoid expressing strong emotions at the other end of the clock, close to bedtime, as it may disrupt our sleep.

Another idea I found helpful: create ways of remembering. For example, try to find ways that help us to recall and honour the person who has died by talking or writing to them, celebrating their birthday, putting up a Christmas stocking, displaying photographs or talking about them.

Here's what we've done in our home. Sitting on a piano near the living room, we have a high-school picture of Lauren holding her cello, and I almost always have flowers in a small vase there next to a large silver-framed photograph of her and Phil's beautiful son. He's wearing a tuxedo and a big, dimpled smile, all dressed up for a wedding. Near the piano is a tall, ladder-style shelf on which we have arranged favourite photos of our daughter as a child and an adult, both with us and on her own. Sometimes I'm a little afraid it comes off as a shrine, but then I ask myself why I should care. After all, it's our home and she is our life, so we pay tribute to her in a way that is somewhat subtle and hopefully elegant, but oh so necessary.

I'm sorry in a small way that we didn't have Lauren buried somewhere that we could go to visit her, sit quietly by her grave and feel as if she is actually someplace in or on this earth. The only location that would have made sense to us was in the graveyard of the tiny church at which she was married less than two years earlier, but now we are several provinces away. There has been a tree planted by a listener in Lauren's memory in an area filled with young trees and small plaques. In another Ontario town, there's a wall for which a woman has purchased and had placed a brick engraved with the words "Lauren PURE JOY." We love that she is remembered in those places and are grateful for the thoughtfulness that accompanied those gestures. In our home we also have a large blackbird urn, a tiny matching one and a box that contains still more ashes. I've no doubt someone out there thinks that this is bad feng shui or is hindering our healing, but we'll decide what to do with those ashes in time, when we're ready. Which may be never, and that's okay too, remember?

Victoria Hospice tells us that a bereaved person may experience hopelessness and despair, in which dealing with grief is harder than we expected or too difficult to put into words. It may even include depression. But we're told—and we know—that these feelings are alleviated as one starts to see some signs of spring in the soul.

The hospice offers tips to help with feelings of hopelessness and despair that include accepting and honouring these emotions. They suggest spending time with others who have gone through a similar experience and survived it, people like family members and friends. Another idea involves joining a bereavement support group. Rob and I were astounded to learn what strength comes from hearing the stories of loss, of love, of grief and of hope. You find help wherever it may be, even in books or films that feature a character to whom you relate.

We are reminded to listen to what we need, to give thought and time to whatever is good for us. That's so counterintuitive for those of us who are givers and doers for others. The strength to say "no," without having to qualify your reasons, is sometimes hard to muster, but its rewards are countless. After all, you're in the very serious business of trying to save your own life, or at least to return to some semblance of the one that has been ripped away from you so brutally.

We must identify what we need, whether rest and quiet time or physical and social activity. Of course, if you or someone you love has had thoughts of suicide, VH advises seeking help as soon as possible from a family doctor or an emergency department. There's absolutely no weakness in saying you're sinking. I know that for a fact.

I never had suicidal thoughts, but two and a half years after Lauren's life ended, I decided I needed help dealing with my deepening feelings of depression. I knew what had brought this on, and it wasn't as simple as the one major life event. You see, not only had Rob and I lost our daughter, but we were also now living in a completely new place. I'd left a high-profile and successful career and we'd moved to the far west side of the country, knowing no more than a handful of people. Talk about a life transformation! I had suffered two huge losses: our daughter and my own identity—not only as her mother but also as a radio host and what I hoped or imagined was my role as a part of people's day. Apart from being Lauren's mother and Rob's wife (and Colin's grand-mother), radio had been my entire life since I was eigh-teen years old. I was missing that purpose, that laughter and adrenalin every morning. Most of all, I missed the feeling of connection—of being able to make a difference in the lives of our listeners. Please forgive me if that sounds as though I have delusions of grandeur, but I really, truly endeavoured every day to do just that: to let people know their world was safe and if, some days, it didn't feel that way, that soon it would be all right again.

So in this new life of staying up until midnight, sleep-ing in until nine, and having few reasons to go out except for dog walks, I began finding it more and more difficult to garner enthusiasm for every day ahead of me. I felt increas-ingly rudderless. The question "What's the point?" began to appear ahead of me at all times, like plumes of black sky-writing. That's when I decided to seek help from my new family doctor.

I'd taken antidepressants in those years of feeling over-whelmed by trying to be all things to all people: mother, wife and a successful woman in a (mostly) man's industry. There was only one Wonder Woman, and guess what? It turned out not to be me. But in the past decade, having given up drink-ing as the way I dealt with the pressure and disappointments, I found my brain chemistry seeming to adjust. I'd stopped taking medication for depression because it didn't exist any-more. But that was then. In 2017, I decided I would seek help where it was available, knowing I'd had success with it in the past. And even with the smallest prescribable dose, Rob and I both noticed an improvement in my outlook, my output and my demeanour. I was singing again. I was feeling able to cope with the stress of my workload and the expecta-tions that had been laid upon me and that I had taken upon myself. I was embracing my vulnerability and getting help, just as I'd recommended to so many of the people who'd writ-ten to me in their own grief. How about that—actually taking my own advice!

Many of us feel guilt and blame when a loved one dies. We were fortunate that we did not (except for wondering if somehow Rob's notably slow heart rate or my heart murmur might have played a role in the reaction of Lauren's own heart). The coroner held on to some of Lauren's tissue sam-ples, so we won't give up hope that, one day, a definitive cause of death for our daughter will be found. But for those people who suffer the added injury of experiencing guilt or somehow believing themselves responsible, we're told these feelings often come with a belief that everything in life happens for a reason. Something life-changing has occurred, and we're try-ing to understand how and why. We're trying to make sense of something that has completely turned our lives upside down with no warning and certainly no explanation. That's why we may blame ourselves or others, even though that may not be realistic. Some things that can help include examining our guilt and looking at what we may feel we're guilty of—the real part—and then deciding what we need to do about it. It is also suggested that we begin forgiving ourselves and others and practising letting go, as we are ready.

We should be doing a reality check and asking trusted friends and family if they have experienced anything similar. If so, how did they handle it? We can also try talking to others who are familiar with the situation we're in. Do they see things differently than we do? How helpful an outside perspective can be! Finally, Victoria Hospice suggests we take action if we find that there really are reasons for our guilt. Maybe we said something we shouldn't have, or didn't listen when we might have. Find ways—if there are any—to make amends, perhaps by volunteering with, making a donation to, or learning more about a cause that mattered to the person who died. They also suggest we might want to make a change in our lifestyle or behaviour based on what we've learned. What more appropriate way to help a loved one's death make sense than to find a way to effect change for the better?

If anger is part of our grief, that's completely normal. Even though Rob and I have often been grateful that this wasn't an aspect of ours—we didn't have anyone or anything in particular to be angry at or about—we've of course felt the inevitable unfairness of it all. And who wouldn't be angry about losing your only child? But we're told that when anger isn't understood or expressed, it can become more intense and unpredictable. We might find ourselves exploding in situations where normally we wouldn't.

What's recommended is that we be safe by taking steps to prevent our anger from hurting us or others. Learn what to do when the feelings surface: take a walk or spend time in a soothing environment. Stop activities like driving; give ourselves a time out. Victoria Hospice recommends that we defuse our anger through things like working out, walking, stretching, swimming or doing things that have repetitive actions like hammering, digging or kneading. Anger can also be diluted by expressing ourselves through letter writing, journalling, taking on arts projects or talking with a counsellor or close friend. That may lend us some perspective as to what—if anything—needs to be done about the source of our anger. VH recommends that we then take constructive action, identifying the steps we need to follow to find peace. Maybe it's writing a letter or working toward creating change. But it may also be a time for forgiveness, letting go or, as the good old "Serenity Prayer" reminds us, acceptance of what can't be changed (and the wisdom to know the difference).

Of course, a trio of troublemakers—fear, worry and anxiety—often accompany grief. I'd be lying if I told you I wasn't more afraid, worried and anxious than ever about anything happening to Rob. Every mole on his skin, every delayed return home, every bump or thump in the house, and my first thought is: *I'm losing him.* That fear, of course, comes from the absolute certainty that he is my world now. There is no one who can take care of me and all the intricacies of our lives, and certainly no one who will love me like Rob has and does. Naming that fear is the first step in helping to alleviate it. Breathing slowly and deeply, asking myself, *What is going on with me right now?* and being aware if I am having a panic or anxiety attack (and seeking professional aid and advice) is helpful. Ask questions and take action, we're told. Identify what would help.

I know that Rob has tried to lessen my fears of losing him by taking care of himself and trying to stay healthy, but as we know (all too well), anything can happen. So he's trying to keep me apprised of what files are where and whom to contact in case the absolute worst happens. Still, "going there"—when "there" is the worst possible scenario—isn't a healthy thing for me to do. I'm told to remind myself that I'm safe, there is no danger and that I'm okay. In addition, sometimes, just as a reminder, we can hold onto a pet, have a hot bath or make this one of those "in case of emergency, break glass" occasions for chocolate. (That last suggestion is mine. You're welcome.)

Thank you to victoriahospice.org for all of the other non-chocolate-based wisdom. You can be sure that there are similar resources in your town or city. They can also be found on the internet, at places like the Elisabeth Kübler-Ross Foundation.

~~~

I'D like to share with you just one more story.

On the morning that Lauren died, three well-known women were having breakfast in a California home. They had gathered to spend another day writing music and lyrics for a new album aimed at comforting and helping those experiencing loss and grief.

As Toronto singer-songwriter Amy Sky checked that morning's news feed, she saw word that Lauren had died. She gasped. Amy and I knew each other from occasions when she'd been on my TV show and our radio station; her daughter, Zoe Sky Jordan, was in a production of *Fiddler on the Roof* with Lauren when they were both teens. Amy looked up, tears in her eyes, and told her writing partners what had happened. Then she added, "I don't know what to say to her. What can you say?"

Amy's songwriting partners had more than their own share of experience where grief was concerned. Beth Nielsen Chapman's husband, Ernest, had died at age fifty of cancer, and it was Beth's achingly beautiful song "Sand and Water" that showed the world just how deeply the loss of her husband had affected her. The other woman in the trio was still grieving the loss of her dear sister, Rona, to brain cancer just two years earlier. Olivia Newton-John answered Amy's question: "Well, what do you want to say to her?"

Amy answered in just six words, and immediately the three women pushed back their chairs, got up from the sun-splashed table and moved quickly to the next room, where a piano awaited. The song "My Heart Goes Out to You" flowed forth, its simple but perfect three-part harmonies layering and lifting with every line.

A year and a half later, Amy reached out to me via email. She wasn't sure if she should tell me, she said, but there was a song on the new *Liv On* album that was inspired by Lauren's passing. I was stunned and most grateful that she had let me know! We agreed to meet in a downtown café to talk about the album and for Amy to give me my own copy.

It was a chilly fall day and we'd both ordered bone broth.

As we sipped from our big cups of comfort, we sat at a banquette, catching up and reconnecting. A steady stream of late-morning businesspeople filtered in and out, heads down, cell phones in hand. We talked, she and I both brushing away tears as our mascara migrated south, and Amy told me of the morning that she, Beth and Olivia had written "My Heart Goes Out to You." Amy made clear at that moment how she felt Lauren had guided the whole endeavour. And just then, something happened.

A young woman's voice on the PA rose above the quiet murmur of the half-filled restaurant. "Lauren . . . ," she said. I stopped what I was saying and asked Amy if she had heard what I heard. Her eyebrows rose as she nodded. I jumped up from the soft leather bench and wove my way through the line of waiting customers to the front counter, where a server stood near a microphone.

"Excuse me," I said, "did you just call 'Lauren'?" She nodded and began to tell me that the order had already been picked up.

"That's okay," I said excitedly. "I just wanted to be sure."

I'm sure the young woman, if she gave me a second thought, figured I was nutty. But I knew what I'd heard, and so did Amy. In a restaurant where no other customers' names had been called since the moment we walked in, suddenly, and at the same moment we were talking about Lauren's contribution and inspiration for Amy, Beth and Olivia, we heard her name.

As a side note, Rob and I had the honour of hearing the song being performed live and dedicated to us at a concert in Tacoma, Washington, in early 2017. It was indeed a surreal experience as "My Heart Goes Out to You" began the show, just as it does the album. I trembled as I stood during a Q&A session to explain to the audience what this song meant to our family, and how grateful we were to Amy, Beth and Olivia for their efforts in helping the grieving, and those who work with them, to move forward and heal through their music. Later, when we met up with the trio backstage, we were able to express our gratitude and humility in person. And each one was just as kind and lovely as you would wish them to be.

And so it is my hope that, just as Lauren may have helped inspire music to aid others in their healing, she has guided me through this book for you. It has been my honour to share with you the story of our family, our lives and especially our daughter. But most of all, it is my deepest and fondest hope that you have seen something in these pages that gives you proof that life can go on after losing someone who means everything to you.

I know it can be done because we are doing it. Our moments of laughter far outnumber our tears now, and we will continue to try to live our lives in a way that would make our Lauren happy and proud. We visit her son and his parents in Ottawa a minimum of two times a year (and plan to extend an obnoxious number of invitations to them to come west when they feel they want to visit our home in British Columbia), and we're grateful for the time we spend getting caught up through short videos sent our way and via live computer visits. How lucky we are to live in this age when thousands of miles dissolve with the click of a mouse. It's not quite as special as having this tall, sweet, brown-haired little boy sitting on our laps while we read to him, but for now it provides some warmth when we're missing him and his folks so terribly.

We cherish the memories and videos of the hours we spent with a young Colin during those early months and years of loss for us all. We would take him for walks and to play in the sprawling, well-appointed park near the home where his mother took her last breath; we'd try (sometimes in vain) to keep him from attempting to join a family's soccer game when he would simply hold on to a ball that had escaped their imaginary pitch. We took this well-mannered little man to family restaurants, to visit a department store Santa at Christmas and to roll on the thick grass on Canada's Parliament Hill in summer. At the end of our full days, I would rock him in the dark for as long as his careful bedtime regimen would allow, tears falling from my cheeks and landing on his soft warm sleeper as I sang to him the same "You Are My Sunshine" I'd sung softly to his mother just two decades earlier. May you never grow too old to cuddle and to rock, sweet boy. Our futures are brightened by thoughts of theme parks, of long visits, of boat rides and plane rides and more precious memories in the making. It's all we can hope for.

Just as Nancy McCartney thought her son, Brennan, would ask how she'd spent the years after his untimely and tragic death, I sometimes imagine an interview where, instead of me posing the questions to Lauren as I did prior to her only Mother's Day, she might have some for me. And perhaps our exchange would go something like this:

LAUREN: *So, Mom, what did you do with your life?*

ME: *We did the best we could with what time was left after losing you. Your dad and I tried to show that life can go on and that there is such a thing as joyful mourning.*

LAUREN: *So now you're stealing my "pure joy" answer?*

ME: *Well, not exactly. I don't know that there's such a thing as "pure joy" when you've lost someone as important and beloved to us as you, but what we could do was not turn our backs on the opportunity, to the idea of being joyful. We continued to find pleasure in the moments and the hours that we spent with your memory, just as we enjoyed the ones where we were being present with each other and taking in a sunset or a full moon or the perfection of a summer day by the ocean or a walk in a late-night snowfall. Best of all, even though I was the one consoled for what seemed like so long through our radio family of listeners and correspondents, I managed to turn things around to the point where I became the one doing the consoling. People would write to me and say that they mourned with me when you died, and then suddenly found themselves in the same unimaginable position, and ask me how I survived. And I actually had answers! It was all for them, just as you said. All of these things—the memories of moments past and the pleasures of the present—plus hopefully helping others move into the future as we made our way there ourselves: these were all our way of honouring you.*

LAUREN: *And my son?*

ME: *And your son. Just as he knew the strength and love of his father in this day-to-day life, he always felt our arms—and yours—around him, even from a distance. We made sure he had everything in this life that you would have wanted for him. And although we never stopped wishing you were here to be his mother, we knew he'd always be surrounded by all the love he could possibly want. And probably a little more!*

LAUREN: *Then why did you leave him? Why did you live so far apart?*

ME: *Your daddy and I made the truly gut-wrenching decision to leave the province and move as far west as we could go in our beautiful country because it just hurt too much to be anywhere near where we'd built our lives with you. If I left radio, which I knew it was time to do, I couldn't still be in the same city, seeing the same sad eyes and hearing those welcome kind, soft words of condolence. We knew that your son and his father didn't need us as they had in those early months after you left us, when we were visiting Ottawa every few weeks to try to lend a hand where we could. You chose wisely. Phil did a beautiful job of handling the impossible. But just as Colin and his daddy had continued to grow and to move on in their lives with a new, loving woman that your son calls "Mommy" (and who swears she feels your presence and sometimes asks for your help), we felt we needed a chance to start somewhere new, where we could try to build a different kind of life—one that wasn't constantly reminding us of how very much we had lost.*

Then we came to awaken (at a much later hour) to the sounds of gulls, the sights of ocean and mountains with deer grazing in our yard and eagles hanging lazily on breezes off our deck, and we came to believe in the power of beauty and nature to heal.

And so it was with this enveloping and comforting backdrop that we continued to hold you close in our hearts, in our dreams. We spoke often to your little boy and his family, and they knew how much we loved them all. There was never enough time, or visits that were not too short. We cherished each one.

Loo, we promised to live out our lives in a way that would make you as proud of us as we were, and always would be, of you. And we waited in joyful hope that when these lives were to be done and our missing you finally came to an end, our souls would be reunited, and we would all know pure joy once again.

LAUREN: *I love you.*

ME: *Oh, and I love you. So much, honey. So much.*

LAUREN *(smiling): I was talking to Daddy.*

The Story of "Our" Hummingbird

YOU'LL NOTICE THAT A HUMMINGBIRD GRACES the cover of this book and several of the pages herein. I wanted you to know the significance of this little bird's presence.

In May 2018, to mark the third anniversary of our daughter's passing, Rob and I decided a change of scenery was in order. Rather than wake up at home on that saddest of days, we boarded a ferry to Friday Harbor, in the San Juan Islands of Washington state, to stay at a quiet inn. Although we could literally see our house from the high points of the island, it was far enough away that we could feel the specialness of the place and its quiet, welcoming charms.

We awoke the next day to a sundrenched room, and I deliberately dressed in a bright fushia shirt (the brand was Lauren). I wasn't going to wear black and allow myself to feel any sadder than the date would dictate. I'd even been told by a medium that our daughter wanted me in more vivid hues.

As we waited to catch the ferry back home, a hummingbird zipped over to me. It hovered in front of my face for what must have been at least five seconds. I didn't breathe; all I could do was take in the brilliance of its colours. Brightest of all were its neck and breast, a deep pink that mirrored the shade I wore.

Perhaps that's what attracted this brilliant little being. Perhaps. But I'd like to believe that on the anniversary of her passing, Lauren made a point of coming by to let me know that she was all right—that she wanted me to find peace in my heart and soul too.

To some, hummingbirds symbolize a lightness of life, a spirit of joy, of playfulness. It is for that reason—and the visit we received on May 11, 2018—that we asked for this tiny carefree bird to grace *Mourning Has Broken*. May it serve as a reminder of these gifts to you too.

Acknowledgements

T HE STORY OF HOW *Mourning Has Broken*
came to be is one of those "God winks" I've heard
about since Lauren left us: Iris Tupholme, who is
senior vice president and executive publisher of Harper-
Collins Canada, was in the studio audience of *CityLine* in
downtown Toronto the day that I was marking my final radio
broadcast and had been asked to appear as a guest on the
popular national TV show. She just happened to be there on
a girls' day out with her sisters and heard me talk with host
Tracy Moore about our lives with and after Lauren. Later,
when Iris emailed me with the words "I think you've got a
book in you," I said she was right. This is that book. Thank
you to Iris and the compassionate and patient team of women
and men at HarperCollins who guided us, and to the incredible Michael Levine for helping us navigate these unfamiliar
waters. Michael, we are so sorry that you personally know
our journey as a bereaved parent through your own family
tragedy. Our hearts are with yours.

Dearest Reader (a term I'm sure no author is supposed to say, but since I'm new at this, I'll be as earnest as I want!), I thank you for sharing our lives—their great joy and deep sorrow—and I hope that this book has made clear that with love, kindness and quiet support, you really can survive anything.

If you promise to remember that, we will too.

I cannot imagine where we would be today without the friends and family who have made us laugh, who let us cry with them and who remember Lauren with such fondness. They will always be in our hearts. My long-time friend, confidante and beloved soul sister, Lisa Brandt, and my actual sister Leslie Davis, who walks this path of grief with us, both showed unwavering support when we lost our girl. We thank the brilliant light of our lives who has been there for almost every moment that mattered both in Lauren's life and ours, Allan Bell. We love you, Ally. Our deepest gratitude goes to Lauren's beloved "surrogate" grandmother, Helen Moase. To Anita Reynolds MacArthur and her husband, Ian: you and your family will always have a huge place in our hearts, and we cherish the closeness you still experience with Lauren and her many hints to you and daughter Ava Erin MacArthur from beyond.

To the family members who wrapped their arms around us when we feared we were lost, we are grateful: sweet Meaghan, also a young mom and her late first cousin's bridesmaid, who felt our loss so acutely; my aunt Laura and uncle Vern and their beautiful family (especially Lauren's fill-in big sister, Karen); Rob's siblings, Doug and Lois, but most of all Lauren's beloved Aunt Susie; and my sisters Heather and Cindy (along with Leslie). To our dad: always know that your daughters are as proud of you as you are of all of us. And Mom—you walk with me daily but I'm grateful you didn't live to share this pain.

Thank you again, Phil Shirakawa, for being the caring and tender father Lauren knew you would be and for so lovingly shepherding your beautiful son through these early years of life. He is the only link we have now to our own beloved child, an attachment that you understand in a deeper way with each passing day. We are so thankful to you for your generosity of spirit in allowing us, indeed encouraging us, to continue to play a prominent role in this beautiful, special boy's life.

To Brooke Russell Shirakawa, whom I'll call my daughter-in-law (but for whom there really is no title), thank you for the love and kindness and guidance you show our grandson, Colin, every day. When you say he is your life, we are grateful that Phil and Colin have found someone who can love and care for them and make a broken world bright again. Thank you, dear Brooke. You didn't have to do this: you could have kept living the life of a young single woman. Instead, you immersed yourself in diapers and sleepless nights, Elmo and school meetings. We adore that you sometimes talk to Lauren and feel her presence; you have earned and will always have our love and respect. You're a wonderful mother.

My radio family—intimate and extended—will forever be one I remember with the greatest gratitude, starting, as always, with the listeners who shared our lives through my journal, through the morning show for a quarter-century, and through twenty-four "Christmas Eve at Erin's" programs on the air with Lauren. You offered such boundless kindness when she died and in the months thereafter—and still do. Thank you, each and every one of you. Rob and I owe you so much.

Of that radio family, my greatest gratitude goes to Mike Cooper. When the unthinkable happened, you helped walk listeners through the days that followed. You carried the show and did so with the perfect blend of grace, humour and tears. My career's favourite dance partner found just the right steps, and I will always be so proud of you. For that, and a million other reasons, Rob and I love you and Debbie with all our hearts.

Also at CHFI, sincerest thanks go to our beloved leaders Julie Adam, Jackie Gilgannon, Wendy Duff and Julie James, Michelle Butterly, Steve Roberts, Gord Rennie, David Lindores and Daisy Yiu and, of course, my dear, sweet friend Ian MacArthur. Thank you also to Steve Winogron and Steve Madely—with whom Lauren and I both had the pleasure of working at CFRA, thirty years apart—and to all of Lauren's fellow employees in Ottawa, for sharing your love and respect for her with us and your listeners. And to Valerie Geller, always a source of strength, wisdom and encouragement.

A special note of appreciation and respect goes to our new Vancouver Island friend Nancy Wood, who has offered counsel and kindness when I was feeling adrift, as I have so often in this new western life. As for this book, Nancy was quick with feedback, advice and input. Her compassion, sensitivity and perspective made the rewrites (and rethinks) so very gentle. Thank you to Marianne Kowalski for retouching some of our family photos for this book. We appreciate your talents and the love for Lauren with which you did this work for us.

To those fellow bereaved mothers who opened their hearts to us and shared their stories here: we so appreciate your helping others who are in pain. Ellen, Nancy, Barbara and again, sister Leslie, may dragonflies, hummingbirds, feathers, dimes and cardinals always bring you messages of hope. Thank you to Marney Thompson and Victoria Hospice for sharing the wisdom behind complicated grief therapy, and to Ellen Wasyl for her help in those early days of our searing grief. Thanks to Laura Abbruzzese for letting us bring to you her blog on grieving via social media.

Rob and I are grateful to the doctors who have helped heal our minds and mend our broken hearts over the years: Alvin Pettle, David Satok, Henry Rosenblat, Randolph Knipping, Barbara Smith and David Singer.

This book would not be here, and I'm quite sure I would not either, were it not for my husband of thirty-plus years, Robert Whitehead. He's been my rock and my blankie, my forever love and my forgiving (and funny) friend. He was also the best father a daughter or mother could ask for, and I will forever be grateful for his dogged and patient participation in this book. As he is in life, he was my sounding board and my sober second thought. Believe me when I say that this book took every bit as much of a toll on Rob as it did on me.

But he would agree with me that every word, every tear, has been worth it. All that we will ever do is in memory of

Lauren, a daughter who was more than we could have wished for, and who gave us such immeasurable joy, laughter and love that some days the only things that keep us going are the moments we can recall that lift our spirits and light up our hearts, and the promise that our souls will be together. We can curse the gods for giving us only twenty-four years with her, or be forever grateful that she was in our lives for that long.

We lean hard toward gratitude: for Lauren, for Colin, for Phil and Brooke, for each other and for everyone who has been at our sides—in person or in thought—offering support, kindness, wisdom and advice.

Thank you. Our appreciation is as deep and comforting as our love for our girl, and as endless as our longing to hear her, touch her, laugh with and hold her.

Our Lauren. Our own Pure Joy.